Acknowledgements and Thanks

There are many people to thank for their contributions to bring this book project to a reality. None is more significant than my wife, Judy, who put up with 18 years as I labored as the Editor of *News & Notes* and then creating the book ready for printing. Other things suffered as the newsletter and book deadlines were met.

Thanks to Frank Dewey for his help in extracting the stories from the newsletters and, most importantly, taking on the *News & Notes* Editor's job so that I could find time to work on this book.

The RABO Executive Committee, including Diane Homburg, Glyn Bailey, Don Imwold, Henry Miller and John Baesch deserve thanks for the tedious job of preparing the index for the entire text of *Rails' Tales*. They also have done all of the work behind the scene to fill and mail book orders and keep track of the revenues and expenses of the project.

Outside of RABO there is a significant group of professional folks that have been of great assistance in guiding the content of the publication. Included are Nick Fry of the Barriger Library in St. Louis and the B&O Railroad Historical Society in Baltimore; Roger Grant, History Professor at Clemson University; Rush Loving, former Associate Editor Fortune magazine and author; and Fred Rasmussen, *Baltimore Sun* writer who have provided valuable advice and assistance.

My right hand man in this project has been Herb Harwood. A longtime associate on the railroad, he has contributed to this project in several key ways. He has provided advice in the editing process; written many of the photo captions, provided from his own collection or supplied from others the majority of the photos included in this book; and he has written a Foreword that describes the content of the book and entices potential readers to take a fun ride.

C. Norman Murphy proof read the stories when they first appeared in *News & Notes* and Ginny Schilt, widow of former member Frank Schilt, did a marvelous job proofreading the entire book.

And my granddaughter, Katie Ashby, created a beautiful dust jacket loaded with information and attractive images.

Most of all, I must acknowledge the many RABO members who wrote their stories for the newsletter and especially those who have had them included in this book. It has been a pleasure putting the collection together for all to enjoy.

E. Ray Lichty, Editor

ISBN 978-1-365-15310-5

Published by
RABO
The Retired Administrators of the
Baltimore & Ohio Railroad

Baltimore, Maryland

First Edition

February 28, 2016
The 189th Anniversary of the Founding of the
Baltimore & Ohio Railroad Company.

Printed in the United States of America
By Lulu.com.

RAILS' TALES

The Baltimore & Ohio
Railroad Company

Edited by E. Ray Lichty

FOREWORD
Herbert H. Harwood, Jr.

Railroading is a business like no other -- and an always fascinating one. One of its less-remarked distinctions is the enormous range of job specialties needed to keep it functioning. In past years the larger railroads have employed within their ranks virtually every profession, trade, and technical skill known to industry – plus many unique to themselves. In addition, much of that work was spread over several thousand miles of scattered locations, often remote from any personal supervision, so that whatever the level of someone's position, a railroader regularly had to make quick decisions that might potentially affect millions of dollars in property, and even lives.

Yet, oddly, very little has been written by or about the people in this huge variety of jobs, both in direct operations and all the support functions. Yes, plenty has been said about the moguls who, for better or worse, built and financed the railroads and those who headed them during their glory years – the Vanderbilts, Goulds, Harrimans, Hills, Morgans, and their like. Then, too, there have been lots of dramatic tales from and about that most romantic of railroad occupations, the locomotive engineer.

But what about all those other railroaders? What about the operating managers at all levels who had to keep the trains running 24 hours a day, seven days a week, often under all sorts of unpredictable circumstances? Who dealt with demanding and quirky freight shippers and receivers, especially at a time when competition from trucks and desperate other railroads was growing? Industrial location specialists? Export-import pier operators? Office workers? Real estate agents? And so on... Here in this book is all of that and more, previously untold tales that illuminate many of the day-to-day details and diversions of railroad work, told directly by those who did the work.

The story tellers in this case are retired officers of the Baltimore & Ohio Railroad, as they relate their experiences to one another through the casual medium of their social organization's newsletter. Thus they tell their stories in their own voices, only minimally edited; you read them as if you are eavesdropping on conversations among veterans who have climbed the ladder within the same company for most, if not all, of their careers, and are talking with the comfort of long-time friends. Their stories take place during the period from about 1950 through the 1970s, in a very different working world from the present day. Then, communications were by telephone, teletype, and even telegraph; operations were mostly managed through on-the-ground personnel manning a multiplicity of stations and towers; great numbers of salesmen scattered all over the country called on freight customers large and small; offices were powered by typewriters, comptometers, and punch-card equipment. The computer age was only beginning, with early mainframes that took up an entire floor of an office building. Passenger train services were diminishing, but still company-run, and in the B&O's case they remained a point of corporate pride.

In one way, the experiences related here typify the wide range of activities on any large railroad in the second half of the 20th century; in another, they reflect the personality and peculiarities of one particular railroad – specifically the B&O. Like many of its peers in the business at that time, the B&O was individualistic and idiosyncratic, with its own particular kind of esprit de corps, and ways of doing things that came out of a mixture of history, traditions, and the all-too-frequent patches of tight times when everyone had to work together to make the best of things.

And times were toughening in the period when most of these stories occurred: truck, auto, and air competition was cutting ever more severely into traditional markets, and Eastern carriers such as the B&O were suffering the most. The B&O's system mileage shrank from a peak of 6,396 miles in 1936 to 5,200 by 1980. The employment drop was far more dramatic and depressing. Coming out of World War II in 1945, the B&O had 64,300 employees; by 1980 that figure was down to 16,000 -- and a short four years later had hit 12,100. Along the way, the B&O had posted an unprecedentedly large (for the time) $30 million deficit in 1961, and that year also got a new president, Jervis Langdon, Jr., who began moving the railroad in new directions. Ownership by the coal-rich Chesapeake & Ohio Railway came in 1963, and afterward new faces and more new ways of doing business appeared – albeit gradually, since this merger was intentionally more measured and graceful than many. In all, this was the challenging environment in which these writers worked.

Some of their experiences are mundane, some comic, a few tragic (and in at least one case, downright horrifying), with many in between. But whatever the subject, they all give an insider's picture of what is was like to help make a large railroad function in the days before megamergers, all-encompassing computerization, stripped-down facilities, and, most of all, the severe diminishment of human contact on and around the rails. So enjoy listening in.

RAILS'TALES
The Baltimore & Ohio
Railroad Company

CONTENTS

INTRODUCTION
By E. Ray Lichty

The Baltimore & Ohio Railroad was formally incorporated in Baltimore on April 24, 1827. While the B&O corporate structure, as the result of mergers and acquisitions, has been folded in to the railroad behemoth CSX, the B&O's former property is still part of the railroad business.

Much has been written about the history and operations of the B&O. This book enhances that work by managers telling the stories of working on the B&O.

The common thread in this collection of 121 short stories is that they were written by retired managers who had worked for the B&O, or its affiliates and successors, and were members of the RABO Club. The stories originally appeared in the RABO (Retired Administrators of the B&O RR) Club's quarterly newsletter, *News & Notes*.

The stories have been arranged by topic into 19 chapters. Although some stories prompted others, each is an independent tale bringing to life the expression "Working on the Railroad." The book can be read front to back, cover to cover. Or it also can be read in any order depending on the reader's interests.

Since the stories were written for the Club's newsletter, the writers' assumptions were that the readers would have an understanding of the many common terms, expressions, names and locations they included in their tale. Such is not the case for all readers of this book. Therefore, a basic description of the B&O's history, geography, operations and organization in the time period of these stories (most are from the early 50s until the late 70s) may be helpful to the reader.

Chartered on April 24, 1827, the Baltimore & Ohio Railroad became the nation's first railroad common carrier company for the transportation of people and goods. There were three groups of investors; the City of Baltimore, the State of Maryland and private investors. The goal was to connect Baltimore and its port to the expanding west, particularly the Ohio River. The ceremonial first stone was laid on July 4, 1828, with Charles Carroll, a signer of the Declaration of Independence, turning the first shovel of dirt.

Ellicott City, Maryland, thirteen miles west of Baltimore, was the first destination and service between those points, by horse-drawn carriages, began on May 5, 1830, and the famous race between the horse and the Tom Thumb steam-powered locomotive allegedly took place three months later according to some historians while others claim the entire story is folklore.

The original mainline crossed the Potomac River at Harper's Ferry, West Virginia, continued on to Cumberland, Maryland, and then via Grafton and Fairmont reaching Wheeling, all three in today's West Virginia, on the Ohio River on Christmas Eve, 1852. The Parkersburg Branch from Grafton to Parkersburg, also in today's West Virginia and on the Ohio River, was completed May 1, 1857.

Acquisitions provided much of the expansion beyond the Ohio River with lines opposite Wheeling reaching Columbus and Cincinnati, Ohio, and opposite Parkersburg reaching Cincinnati by way of Chillicothe, Ohio. Ferry services operated across the Ohio River at Wheeling and Parkersburg until the two river bridges were completed in 1871. A line was acquired from Newark, on the Wheeling-Columbus-Cincinnati line, north to Sandusky on Lake Erie. From Chicago Junction, later named Willard in honor of B&O President Daniel Willard, 28 miles south of Sandusky, a line was built reaching Chicago in 1874.

The B&O built a line west from Cumberland to Pittsburgh and through acquisitions and construction joined the line at Chicago Junction, in 1891, providing an improved route to Chicago from the east.

The Ohio & Mississippi Railroad was acquired in 1893 which provided a direct route from Cincinnati to St Louis. Other acquisitions provided routes from Cincinnati to Toledo and to Beardstown, Illinois by way of Indianapolis.

The Washington Branch was built from Relay, Maryland, to Washington in 1835 and in 1873 the Metropolitan branch was built from Washington to Point of Rocks where it joined the mainline from Baltimore to Cumberland.

The B&O crossed the summit of the Alleghenies at Terra Alta, on the southwest line, at an elevation of 2,686 and at Sand Patch, Pennsylvania, elevation 2,258.

In 1886, the B&O opened a line between Baltimore and Philadelphia, and extended its service to New York Harbor over

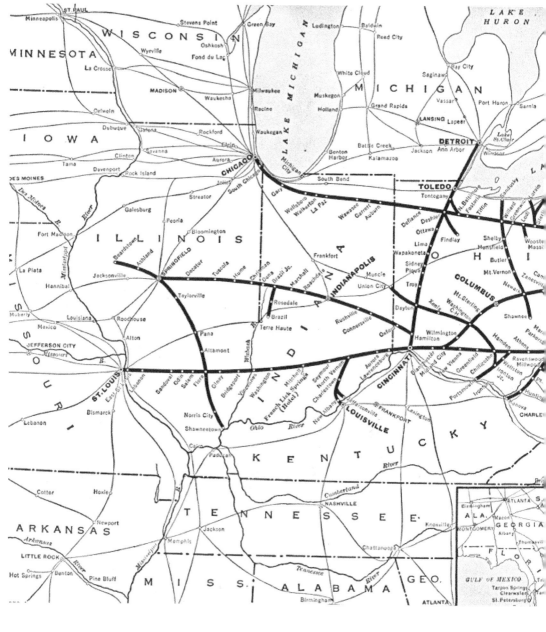

this route by using lines of the Reading Company and Central Railroad of New Jersey between Philadelphia and New York.

The Baltimore Beltline opened in 1895 with its Howard Street Tunnel, at 1.4 miles, the longest tunnel on the B&O.

The last major acquisition by the B&O was the Buffalo, Rochester and Pittsburgh in 1932. At its peak in 1936, the B&O included 6,396 miles of road and, as its public motto claimed, "Linking 13 Great States with the Nation."

April 25, 1954, B&O public timetable map. Ray Lichty collection.

Geography

The B&O Railroad system extended from Philadelphia through Baltimore and Washington to Cumberland, Maryland, where the main line split into the St. Louis and Chicago main lines; each crossing the Alleghany Mountains west of Cumberland and serving the coal fields of those areas. The Chicago main line passed through Pittsburgh, Youngstown and Akron with branches to Buffalo, Rochester, Cleveland and

Toledo/Detroit. The St Louis main line crossed the Ohio River at Parkersburg, and passed though Cincinnati and had branches to Huntington, West Virginia, Indianapolis and Louisville. In the middle of the railroad between those two main lines was a network of lines serving Wheeling, Columbus and Dayton.

The B&O had a interline agreement with the Reading and Central Railroad of New Jersey to serve beyond Philadelphia to the New York City metropolitan area and the B&O owned lines in New York City including the Staten Island Rapid Transit lines in New York and New Jersey.

Passenger Trains

In this time period and before the Arrival of Amtrak in 1971, the B&O operated premier passenger trains between New York City, via Baltimore and Washington, to Pittsburgh, Akron, Cleveland, Toledo/Detroit and Chicago and between those most eastern points and Cincinnati, Louisville and St. Louis. Service was also provided between Detroit, via Toledo and Dayton, and Cincinnati. Commuter services were provided between Baltimore and Washington and Brunswick, Maryland, and Washington and from Versailles, Pennsylvania, and Pittsburgh.

On these passenger routes, the highest priority trains were between:
Jersey City and Washington
Nos 27 and 28   The Royal Blue
Baltimore/Washington and Chicago
Nos 5 and 6   The Capitol Limited
Nos 25 and 25   The Columbian
Nos 7 and 8   The Shenandoah
Baltimore/Washington and St Louis
Nos 1 and 2   The National Limited
Baltimore/Washington and Cincinnati
Nos 75 and 76   The Cincinnatian (1947-1959)
Detroit and Cincinnati
Nos 53 and 54   The Cincinnatian (1950-1971)

Freight Trains

Generally speaking, B&O's eastbound freight trains carried higher valued commodities and were of a higher priority than westbound trains.

Into the mid-20th century, B&O's passenger trains were typically dominated by heavy but smooth-riding and comfortable modernized 1920s-era cars -- even so when the entire train was streamlined. Such was the case with the fondly remembered Columbian, a luxury coach train created by completely rebuilding older equipment in B&O's Mt. Clare shops in Baltimore. First assigned to the New York-Washington run in 1937, it was subsequently refurbished and expanded for service as the premier overnight all-coach train between Washington and Chicago. Here on its original New York run, the Columbian storms through Hopewell, New Jersey, in about 1938.
W. R. Osborne photo, H. H. Harwood, Jr., collection.

Key eastbound trains were the "94s" from Chicago named for their primary destination: Baltimore 94, Philadelphia 94, New York 94, etc. From St Louis the best train was No. 88. 396 was the auto parts train from Toledo to Baltimore and Wilmington, Delaware.

The LCL (Less-Than-Carload) trains of consolodater freight from the New York market moved on hot-shot trains; the Time Savers. These westbound trains were destined for Chicago and St Louis with stops at intermediate cities.

In the later portion of this time period, the solid piggyback trains became the highest priority. They were the "Jets" and their destination city identified the particular train; New York Jet, St. Louis Jet, etc.

Organization

In addition to the headquarters' staff areas of responsibility, the B&O Operating Department was organized into the three main functions, Transportation, Mechanical and Maintenance of Way. Geographically, these three functions were organized into Regions and Divisions. During most of this time period, the Regions were based at New York City, Baltimore, Pittsburgh and Cincinnati. The Baltimore and Ohio Chicago Terminal Railroad in Chicago was treated as a separate company.

The Divisions were largest in number at the beginning of the period and diminished in number as time passed. It seems that over the years, the B&O division structure was constantly changing. Also the arrival of the C&O changed the regional structure and some division structure. At one point, the B&O divisions were located as follows, named for their city headquarters except as shown;

Eastern Region (Baltimore)
New York City, New York (SIRT)
Baltimore, Maryland
Baltimore Terminal
Cumberland, Maryland
Grafton, West Virginia (Monongah Division)
Central Region (Pittsburgh)
Pittsburgh, Pennsylvania
Punxsutawney, Pennsylvania (Buffalo Division)
Akron, Ohio
Garrett, Indiana (Chicago Division)
Wheeling, West Virginia
Western Region (Cincinnati)
Newark, Ohio
Cincinnati, Ohio (Ohio Division)
Cincinnati Terminal
Dayton, Ohio (Toledo Division)
Washington, Indiana (St. Louis Division)
Indianapolis, Indiana
Baltimore & Ohio Chicago Terminal (Chicago)

Regions were under the authority of the General Manager and later titled Regional Manager. Divisions were under the authority of the Superintendent and later titled Division Manager.

Overall, the highest railroad position was the President.

Reporting to him were Vice Presidents for the key departments including the Operating Vice President who had the responsibility for running the railroad. Since 1941, B&O Presidents were as follows:

Roy B. White	1941-1953
Howard E. Simpson	1953-1961
Jervis Langdon, Jr.	1961-1964
Walter Touhy	1964-1965
Gregory S. DeVine	1965-1971
Hays T. Watkins	1971-1972-
John W. Hanifin	1972-1975
Hays T. Watkins	1975-1978
John T. Collinson	1978-1987

Headquarters

Going way back in time to 1857, the B&O's headquarters was at Camden Station in Baltimore. It remained there until the elegant headquarters building was built at the corner of Baltimore and Calvert Streets, it was destroyed in the Great Baltimore Fire in 1904. To replace that building, the new thirteen story headquarters building was constructed at the corner of Baltimore and Charles Streets. It too was an elegant structure and included some very nice offices for senior managers which included private toilets and fireplaces. The President's office and Board Room were on the third floor and the Operating VP's office was on the 5th floor and the transportation officers were on the sixth floor.

1962 was the beginning of decade long movement of the headquarters one block north to the One Charles Center building. B&O/Chessie was the largest tenant in that modern 22 story building. However, the advent of the C&O's control of the B&O resulted in the President and senior management positions being located in Terminal Tower in Cleveland, Ohio. Also, the arrival of the C&O brought into the picture the combined C&O/B&O Engineering Department located in the OH Building (Operating Headquarters) in Huntington, West Virginia.

1980 was the year CSX Corporation was created and more location changes affected the old B&O. The CSX Corporation corporate headquarters (the holding company) was established in the James Center in Richmond, Virginia. The railroads, under the

For 60 years, whenever employees anywhere on the B&O's 6,000 -mile system reverently (or not) spoke of "Baltimore," they meant the wisdom and ukases emanating from the impressive headquarters building at 2 North Charles Street. Completed in 1906 to replace its incinerated predecessor, the 13-story structure, known by its workers as the "Central Building", was gradually vacated during the 1960s and '70s in favor of more modern facilities a block away at One Charles Center. It still contained some active railroad offices in this 1970 photo, but by then had lost most of its important functions. It still stands today, now adapted for other uses and designated by the Maryland Historical Trust as one of the city's most historically significant buildings. H. H. Harwood, Jr., photo.

CSX Transportation banner, initially continued to use the former railroad headquarter locations; Cleveland, Baltimore and Jacksonville, Florida. Later, the Cleveland and Baltimore offices were closed and the CSX railroads, including the B&O, were headquartered in Jacksonville. After CSX Corporation sold off some of its non-rail subsidiaries, the Richmond offices were closed and all of the CSX-CSX Transportation offices were consolidated in Jacksonville. The B&O corporation was merged into CSX Transportation in 1987.

Railroad Company Abbreviations

Many railroad company abbreviations are in this book. They are listed in the Appendix at the back of this book in two sectons in the first group are those with a B&O ownership or financial interest. The second group includes other carriers that were mentioned.

Fair of the Iron Horse

The B&O Railroad proudly claimed to be the first railroad in the United States, chartered in February 1827. The 100th anniversary of that occasion was marked by the railroad with the Fair of the Iron Horse.

It was a two month event staged at the fairgrounds built by the B&O specifically for the occasion. The site was at Halethorpe, Maryland. It featured a parade around the ground's oval track of replicas of historic equipment and examples of modern 1927 engines and cars.

Writers of the stories in this book may refer to the Fair of the Iron Horse merely using the nickname "The Fair".

In 1970s and beyond, the railroad had division offices and a dispatching center across the street from the site of "The Fair".

The above brief history of the B&O Railroad is good background information, especially for non-B&O railroaders, to put into context the collection of short stories that are to follow. The stories, as written by the authors who lived them, provide great insight as to how parts of the railroad were run. But they are more than that as you gain insight into the lives of the people who actually ran the railroad.

If one looks at many of these stories as a group, it becomes obvious that, over time, the work environment and permitted personal behavior have changed. The abuse of alcohol, on and off of the job, may have been tolerated sixty years ago when some of these stories took place but not today. Likewise, what once were acceptable practices by managers in dealing with subordinates, especially women, are unfathomable today. Social norms and work practices have changed which makes some of these stories remarkable by highlighting those changes over time.

These tales run the gamut of emotions from the joy of success to the pain of failure. Some are funny, very funny, and some are sad. Also, a picture is painted of the impact on the families of the managers and how the demands of the job and household moves impact them all.

Read on and enjoy

During September and October 1927, the B&O celebrated its 100th birthday in the grandest possible style with an elaborate, three-week-long public outdoor celebration it called "The Fair of the Iron Horse." Staged at a thousand-acre site eight miles outside Baltimore in Halethorpe, Maryland, the fair included a huge exhibition hall containing historical artifacts, various smaller exhibit buildings, and, as its star attraction, a 12,000-seat grandstand where fairgoers regularly witnessed a dramatic pageant covering the entire span of transportation history – "performed" by genuine locomotives and trains, both antique and modern. By the time the fair closed, over 1.3 million people had passed through its gates -- an average of 50,000 each day. Many of them remembered it for decades after.

RAILS' TALES
The Baltimore & Ohio Railroad Company

Section A
CONDUCTING TRANSPORTATION

Chapter 1   Keeping the Railroad Running

We Don't Want Any Cornfield Meets!
By Gifford Moore
July 2008

In the early days of railroading, opposing trains on a single track would meet at an agreed-upon point. One would be on a siding so the other could pass on the main track. No one controlled this! The two trains would wait for each other, whether five minutes or five hours.

Next was the timetable which conveyed superiority, in some cases to trains because of "class" (first class, second class, etc.) or "direction" (usually eastward trains were superior to westward trains). Thus, an inferior train could move against a superior train by observing the operating rule and the provisions of the timetable schedules.

Soon, it became obvious that, like anything in life, nothing works perfectly and often not at all, so there had to be human control. Thus was born the train dispatcher. Using the framework of the timetable, the established operating rules, and train orders and messages, the train dispatcher was able to "move" the trains over the far-flung railroad and keep them apart.

Understandably, you have read about awful railroad wrecks, collisions and accidents that occurred. Many were caused by "man failure" but very, very few by the Train Dispatcher. Yet the train dispatcher was then, and even today, at the apex of responsibility for oversight of railroad train movements.

The so-called "cornfield meet" was the label applied to a head-on wreck, often out in the middle of nowhere, caused by someone's mistake.

The Baltimore Division dispatcher's office was on the 2nd floor of Camden Station in downtown Baltimore at the west end of Howard Street Tunnel. When the Baltimore East End and the Old Main Line were single-tracked in 1960, a CTC machine was installed there. Shown here is dispatcher, La Vere Neal, at the model board; to the left is the Old Main Line and to the right is the Baltimore East End. In the center, the rows of buttons are the phone "call system." Punching the appropriate button would ring a location's phone, such as a yardmaster's office. The small chrome handles remotely operated the switches and signals along the line. The large piece of paper on the desk is the "train sheet" on which the dispatcher recorded information about a train; its conductor and engineer; train consist; and a chronology of the trains' movements. The machine was manned 24/7. The office also had another dispatcher for the Washington and Metropolitan Sub Divisions and Baltimore Terminal. The Chief Dispatcher had overall responsibility for the dispatchers working on his shift and for the movement of traffic, loaded and empty, over the division.

B&O Railroad Historical Society collection.

THINK

SPEAK

ACT

with caution!

Your life, as well as the lives of others, depends on YOUR attitude and action with regard to safety.

Safety is everybody's job on the B & O (from the President down) . . . but, it begins with

You

THE BALTIMORE & OHIO RAILROAD COMPANY

CENTRAL REGION

SAFETY ABOVE EVERYTHING

AKRON-CHICAGO DIVISION

81

TIME TABLE No. 81
EFFECTIVE 12:01 A. M.
EASTERN STANDARD TIME
SUNDAY, APRIL 26, 1964

C. E. HECK,
Superintendent

Most folks are familiar with the public versions of railroad timetables. They contained the train schedules, information about services offered, onboard sleeping accommodations, ticket prices and system maps. Far less familiar are employee timetables. These booklets are the instructions used by the employees who are involved with the running of trains; freight and passenger, over a segment or division of a railroad company.

For the B&O, each of the divisions had an employee timetable. Most were issued twice a year when daylight savings time began or ended. Shown here is the front page of the Akron Division employee timetable that was effective on April 26, 1964.

The contents were, for the most part, laid out in a two column format. Typically, the employee would vertically fold the timetable so that it would fit in a back pocket. *Ray Lichty collection.*

3

For the first few weeks, perhaps even months, the job can be a "pressure cooker". New dispatchers feel the responsibility to be very careful. The fear is making a mistake that would or could cause damage to person or property. Occasionally, a new dispatcher would quit because the tension of the job was overwhelming.

When I hired on the railroad, the train dispatchers used Morse Code, not telephones or radio, to communicate with the operators located in towers along the railroad to transmit train orders and messages to the trains. The operators constituted the eyes and ears of the train dispatcher. After World War II, the "dispatcher's wire" was replaced by telephone. There was an awkward situation created when the dispatcher's phone was partially gone, usually due to weather problems, because the dispatcher must fall back on Morse Code for some of his communications. Further frustration.

I started in the train dispatcher office in 1948 on "third trick" (the night shift). I was apprehensive for a long time about how I would be accepted by the old timers there. My principal fear was that I would overlook some important fact and forget to tell the dispatcher who relieved me. I would lay awake and worry about it. Occasionally, I would have a bad dream: a mini-nightmare.

Fortunately, I did not make an error that did any harm or damage. Yes, I did commit some mistakes in judgment and received some reprimands (a couple written on my service record). I learned that good judgment is the result of experience which, in turn, is the result of bad judgment. It was said that "You're not worth your salt unless you have several reprimands on your record!"

As the months and years rolled on, the fears diminished but the pressure was sustained. One observer said the work was akin to a General in battle. The tasks become routine but always serious and demanding. I did not make any unpardonable mistakes, although one night I overheard another young dispatcher about ready to issue orders that might have resulted in a "cornfield meet". Fortunately, he recognized what he was about to do and corrected the plan.

It was my fear of something that never happened... a long time ago.

The Demise of "DS" Tower

By Bill Lakel
January 2003

Recently, while sitting around the table of our cabin in Canada, swapping railroad tales, my son, Bill Jr., Engineer on the Trailer Train, Cumberland to Philadelphia, asked me a question probably only two people could answer, myself and A. W. Johnston ("Peanuts," in the old B & O days).

I was first introduced to "DS" Tower, Boyds, Maryland, on the Metropolitan Branch to Washington, around 1950. Ross Schenck, Division Operator, sent me a work message, "Commence 2nd trick 'DS' tower until further notice." "DS" Tower sat on the fill between Buck Lodge and Boyds, Maryland, on the Metropolitan Sub Division, between "QN" Tower, Washington, D.C., and "KG" Tower, Point of Rocks, Maryland. It was a lever-operated interlocking, consisting of double crossovers and passing sidings in both directions. There was no road to the tower. Weather permitting, we could drive through a farmer's field. Any rain or snow, and it was a ¼ mile walk from the road.

There are many words to describe "DS":

Proud, absolutely, for she controlled everything in both directions between "QN", in D.C. and "KG" Tower, Point of Rocks, where the Old Main Line joined. Many an evening, a P-7 steam passenger locomotive would blow the six shorts ordering the "Protect Engine" out at Brunswick. "DS" had done her job for that day.

Sturdy, you bet, for she was constructed completely of poured concrete and faced with red brick. I remember on one derailment a loaded 'reefer (ice refrigerated car) hit the front porch and actually wrapped around the west corner of the building. Total damage was several bricks off the facing. The roof was built as a reservoir for the steam boiler in the basement, which never produced enough water to work properly. The old caboose stove kept her warm and comfortable.

Lonely, definitely so, isolated completely. At night when coming to work, the "goose neck" porcelain light over the door produced an eerie glow of light, the only light you could see in that direction.

The Metropolitan Sub Division, opened as a single track line in 1873, extended from QN Tower, the junction with the Washington Branch from Baltimore and the entrance to Washington Terminal, to Point of Rocks where it joined the Old Main Line from Baltimore to Brunswick, Maryland. It was built to provide a more direct route connecting Washington to and from the west. Also, when used in conjunction with the Washington Branch, the line provided a longer but easier grade double track route to and from Baltimore.

Boyds Tower was built when the line was double tracked in 1928. The tower was unusual for the B&O as it was an armstrong interlocking but not a two story building as was normally the case. Also, it was built of concrete with a brick façade. When constructed, the location was in the rural countryside.

The interlocking controlled a set of crossovers and the entrances to eastbound and westbound sidings. As freight traffic grew on the line, so did the number of passenger trains. Then as the area became urbanized, commuter traffic to and from Washington grew. As late as 1958, the tower was open two shifts a day to handle the heavy traffic including commuter trains. Today, the Metropolitan Sub Division is double tracked signaled in both directions and operated remotely from the dispatcher's office at Halethorpe, Maryland. All of the towers on the line have been closed, including Boyds.

E. L. Thompson photograph, John King collection.

Memories, there are many, as in every telegraph office, but some at "DS" are forever etched in my mind.

"Suzie," the resident cat belonging to first trick operator, Eweil Shewbridge, had produced a total of 74 kittens under the desk. Ewell kept a record on the wall. She would bring live mice to her

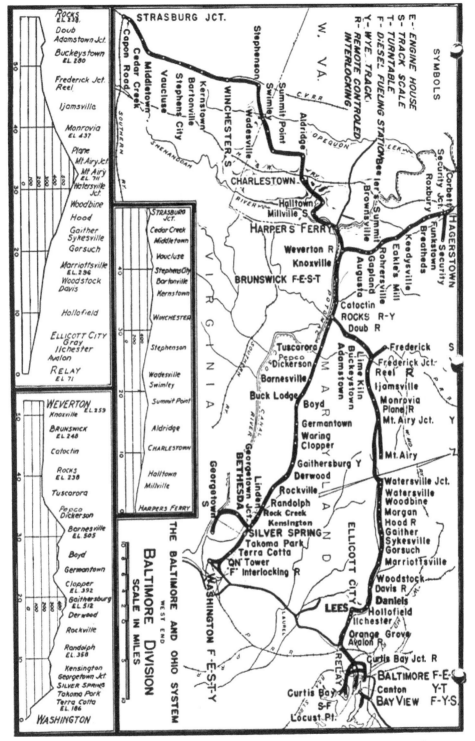

Baltimore Division West End October 27, 1963, employee timetable map showing the main line from Harpers Ferry to Washington and Baltimore.   *Ray Lichty collection.*

brood to train them. There was always someone waiting for her kittens. Kitten No. 4 ended her career at the Eastbound Home Signal when she waited a second too long to get off the rail.

"Monty Sanbower," the signal maintainer stocking rabbits in the spring to assure fantastic hunting in the fall season.

"A. W. Johnston," Assistant Trainmaster from Brunswick, coming down to meet the "Met" way train to switch out shopped N-41 hopper cars scattered throughout the mess stored in the eastbound siding, by number of course. I kept an accurate "check" which always helped. "Bill" had legs like a giraffe and could span three ties with his stride. I probably looked like a ballet dancer trying to keep up. This situation prevailed throughout our long careers.

"The Strawberry Pickers in June," the hollow behind the tower was solid strawberry plants and provided the locals with buckets of fruit.

"The Resident Raccoon," who would eat his sandwich and scratch on the screen door for more.

Getting back to Bill, Jr.'s question. After countless buckets of water over the spillway, Bill Johnston was Superintendent of the Baltimore Division and I was Division Operator-Rules Examiner. "DS" tower had long been closed, the pipelines removed and switches modified. "DS" was a lonely shadow still sitting on the right of way. AWJ had me setting up temporary offices at "BN," East Brunswick, and "KG" Tower, Point of Rocks, for single track operation. It seems we were blowing down the mountain at Point of Rocks Tunnel to move the eastbound track outside the tunnel. The westbound track was to be moved to the center of the tunnel to accommodate high cube boxcars and auto racks.

AWJ suggested I contact the superintendent of the project to see if "DS" Tower could be removed. He was right, as usual, for when we took the "Powder Man" to "DS" he said, "No Problem." He would set three charges under the foundation caissons and one under the front of the building. The front charge to be set off several seconds after the rear charges were detonated.

When he did the job, "DS" went over backwards, ever so slowly into the hollow. The relays and signal equipment in the basement, the old files, stove and furnace remained with the building.

To answer Bill, Jr.'s question: "Son, she is still there." Yes, now completely covered with honeysuckle, brush and trees. Totally invisible to the passing trains, forever hiding the once proud tower and her many memories.

Nightmare on the Rails

By Bill Lakel
April 2004

It was New Year's Eve Day, 1957, in the dispatcher's office at Camden Station in Baltimore, Maryland. I was 3rd trick Train Dispatcher working the "West End CTC," Philadelphia, Pennsylvania to Harpers Ferry, West Virginia. I had not been on duty long when Chief Dispatcher Roy Barret told me to plug into the Cumberland Division dispatcher line. It seems that there were two trains, a westbound empty coal train and an eastward "Brunswick 96" merchandise train running head-on on the "lowgrade," a 11.6-mile single track line running from West Cumbo Tower, (W Tower) West Virginia, five miles west of Martinsburg, to R Tower at Miller, West Virginia. Eight tenths of a mile east of Miller on the lowgrade was the connection to the Western Maryland Railway at Cherry Run. The lowgrade was signaled for eastbound movements only. A westbound train had to operate in a manual block with 'rights over opposing trains' conferred by train order The westbound empty coal train had such an order and a Clearance Card Form A showing they had a clear block West Cumbo to R Tower, Miller.

It was transfer time at Cumberland and also at R Tower at Miller, when the Operator at Miller asked Dispatcher D. Courtney at DU office in Cumberland for instructions for "Brunswick 96." Courtney said, "lowgrade with a highball." The highball was because the westbound passenger train #7 was due shortly and he wanted the 96 to cross the westbound main without delaying #7. The Operator then lined 96 up for the lowgrade and 96 entered the single track with an Approach (yellow) signal setting up a collision.

Investigation revealed that the 2nd and 3rd trick operators at R Tower, Miller, were not speaking and made no transfer. The 2nd trick Operator also failed to display a Red Order Board and Stop Signal eastward on the lowgrade as required by the rules.

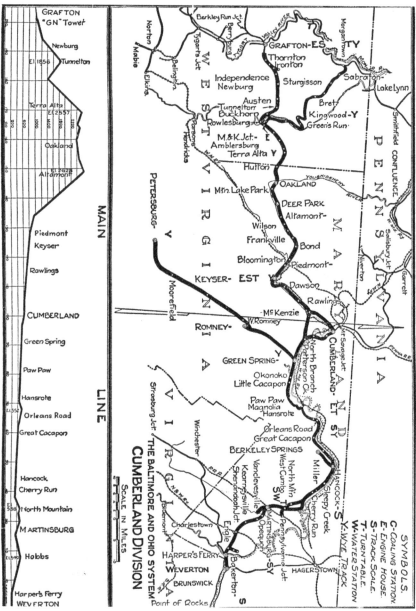

The map shown is the back cover of a 1963 Cumberland Division employee timetable. At that time, the division headquarters in Queen City Station had been moved to Cumberland Yard. Key locations shown on the map are the east end of the division at Harper's Ferry; Martinsburg, which was the location of major shop facilities and an

(Continued on page 11)

(Continued from page 10)

engine roundhouse; the line of the Patterson Creek Cut-Off between Patterson Creek and Rawlings; Keyser Yard which was a major coal car switching yard; Deer Park, the source of the Deer Park Spring Water served on the B&O passenger trains; Rowlesburg, the important helper station for the trains operating on the mountain grades and Grafton, the west end of the division. The grade diagram at the bottom on the page is significant as it shows the ruling grades for trains from the Monongah Division coal fields and traffic to and from Cincinnati and St Louis.   *Ray Lichty collection.*

The westbound coal train, with 175 empty coal cars powered by two GP type diesel locomotives, had been delayed by air trouble at West Cumbo Yard for several hours, probably contributing to the situation being overlooked by the dispatchers at Cumberland. The engineer on the coal car train was running the train from the second unit, GP 6500, because the lead engine would not make transition, an electrical problem similar to shifting gears on a truck. This fact could have very well saved his life.

The eastbound Brunswick 96 was powered by a three-unit F7 diesel consist and had a deadhead crew riding in the cab of the rear unit. Directly behind the engines was a cut of covered hoppers loaded with sand. The estimated speed of both trains was 25 MPH. The weight and momentum of the eastbound greatly exceeded the westbound empty coal cars.

The "head on" situation was almost immediately recognized and every effort was made to prevent a collision. Local police, ambulance services and fire departments were notified to try and contact the moving trains. The short distance the trains had to travel and the isolated area prevented stopping the trains and they collided head on about 25 car lengths west of the west switch of Halfway Siding. Knowing the trains were on a collision course and realizing there was nothing anyone could do to stop them created a feeling of complete helplessness and despair.

Shortly after the collision, the Operator at HF Tower, Harpers Ferry, told me he had a member of the deadhead crew on the block phone at Halfway Siding and he hooked me up to him. I asked him if he knew the condition of the eastbound crew and he

A communications lapse between the operators at Miller (or "R") Tower at Cherry Run, West Virginia, set the stage for a catastrophic head-on collision that claimed three lives. While not the railroad's worst wreck, it was probably the most horrifying in its way, because operating employees recognized the impending collision in enough time to prevent it -- but could not, and could only wait helplessly for the inevitable. The tower, seen here in 1987, also controlled a key connection to the Western Maryland Railway's main line to Hagerstown, a heavily used alternate route to many eastern points. H. H. Harwood, Jr., photo.

said no. I asked him why and he said there was no crew compartment left on the lead F7. He did say that the Head Brakeman of the westbound empty coal car train had jumped when they saw the headlight of the eastbound shining on the trees saying, "Someone _____ up!" An empty coal car had partially fallen on the brakeman and they rescued him by digging him out of the cinders with their bare hands. He was injured but recovered OK. Help was arriving through the woods and treatment being provided to the engine crew on the westbound who were not seriously injured. The three crewmembers of the eastbound 96 were killed instantly for the nose of the lead engine on the westbound had buried itself in the high tension panel of the lead F7 engine. The windshield and door frame of the Brunswick 96 had opened like a can and was sticking out of the wreck but could be easily recognized. The engineer of the eastbound 96, B. F. Phillips, was the husband of "Pepper," the 1st trick Switchboard Operator, who was scheduled to work 7 AM at Brunswick. General Yardmaster Lawrence Nelson went to her home and told her of the accident.

When I was relieved at 7 AM, I went home to Frederick, got my camera and my airplane and took aerial photos of the wreck. These snapshots clearly showed the roadbed which followed the Potomac River bottom and showed the long sweeping curve restricting any real warning of the impending collision.

I then drove to the wreck, arriving about noon. The scene was almost unbelievable. The two locomotives were lying slightly on the right side. It was very difficult to distinguish the Jeep from the F-7. The westbound Jeep had completely penetrated the eastbound F-7 cab and was extending through the high tension panel

Empty coal cars were stacked seven high behind the 6500, the 2nd Unit of the westbound, and were stacked four deep on top of the 6500 completely stripping the engine down to the diesel and main generator. The cab of the 6500, from which the engineer was operating the train, was almost unscratched with most of the windows intact although coal cars were on top of it four deep.

I met the crew member I had talked to the night before from Halfway Siding and he provided more information. He had an abrasion on his forehead and was working on the work train crew on the east end called out of Brunswick. The loaded sand cars head out on the Brunswick 96 had sandwiched sideways completely filling the cut and preventing extensive damage to rear unit and serious injury to the deadhead crew.

The bulldozer was on the scene along with an ambulance from the Ryneal Fire Department. Crews were busy with torches dismantling the F-7 and using log chains and the dozer to pull parts away. The high tension panel had to be removed before crews could get to the bodies of the crew.

Engineer Phillips' blue sweater was partially visible. He was pinned in the wreckage from the waist down. The Fireman was also pinned in the wreckage. Both would have to be cut out by torches later on. The Brakeman was not found until much later. His body was under the traction motor of the F-7 Locomotive.

Engineer B F. Phillips was removed at 3:00 P.M. that day while I was still at the scene. I talked to the worker who was cutting the bodies out of the wreck and he was visibly upset. He told me it was the worst job he ever had to do. Even though he knew they could not feel any pain, burning steel that close to a fellow worker was extremely difficult.

I never went back to the scene but it was eventually cleaned up. The lowgrade is still in use today but it was signaled in both directions as a part of the signal upgrading that closed the towers in that area.

Dispatcher Doug Courtney later went to Brunswick and personally visited the families of the three men killed. I do not recall the results of the hearing held or any discipline rendered in this case.

While my 50-year memory of the incident is very vivid, I wish to thank fellow RABO members, Bill Johnston and Walt Vander Veer, for their assistance in this story. Also, I realize that the radio network that we now have would prevent a recurrence of this type of accident.

Written in Blood

By Ray Lichty
April 2004

Bill's story brings to mind my exposure to this fatal accident. When I was learning the road to be a Train Dispatcher in 1957, I convinced the Division Operator, Walter Paull, that it would be beneficial if I traveled the system to see how other parts of the railroad dealt with various operating situations. While doing so, I rode the engine of No. 7 from Washington. As we approached Miller tower, the head-end crew told that they had been on the same No. 7 run the night of the New Year's Eve accident. They told how they had seen the westbound train leaving Cumbo on a reverse on the lowgrade. As they approached Miller that night, they got a big highball from the operator and, as they passed the

"Tower" is a misnomer when applied to XN Tower. The office, with telegraph call letters of "XN", was a small one-story structure in Cuyahoga Falls, Ohio, on the Akron Division mainline, just a few miles east of Akron. It was an interlocking as the operator controlled the signals but the switches were hand-thrown by the operator. Those switches included a set of crossovers, the exit from the eastbound siding and the entrance to the westbound siding. Until the steam engines disappeared in the late 1950s, there was a water penstock between the eastbound siding and the eastbound main for filling the tenders.

The main purpose of XN Tower was to handle trains working at Akron Junction yard and trains going to and from the CT&V Sub Division at BD Tower (an unattended location) at the east end of Akron Junction Yard. This included the passenger trains, #17 and #18, to and from Cleveland. There was a steep grade from BD Tower to XN Tower and the heaviest freight trains used helpers to get up the hill. If the helpers were on the head end of the train, it was XN's job to get them back down the hill to the yard. If a train stalled coming up the hill, the Akron Division could become a mess in very short order.

Barnard photo, B&O Railroad Historical Society collection.

When a Telegraph Operator had orders for a train, the Book of Rules required that the train order board be displayed for the train or trains travelling in that direction. The board was actually a sheet of metal about 1 1/2 feet by 2 feet that was hung outside the telegrapher's office on hooks built into the wooden display board. The metal sheet was painted yellow on one side and red on the other. The operator would hang the metal sheet on the hooks displaying the proper color; yellow for "19 Orders" that could be picked up by a train without stopping or red for "31 Orders" for those trains that needed to stop to pick up their orders.
The display board was equipped with the lights to illuminate the train order board. If a light was not available, a lantern with the appropriate red or yellow colored globe also had to be displayed at night.   *John King photograph.*

tower, they saw Brunswick 96 waiting to cross over. They assumed it was a CSD (Central States Dispatch train routed to the Western Maryland Railroad) man that would branch off at Cherry Run, realizing it could not be a lowgrade train as there was a westbound headed their way. Unfortunately, they were wrong.

As to the train order board matter, the rules said that if you had orders at a tower, you displayed the yellow or red board for trains in the direction for which you had any orders. Trains that were not addressed on any of the orders were delivered a Form A stating that you had no orders. This meant holding the signal until the order board was acknowledged and the train then passed the tower at a slower speed to pick up their orders or stopped in the case of a "31" order.

Prior to the lowgrade accident, it was the practice on the B&O, although not officially blessed, to not display a train order board, yellow or red, for any train for which you didn't have orders.

XN Tower, in Cuyahoga Falls was one of my favorite jobs. That one-floor "tower" had an old ice box fastened into a back window. When we had orders that we didn't need to deliver to some trains, we would put the orders into the ice box, just in case an official stopped by. A similar practice was surely in effect at Miller Tower on the night of the fatal accident.

This all came to a halt after the accident. Some towers, where there was a diverging route, established two order boards. One was designated for the diverging route and it didn't apply to through trains.

At locations where trains could originate, the practice was established of having the operator saying "FANI" (Form A not issued) before the Train Dispatcher would issue an order. FANI meant that no Form As had been issued and the order about to be copied would be delivered to all addressed trains or engines.

It has been said that the Rule Book was "written in blood" meaning that experience gained from accidents resulted in new rules. That clearly was the result in the case of the unfortunate lowgrade accident.

Allen Brougham, Editor of *The Bull Sheet* and a former operator at Miller, helped me recall some of the details associated with this story.

A Flagging Incident

By Gifford Moore
January 2003

Early on, I learned a little something about then flagging rules 100 (A) and 100 (C). The former read: "Flagmen must not be instructed to flag certain trains. They must flag all trains." The latter rule read, in part, "Flagmen must not attempt to inform the engineer why he is flagged until the train has been stopped or

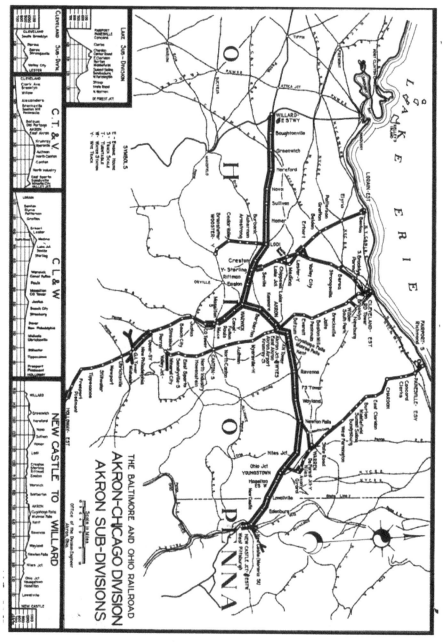

This 1964 employee timetable map for the Akron-Chicago Division showed the Akron Sub-Division double track main line between New Castle and Willard and the single track branch lines. Shown are the Pittsburgh Division going east of New Castle and the lines of the former Wheeling Division joining the main line at Warwick and Sterling and the Chicago Sub-Division connecting at Willard. The division headquarters was in the Metropolitan Building in downtown Akron. Ray Lichty collection.

speed reduced so that instructions can be plainly understood"....
(and)..." A flagman picked up by a train will ride the engine of
that train."

I was working third trick at Nova, Ohio, (VN Tower) on the
Akron Division. The year, as I recall, was 1946; summertime. A
steam powered westbound freight train stopped for water and then
passed the tower headed for Willard at about 1:30 am.

About an hour later, perhaps less, I heard someone coming up
the steps of the tower. As I recall, the door had no lock on it and I
was uneasy about it. A man came in and I said, "Who are you?"
He told me he was the Flagman off the earlier westbound freight
and got left; he had some "choice words" for the engineer. He
asked what the next train was going to be and I told him it looked
like No. 5, the Capitol Limited, the premier passenger train. He
replied, "That was fine. I'll flag that." I told the dispatcher on the
phone (it was Morse only on the dispatcher's wire when I worked
Nova once during the war but now the dispatcher was on phone)
and he replied something to the effect that, "If you have to, I
guess you have to!!" The "DI" was L. M. Eberhard (Ebby) who
was a good train dispatcher but rather grumpy and was definitely
not pleased about the situation.

So as the Flagman requested, I held the block on No. 5 until he
stopped. The Flagman had busted a fusee at the home signal just
to play it safe. As soon as No. 5 stopped, I gave him the block and
away they went. Presumably, the Flagman got back with "his
train" at Willard which, by this time, was yarded and the rest of
the crew off duty.

I thought about it later. The rules don't seem to be clear about
that: Should he have ridden No. 5 to Chicago looking for the
markers of "his train"? I also thought that was pretty neat that the
Flagman and I had that much "control" over No. 5 for a short
period of time....without retribution.

A "Heart in your Mouth" Moment
By Gifford Moore
October 2008

I recently saw in the news the report of a terrible railroad
accident on the West Coast. It was a head-on collision between a

Failes Spur was a flyspeck operating point in northeastern Trumbull County, Ohio, where once helper engines awaited westbound trains to aid them up the twisting grades through adjacent Geauga County on their way to Lake Erie at Painesville. Here in 1950, a misaligned switch caused a fatal headon collision when an eastbound freight entered the siding already occupied by a hapless helper engine. This was the scene, shown here with the eastbound local freight from Painesville (safely) passing a waiting EM-1-class helper at the right.

H. H. Harwood, Jr., photo, 1956.

passenger train and a freight train on a stretch of single track. Many people were killed and injured. The cause will be determined, perhaps months from now, but I think one can assume that a head-on collision in railroad operations can safely be attributed to man-failure.

The year was about 1950 and I was working as a Train Dispatcher on the Baltimore and Ohio Railroad's single-track Lake Branch on the Akron Division. This was a stretch of railroad extending from the Youngstown, Ohio, area to Fairport Harbor, Ohio, on Lake Erie. Operations were governed solely by railroad timetable and train orders issued by the train dispatcher.

I was working third trick (11 pm to 7 am). Soon after I came to work, I issued a train order for a single helper engine to "run extra (eastbound) Painesville to Failes Spur", located near West Farmington, Ohio, 35 miles south of Painesville, and other appropriate orders. The helper engine, headed west, ran backing up eastbound to Failes Spur. At that point, the helper would enter a short track, not connected on the east end and just big enough for one large steam locomotive and stay there until the westbound train, which it would help up a long grade starting at Failes Spur, had passed by. The helper was manned by an Engineer, Fireman and a Brakeman who would throw switches and serve as a Flagman as necessary.

Later, I issued the appropriate orders for a scheduled freight train, No. 90, to operate in two sections, 1st and 2nd 90, from Painesville to Ohio Junction. 1st No. 90 had operated earlier the evening before and had cleared the railroad. About 2:30 am, the Brakeman on the helper engine called in on the telephone at Failes Spur to report "in the clear"; meaning clear of the main track. In the meantime, 2nd No. 90 had left Painesville and was moving east.

Then, suddenly at about 4 am, a loud voice came on the telephone from Failes Spur, "We hit the helper... we hit the helper!" I asked, "Who is this?" and the answer came back, "This is Engineer Lockwood on 2nd No. 90. We hit the helper head on! Engineer Mills on the helper is badly hurt, maybe dead! The helper is derailed along with some cars! Send help right away!"

My heart was in my mouth. Then it sank to the bottom of my stomach! Had I done something wrong? Were the train orders ok? Had I overlooked something?

After some further conversation with Engineer Lockwood and later with a railroad officer who gave me more information, it was obvious it was a case of an open switch. The heavy freight train, 2nd No. 90, moving at a good clip, had simply run in the open switch into the spur track and collided head on with the helper.

A few weeks later, the government investigation by the Interstate Commerce Commission (ICC) confirmed that the main track switch was not closed by the helper's brakeman, who was hurt in the accident. The helper's engineer, who was ultimately responsible, was dead—crushed to death while getting off the helper engine.

A very unfortunate man-failure incident which I remember so well, ranking at least in second place on the "heart in your mouth" scale.

Tit-for-Tat

By Ray Lichty
January 1996

In the late 50s, I was a telegrapher at "RN" Tower in Ravenna, Ohio. There was a PRR connection at that interlocking where PRR trains had access to the joint trackage, along with NYC, over the B&O line to Niles Jct., Ohio. PRR ran many ore trains from Cleveland to the Youngstown steel mills. The run from Cleveland was just long enough that the axel journal bearings warmed and sometimes got hot while on the B&O joint trackage.

To avoid tying up this busy line with a train setting off a hot box, a car with an excessively hot journal bearing, the Chief Dispatcher's office in Akron, probably under directions from Superintendent H. I. Walton, issued instructions that PRR ore trains must stop on PRR tracks at Ravenna, inspect their train and proceed only when they advised everything was OK.

One night, soon after these instructions were issued, the PRR Cleveland Movement Office called me at Ravenna to complain about the arrangement. On their behalf, I called Akron and appealed to Chief Dispatcher Jack Humbert. He had no sympathy for them and told me, in no uncertain terms, that he would not take down the instructions. I passed the bad news on to Cleveland. (My wife's uncle was a dispatcher in that office.)

About an hour later, the operator at Akron Jct., the tower where B&O entered PRR trackage through Akron to Warwick, announced the arrival of Number 5, the Capitol Limited. The B&O dispatcher, expecting an "OS" (telegrapher's code for 'on sheet') by the tower asked, "Arrived?" The operator said, "Arrived ! And as soon as the crew inspects the train and tells us all is well, it can proceed."

The Ravenna ore train instructions were taken down before #25 got to Akron Jct!

RN Tower at Ravenna, Ohio, is a typical armstrong interlocking plant. The term "armstrong" comes from the manual force required of the Operator to move the levers that controlled the switches. Switches were moved by means of a series of rods and mechanisms connecting the levers on the second floor of the tower to the switches on the tracks.

Ravenna was an important location where PRR and NYC trains entered or left the B&O line on trackage rights between Ravenna and Niles Jct., 23 miles to the east. The Operators, who worked in three shifts, 24/7, routed the trains' movements as directed by the Train Dispatcher at Akron. Instructions were received over telephone or telegraph lines. The train order board was outside the window in front of the Operator, facing the east-west direction of train movements on the tracks.

H. H. Harwood, Jr., photo, 1956.

Baltimore & Ohio New York Merchandise Piers' Operations

By Bob Patterson
January 2005

In 1961, the Baltimore & Ohio Railroad was on the verge of bankruptcy. B&O lost $31,300,000 — a staggering amount by 1961 standards. Obviously, it was necessary to rein in excessive costs in all areas of operations. With Jervis Langdon as President, department heads were charged to immediately investigate all areas under their jurisdiction to seek out cost reductions. One area, under the jurisdiction of Mr. Walter L. Pfarr, Manager-Station Operations, was our New York piers, which operated 24 hours/day, 7 days a week.

B&O had a car float operation on the Hudson River from Staten Island to Piers 20, 21, 22, 23, 45, 52, 63 and 66, plus our West 26th Street land operation, all on Manhattan, to support various freight forwarder operators. Carfloats consisted of a center platform with rail tracks on each side holding twelve 40 ft rail cars. Tugboats were used to push carfloats across the Hudson and spot them at the above named piers. A special carfloat with multiple tracks was used for the Pier 66 operation and a trackmobile would pull cars from the carfloat across 12th Avenue and spot the cars at the West 26th Street facilities.

Merchandise from the New York City garment industries was delivered to the freight forwarders, companies that consolidated LCL (less than carload) shipments into carload quantities, at West 26th Street as well as the other piers, as noted previously.

B&O employees (railroad clerks) loaded the merchandise into the designated rail cars. The pier operations were somewhat unique as the merchandise was accepted at the platform, loaded onto 4-wheel trucks and pulled by a towmotor onto the carfloat where the employees transferred the goods to the designated rail cars destined to various locations (Baltimore, Chicago, Detroit, Louisville, St. Louis, Washington, DC, etc). In the early evening, the carfloats were pulled from the piers to Staten Island, where the cars were classified and moved in special merchandise trains

Like most railroads serving New York City, the B&O's trains ended their runs on the west side of the harbor at Jersey City and Staten Island. In order to reach the multiplicity of freight terminals, steamship piers, and railroad interchanges in Manhattan, Brooklyn, Queens, and the Bronx, freight cars were floated across the water on barges equipped with tracks, called "carfloats." Often, a tug would jockey two carfloats at a time, lashed together, as seen in this scene on the East River approaching the Brooklyn Bridge. Not surprisingly, performing this work in a crowded harbor in all kinds of weather required a high degree of very specialized skills on the part of the tugboat crews -- now virtually a lost art in railroading.

H. H. Harwood, Jr., photo, 1967.

Although B&O could not directly serve Manhattan by rail, it nonetheless maintained a compact freight terminal there next to the waterfront at West 26th St., reached by cars ferried across the Hudson River on carfloats. At West 26th Street, the cars were rolled on and off the carfloats at this transfer pier, or "float bridge," designed to adjust to the ever-varying levels of the river. In this scene the Manhattan-based diesel switcher is reaching onto a carfloat to pull cars off and haul them across 12th Avenue to the yard.   *H. H. Harwood, Jr., photo, 1955.*

via Central Railroad of New Jersey (CNJ), Reading (RDG) and Baltimore & Ohio (B&O) to their billed destinations.

The cost for loading merchandise was $4.09 per net ton and an additional unloading charge of $4.09 per net ton billed to the various freight forwarders. It was concluded that we were losing quite a bit of money on the overall operation; however, we needed to know "how much".

Mr. Pfarr decided to conduct a full investigation and appointed me to head the study team. Included in the study team were Joe Camas, Bill Gross and Denny Kirkwood. We would alternate working 13 days straight with weekends off, from the latter part of 1962 through June, 1963. Pilferage of merchandise was out of control, based on our observations and the complaints received from destination unloading points. Destination customers were advising that cartons containing valuable garments were opened and items missing, etc. For example, we would stop and engage a towmotor operator, lift up the seat and find a number of Chanel #5 perfume bottles; however, he would merely say, "I just drives — don't know how they got there." Or, hundreds of cases of AC Spark Plugs disappeared from the storage area and obviously this had to involve railroad employees and freight forwarder truck drivers.

Based on all of the information we collected, as well as the report of our Freight Claim Department as to the number of freight forwarder claims, we determined that our cost of operation was quadruple the $4.09 per net ton that we were charging. A full report was made to Mr. Langdon's staff and it was decided that we would bring in the management firm Booz, Allen & Hamilton to investigate and prepare a formal report to B&O management for further action. I was assigned to work with Pete Yocum of Booz, Allen & Hamilton for an on-the-ground survey of the New York operation. Their final report to senior management was that our overall cost of the operation was approximately $25.00 per net ton!

As the result of these findings, Charlie Bertrand, Clarence Jackman, Walter Pfarr, Manager Station & Warehouse Operations, and I met with the freight forwarders' presidents and presented the results. We told them we would cancel the tariffs and, if they wanted to continue operations, they would be responsible to lease the piers and furnish their own labor.

This was accomplished, I believe, in May, 1963. At that time, the tariffs were canceled and we terminated the employment of 850 railroad clerks. The freight forwarders not only hired many of the clerks but also immediately reduced the hours of operation, closed during the lunch period, etc., as well as implementing many of the cost savings that they refused to accept previously.

Mission accomplished!
Accuracy! Accuracy! Accuracy!
By Van Vander Veer
January 1996

In 1972 as Superintendent of Transportation, I felt a need to improve the timely input of the agency data on car movements in order to have Chessie System enjoy better cash flow from customer car movements, improved per diem information on foreign cars and faster turnaround of Chessie equipment. With the approval of Dick Rayburn, to whom I reported, we arranged for a one-day meeting at Baltimore in the Operations Conference Room to review these subjects with the major agency officers, data input department personnel, car service department officers and other key transportation officers.

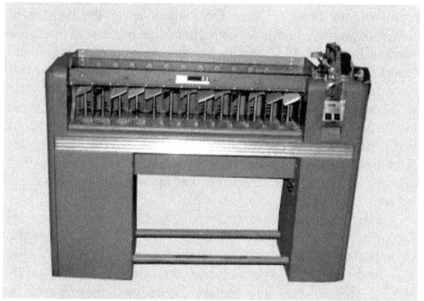

An IBM card sorter of the type used by the B&O.

We spent the entire day going over the details of the forms and input equipment, discussing various problems and how we could improve the input data to avoid errors, have more timely input and improve our contacts with the customers. Mr. "Buck" Weaver, Assistant Vice President Operations, while not invited to the meeting, felt he should sit in on this important discussion and offer his comments to the group. Thus, near the close of the meeting, at approximately 4:30 PM, I noticed that Buck had not said one word during the meeting and I called upon him for a few final remarks.

Buck's inspiring words to the group were, "Now I want you gentlemen to go back to your agencies and make sure WE CROSS OUR I's AND DOT OUR T's!!!"

Memories of the Curtis Bay Coal & Ore Piers
By Van Vander Veer
January 1998

I was appointed to the position of Superintendent of the Curtis Bay Coal and Ore Piers in Baltimore upon the death of Buddy Day, in 1958. At that time, during the cold war with Russia, the US government was stockpiling essential defense ore at the Curtis Bay Ordnance Depot. As the ore arrived by vessel, we loaded it into gondola cars and moved it by rail to the storage area. This was a great idea except all the gondola cars of the B&O were being tied up in this service and causing serious problems with other customers. Ted Klauenberg, Assistant to General Manager, who was actually my boss (although, technically, I was supposed to report to Baltimore Division Superintendent, Bill Murphey) suggested we use trucks to transport the ore. A great idea and we got Joe Hock, owner of the trucking outfit J. J. Hock Company, to supply about 35 trucks for hauling the ore by highway to the storage area.

However, we did develop a few problems, initially, such as dropping 25 tons of ore on the cab of the truck, instead of in the truck storage body. The driver was a little upset! Then, as we worked around the clock unloading the vessel, the citizens of Curtis Bay were upset about the Mack trucks driving through the streets during the night, shifting gears and making quite a bit of noise. At first, we told the local police that this was government ore and we had to unload it as quickly as possible. However, on the third vessel and future vessels, "Washington" told us it was OK to stop trucking between the hours of 11:00 PM and 7:00 AM; thus, the citizens of Curtis Bay got some sleep.

When the steel workers went on strike in 1960, Bethlehem

Top photo: B&O's ore-unloading facility at Curtis Bay in Baltimore includes a traveling crane that brings the ore out of ship holds and transfers it to awaiting railroad hopper cars or trucks for transferring to ground storage pads.
The system is shown here at rest   *W. D. Edson photo, 1953.*

Bottom photo: The ore machine is working an ocean going bulk carrier moving the ore from the ship's hold to the waiting railroad hopper cars.   *H. H. Harwood, Jr., photo, 1979.*

Steel had contracts for iron ore from South America and no place to store it because of the strike. We agreed to put the ore on ground storage at Curtis Bay, but it had to be stored on a black-top surface (bituminous concrete) and we had Joe Hock's company do the work. This all happened as the vessel was coming up the Chesapeake Bay and Joe and I, and our respective people, found ourselves constructing the ground storage pads as the trucks were dumping the ore. The pads were finished minutes before the trucks arrived. It was a wild night or two. I remember calling Norm Murphy in the Real Estate Department and asking him to have an outdoor advertising sign removed from a storage area and he asked, "What day do you wish the sign removed?" I said, "Today; in the next two hours." Norm, as usual, came through and by midnight, we had several thousand tons of ore at the sign location.

During this period, the Environmental Protection Agency was just starting to enforce the new Federal laws. One rainy day, an agent came to the pier and told me to stop the operation because the ore being carried by the truck tires was staying on the streets at the storage areas and the nearby locations. The runoff of rain water from the storage areas was a problem. I told him in no way was I stopping the operation and I suggested he leave our property. His boss called me later that day and said the existing regulations did not cover this type of operation and I could continue the unloading. However, they changed the law shortly thereafter to cover this type of so-called environmental concern. Credit must be given to Walt Webster, Senior Engineer, who arranged for the rain water run-off so we wouldn't have any more problems.

Another favorite memory is that of U.S. Steel requesting ground storage of ore during the same steel workers' strike. Bill Zoller of US Steel called and asked for ground storage with the usual request for the ore to be put on a paved surface. I inquired through the ranks to find out if the B&O was agreeable and John Collinson, Engineer Maintenance of Way, said OK but the railroad had no money for paving the pads. To make a long story short, I spent one entire morning negotiating with U.S. Steel and Joe Hock and we arranged a solution. Joe Hock's Company would build the paved storage areas and U.S. Steel would pay back the cost of the pads plus Joe Hock's revenue on a basis of additional cents per ton as the ore was stored and finally shipped to the U.S. mills. Thus, the B&O received ground storage income without paying for pad costs.

Footnote; I was happy to receive a call from Jim Caywood, Assistant Chief Engineer, appointing me Division Engineer on the Wheeling Division a few weeks later.

Harry Tales

By Frank Dewey
October 2008

Being in railroad management requires a unique ability to be able to turn a bad situation into, at least, a workable situation. While I have met numerous such officials in my 36-year railroad career, one individual comes to mind because of the number of stories I heard about him that built a legend on the west end of the old B&O. That man was H. K. (Harry) Picklesimmer, the Trainmaster at Garrett, Indiana in the early 70s.

Harry had to run a long piece of very important railroad for the B&O – from Pine Junction, Indiana, just east of Chicago, to J Tower, Ohio, at the west end of the Willard, Ohio, yards. That was 249 miles of railroad with only the help of an Assistant Trainmaster at Defiance, Ohio, and sometimes a Road Foreman of Engines stationed at Garrett.

One story about Harry that I heard, and Harry admitted to me as true, concerned the closing of the cleaning track at Garrett. The track was on the southwest corner of the yard. This was when the railroads carried a wide variety of things in box cars, gondolas, hopper cars and covered hoppers. So the clean-out tracks were pretty much a dumping ground for materials ranging from rusting metals to rotting food stuffs. Thus, it is not surprising they attracted rodents along with other beasts and smelled much like a city dump.

Garrett, being a railroad town, normally did not have problems with the city fathers as they often worked for the railroad, were part of a railroad family or supplied services to the railroad. However, a new ambitious city official decided that he wanted to take on the railroad to clean up the area around the clean-out

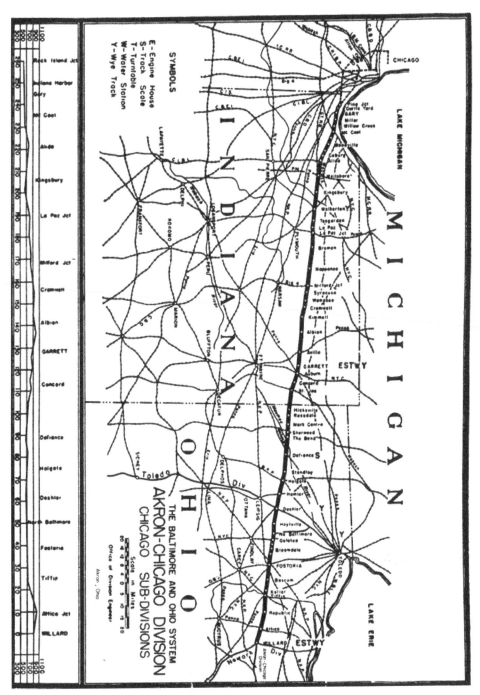

Akron-Chicago Division Chicago Sub-Division April 26, 1964, employee timetable map.   *Ray Lichty collection.*

track. He threatened Harry with closing down the track if the railroad did not clean it up.

Now this was an opportunity for which Harry had been waiting. Clean-out tracks tied up at least one track in the yard, used up engine time and tied up car days. They were just expensive. All these are things that Harry did not want.

So, Harry posted notice to the railroad employees on the clean-out track that their jobs were being abolished and closed the track down. His public relations coup came when the local Garrett newspaper came out with the headline--"Local City Official Forces Railroad to Lay Off Employees". Now that is the creative use of the public media and I doubt if that public official had a long career in Garrett politics.

Another story about Harry concerns how he was able to keep his 60 mile-per-hour railroad relatively free of slow orders. During much of Harry's time as a B&O official, the railroad was very tight on cash, to say the least. That meant ties and other track materials were hard to come by, especially on a stretch of railroad at the western edge of the system, far from the thoughts of those in Baltimore. Strangely enough, any car of ties that came by Garrett got set out of passing freight trains to be shopped for "repairs" and the top layer of ties was removed prior to the car being released by the Car Department. This was also true for cars of spikes, anchors, etc., that might have been passing through Garrett. Harry just placed orders with the "storerooms on wheels".

The railroad rule book stated, "Citizen Band (CB) radios will not be used for railroad operations". This was to comply with the FCC regulations assigning specific frequencies to the railroads. However, the B&O, even though it was one of the pioneers in the use of railroad radios, did not furnish "walkie talkies" to the train crews. Harry knew that radios would speed up moves, so he required his crews to furnish and use their own CB radios. He even had a base station in the yard office at Garrett and, likewise, at several of the towers and depots along his territory. The storekeeper even furnished batteries to use in the crews CBs. Harry knew he could not enforce his requirement but all, except one crew, did have and used portable CB radios. That one crew Harry referred to as the "Bolsheviks" and did everything he could to make their lives miserable. If there were a chance that their pool would catch an intermodal train or a local, they were sure to get the local. I do not think that Harry ever won that particular battle.

Memories of the Monongah Division; 1963
By Van Vander Veer
April 2000

During the coal miners' holiday each summer, it was the practice to send every foreign (non-B&O) hopper car back to the parent railroad, to avoid Per Diem charges (daily car rental). In those days, the B&O had a reputation, and rightly so, for not returning foreign hopper cars to the owners but sending them to the coal fields for coal loading. In 1963, John Edwards, General Manager-Baltimore, instructed me, as superintendent, to ground-inspect every siding, every yard and all coal mines and to send all foreign cars home.

Thus, all division officers and I spent several days at the start of the coal miners' holiday inspecting the division to see that only B&O hoppers were on the property. After being successful (in my opinion), I advised John that we had accomplished our assignment.

The next problem was the storage of B&O hoppers as they flowed back to the division waiting for the mines to reopen. This was a serious problem for the Monongah Division but we always found the ability to handle the returning cars.

One morning, sitting in my office at Grafton, I received a call from Trainmaster Dick Shindler that he had a problem on the Strouds Creek and Muddlety (SC&M) Railroad, a B&O subsidiary. He had put too many cars on a dead-end siding and had shoved several cars off the end of the track into a swamp. That certainly was upsetting news but obviously a human error that one could live with at this time.

Upon asking Dick for the car initials and numbers, he proceeded to advise me the cars were NYC, PRR, P&LE., etc. They say to this day that the explosion in the superintendent's office was one of the highlights of the 1963 year in Grafton. I then had to call John and advise him of the problem. Needless to

A 1975 view of downtown Grafton, West Virginia, is dominated by two buildings, whether seen from the street, one story above the tracks, or the railroad tracks as shown here. The Division Offices and passenger station, built in 1911, are on the left and the Willard Hotel, finished a year later, is on the right. At one time 33 passenger trains used the B&O station. Grafton was a crew change point so all passenger trains stopper there. The division office remained in the station building well into the modern day CSX era.

Baltimore & Ohio Railroad Historical Society collection.

say, John was also somewhat upset about this news.

In the best interests of the Monongah Division, we transferred Dick to Indianapolis where we felt he had a better opportunity to avoid problems.

One other comment on the SC&M Railroad: When I first went to Grafton as Superintendent, we had a Trainmaster on the SC&M Railroad who stated that when the B&O took over the SC&M it was understood he would never have to work on the B&O. This did not set too well with me so I told him he had to perform other duties on the division as one train a day on a 23-mile railroad was not a full-time job.

In Baltimore the following day for a staff meeting, Ray Pomeroy called and said this gentleman was going to resign unless he went back to being just a trainmaster on the SC&M. I told Ray to accept his resignation immediately. That was the last contact I ever had with the ex-trainmaster of the SC&M.

Talking about Ray Pomeroy, I wish to state Ray was one outstanding railroad operating officer and it was always a pleasure to be associated with Ray and his lovely wife, Betty.

One other story is that we had a coal train derailment on the Cowen Sub-Division of about 76 cars of coal and two locomotives. It was caused by a broken rail on a downhill grade. I always felt I had set the record for total cars derailed. Then, when Ray was Superintendent of the Monongah Division, he advised me he had broken the record with another coal train derailment. In those days, the B&O maintenance was very much handicapped by lack of maintenance money. In fact, we even took the guard rail off several bridges to use as rail on the main line in the coal fields.

Some Things Just Don't Make Sense
By Fred Yocum
July 2010

One of my assignments while in Schedules and Classifications in the Operating Department was to set up and monitor the performance of special trains carrying spent poisonous gas. This was gas that had been produced for use during World War II; had never been used; and was to be disposed of by burying it in the Atlantic Ocean.

There was a particular incident which occurred in May (year?) that I still remember. The government had been very sensitive as to the route of these special trains because it wanted to avoid population centers. We received some of them through an obscure interchange at Beardstown, Illinois, on the end of one of our branch lines. A demand had been made that we run the trains over the Patterson Creek Cutoff in order to avoid going through the city of Cumberland, Maryland. At that time, the Patterson Creek Cutoff was still in place but was out of service, so using it for these trains required some work and expense to put the line back in service.

I received a call lining up a train to come to us at Beardstown. While the line it would initially travel on us was a branch line, the trains would go through Indianapolis, Indiana. Based on the time that we were to get the train at Beardstown, I figured that the train would go by the Indianapolis Speedway at about noon on the Sunday before Memorial Day, the day of the running of the Indianapolis 500 auto race!

I played my cards slowly in our phone conversation. I had the

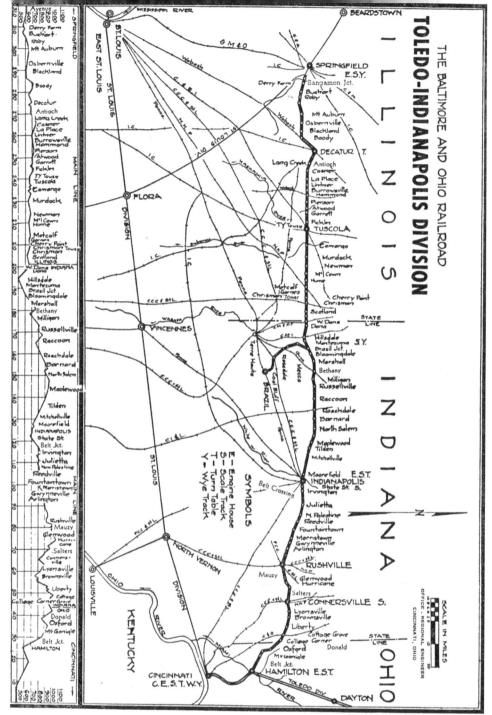

Toledo-Indianapolis Division Indianapolis Sub Division employee timetable map showing the main line from Hamilton, Ohio, to Springfield, Illinois.

Ray Lichty collection.

38

official repeat his demand that we use the Patterson Creek Cutoff in order to avoid the concentrated population center of Cumberland and then calmly pointed out that his proposed schedule would have the train go by the Indianapolis Speedway at a time when the greatest concentration of humanity anywhere in America would be present. He hastily got off the phone and subsequently rescheduled the train.

Telephone Calls

By Van Vander Veer
October 2010

During my employment with B&O-Chessie-CSX, one of the things that I remember as a field officer was receiving telephone calls when there was a major derailment, or other problem such as a road crossing accident blocking the main line and causing delays to the train operations. This required an immediate response and often a fast trip to the location of the accident. It was not too bad receiving calls in the daytime but a night call was not pleasant. When one went to the accident location, you never knew how many hours you would be there—a few hours or maybe over 24. There was also the problem of trying to keep headquarters advised by telephone of the time train

The B&O Central Building telephone switchboard.

operations could resume, cause of the accident, etc. In my time, we did not have the excellent communication systems that now exist for field operating officers and finding a telephone at times was a problem. I must say that I appreciate and applaud all field officers, past and present, who have handled field accidents and quickly restored train operations.

Some Interesting Comments on Telephones:

Now that I have retired from CSX and am enjoying life in Williamsburg, Virginia, I occasionally mention to my friends my experiences as Superintendent of the Monongah Division of the Baltimore and Ohio Railroad. As information, I was assigned twice to the Monongah Division at Grafton, West Virginia, first as Assistant Division Engineer and later as Superintendent. Jean and I enjoyed our time in Grafton and consider it one of the nicest towns we have lived in and a highlight of our railroad career.

One story I like to tell is the time when I was in Fairmont Yard reviewing the operations and realized I would not be able to get home to Grafton until late in the evening. At that time, the telephone system was not as modernized as it is today and you had to ask the operators to handle your telephone calls. Grafton was one of the last communities to modernize to electronic communications. Upon reaching the operator, she proceeded to inform me that there had been a fire in my home but my family was safe and the fire was not serious. She went into great detail about the fire and how the Grafton Fire Department handled the situation. The fire was started by my second oldest son playing with matches in the bedroom on the second floor while my wife was in the living room playing bridge with neighbors. My son informed his mother that the bed was on fire and a call went at once to the Fire Department who arrived quickly and threw the burning mattress out the window. Thus, this was not a very serious fire. When the operator finally connected me to Jean, I knew all about the situation and advised her, before she could mention it to me, that I knew the details of the fire. (A good example of living in a small town.)

Another story about telephone calls: I decided one night to visit the night train order stations on the Cowen Sub-Division from Berkeley Run Jct. to WN Tower (location), such as Buckhannon, Burnsville Jct. and WN Tower. The Chief

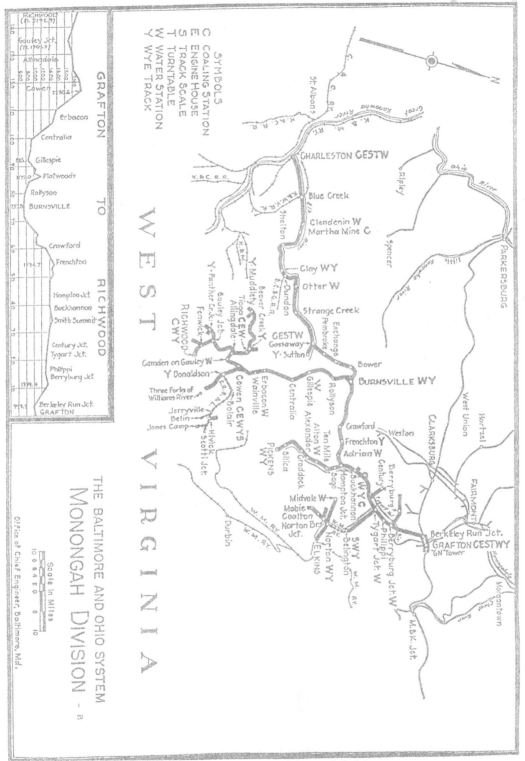

Monongah Division employee timetable coal fields map.
Baltimore & Ohio Railroad Historical Society collection.

Dispatcher at Grafton, Sid McKinley, was on duty on the Third Trick and I remember that he was wondering what I was doing out in the night hours. In my opinion, it was just a normal inspection but I did feel the third trick train order station operators should meet the superintendent and understand that they were an important part of the division team. At each open telegraph office, the operator was surprised to see me but we always had a pleasant conversation. I checked into the dispatcher's office at Grafton from each open telegraph office to learn about the division's night operation and how many coal trains we were dispatching to the Cumberland Division. It was an interesting night and Sid always commented on it when we met at later times.

Another interesting comment on telephone calls was trying to call my home in Grafton when I was not in West Virginia. For example, at night after a staff meeting in Baltimore, I would call my wife and ask for the number 43 (at that time my home telephone number in Grafton). The Baltimore operator would always say I had to give her the seven digit number, area code and house number, which I could not do. After the first attempt and failure, I learned to ask the Baltimore Operator to call Operator # (I forget the number) at Pittsburgh and have her handle the call to my home in Grafton. Thus, the problem was solved. I assume Bill Shaw and Ray Pomeroy may have had the same problem when they were Superintendent of the Monongah Division.

A major concern I faced as Superintendent of the Monongah Division was the interruption of staff meetings by the staff officers from Baltimore. In order to save money, I held the division staff meetings in the former hotel that was part of the Division headquarters. I felt that some staff officers believed they knew more about the operation of the division than I did. At the staff meetings in the Grafton Hotel meeting room, I often received telephone calls and the caller would tell my Chief Clerk that he (the caller) must speak to me at once. The Chief Clerk would explain to the caller that I was conducting a staff meeting but the caller cared less for this comment. This, of course, disrupted the staff meeting and was counter-productive to the desires of the superintendent. To avoid this problem, future staff meetings that I conducted were held off the property at a local restaurant.

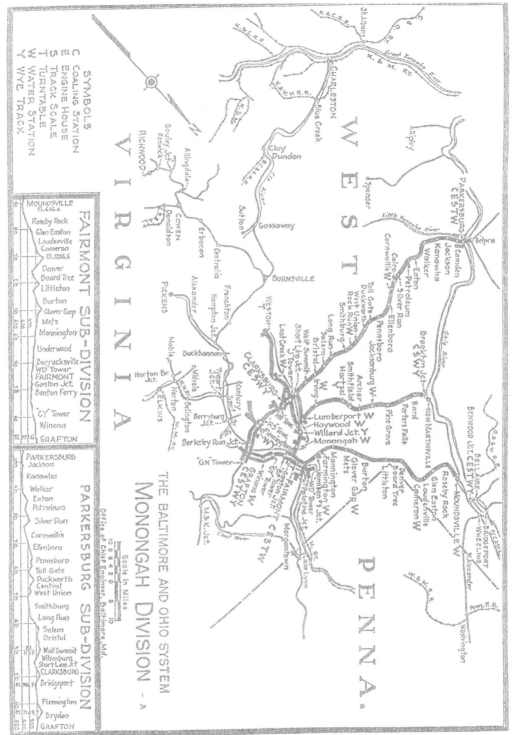

A Monongah Division employee timetable map showing the main line from Parkersburg to Grafton, West Virginia.
The Baltimore & Ohio Railroad Historical Society collection.

43

Telephone calls in this situation were counterproductive to achieving improvements in division operations. In my opinion, the headquarters staff was not in daily touch with field operations. I know this may not be agreed to by some of my friends who were staff officers but that is my opinion.

Another Telephone Problem in Michigan:

Later in my career, I was promoted to Division Manager of the Michigan Division at Detroit, Michigan; and in the first few years, I had another telephone problem. At that time, our trains were being equipped with radios for communication with the Division Dispatchers' offices at Grand Rapids and Saginaw and often, while in transit on the highway, some miles from the railroad, to and from my office, I would pick up a radio call that was relayed to me by a train crew to call the Dispatcher at Grand Rapids or Saginaw as the dispatcher had a message for me. I would thank the train crew and, if able, (my company car radio was very limited if not near the railroad) proceeded to try and find a telephone, such as at a highway rest stop or a fast food location, where I could call the Dispatcher. However, in the winter, with lots of snow and below freezing temperatures, this was at times a problem. This problem was finally solved when my company car radio was replaced with a new radio that allowed me to call directly to the Dispatchers' offices or any other location, such as my home, from any location.

I remember one time I was in the Hi-rail car with General Manager Maurice Good on the Manistee Subdivision of the Michigan Division in the winter, with deep snow on the ground and temperatures below freezing. We received a radio call that Vice President Dick Rayburn wanted to talk to Maurice Good. Our next problem was to find a telephone that was not in the open but in a building with heat, so the two gentlemen could have a private conversation. Obviously, it was not a good move to have your General Manager talk on an outdoor telephone. After some searching, we did find an indoors telephone that avoided Maurice having to talk to Cleveland headquarters out in the low temperature or standing in the snow.

In conclusion, communication today is far superior to my field days on the railroad but my predecessors had many more communication problems then I had and they deserve credit for running an efficient railroad.

Chapter 3   It Happened in the Terminal

A West Virginia Trio

By James E. Sell
October 1995

By far, the time spent railroading is serious, but occasionally there are humorous moments. Three that I remember are one at the beginning of my railroad career and two about midway of my railroading days.

During the summer of 1937, I was yard-checking in the High Yard at Parkersburg, West Virginia, on the 12 Midnight to 8:00 AM shift. As I recall, many things went wrong that night and the Night General Yardmaster was beside himself. (This particular gentleman was an artist in the use of profanity - never during my three-year Navy stint did I hear profanity that in any way approached his talented use of profane words I had never heard before and some I have not heard since!) Anyway, he was in rare form that night. The crew in the West Yard had shoved a car over the derail on #5 track and it sideswiped #6 track. Number 4, the Diplomat, had parted on the East Main track because of a defective anti-coupler device, and the first 97 had derailed a car in the extension arriving Parkersburg's West Yard. I stayed out of the General Yardmaster's way as much as I could. However, I had to deliver the 97's bills to the office for listing. As I was coming by the local stock yards, next door to the yard office, with 97's bills, I noticed there was something unusual going on there. As I trotted by the stock yards, I hollered to one of the employees, "What's going on?" He yelled back, "Oh some stock busted loose." As I was listing the 97 on a switch list, a brakeman ran in the office and said, "A car of coal is derailed on the coal tipple!" The General Yardmaster had just started his litany of profanity when in walked a Billy Goat and let go with a long and loud bleat. The General Yardmaster's eyes got big, his face turned ashen - I thought he was going to cry - he sat down, put his head in his hands and kept repeating the Lord's name over....and over....and over and over.

In 1956, I was Assistant Trainmaster at Cowen. If you have never been to Cowen, it is difficult to explain. Five hundred people, mostly coal miners, a company store, one traffic light and when they decided on the West Virginia Motto - "Mountaineers are Free" they certainly had the folks of Cowen in mind. Fred was a Flagman on an assigned turn. He showed up for his turn each day. No one really knew where he lived, except it was a dirt road somewhere "off the straight". And like most local crews, he had no telephone. One summer afternoon, it was decided an extra turn was needed and Fred stood to be the Conductor. So, he had to be called. There was a lot of discussion as to how to call Fred. Finally, the trainman who would be the flagman on the extra turn arrived and said "I think I know where Fred lives. I will go get him." He had no problem finding Fred's house and when he got there, Fred was sitting out under a large tree drinking mason jars full of home-brew. Of course, Fred offered the trainman a drink and one drink led to another until now the extra turn was short not one man but two. Neither Fred nor his flagman-to-be showed up. Some hours later, the extra turn was cancelled.

In 1959, I was Terminal Trainmaster at Fairmont, West Virginia. One afternoon, a yard turn was doing switching at the shops and the storeroom. The storeroom was part of the shop facility and there were tracks into the roundhouse and the storeroom and many stub-end tracks that went toward the shops on which engines were to be set.

I was at my desk, in the yard office. The phone rang and it was the General Roundhouse Foreman, Arch Vaughn. He said, "Jim, do you have a switch order for the storeroom?" I said, "Yes I do." He said, "Does your switch list say spot car B&O (car number) at Spot 2 in the storeroom?" I said, "Yes it does." He says, "Does it say anything about spotting it thru the roundhouse wall?" I said, "What in the hell are you talking about!" He said, "Your crew forgot to line the switch for the storeroom and instead shoved the car up one of the stub-end tracks, over the end, thru the roundhouse wall and into the shops." It took me very few minutes to race the half-mile from the yard office to the shops; and as I was standing looking at a very large hole in the roundhouse with bricks and glass all over the place and the box car, that was to be spotted at the storeroom, sitting very close to one of the engine pits, Arch sauntered over, tapped me on the shoulder and said, "They missed number 2 spot two tracks." At the time, I did not see the humor in it.

No Excuses Will Be Accepted

By Ed Willis
October 1997

In my early years on the B&O Railroad, I worked in train service. At the time the incident I am about to relate occurred, I was the Yard Foreman on a job at Camden Yard, going to work at 11:55 PM. Our work days included the weekend.

On Sunday night, the most important job we had was to set up the Bozel Meat Company, which was located parallel to the old B&A track at Camden Station.

The set-up of Bozel cars consisted of eight or nine cars, which arrived over the weekend and were supposed to be placed in the order designated by Bozel, no later than 3 AM Monday, without fail!

There was no problem with the 3 AM placement except the Yardmaster always had two or three little jobs to do before we spotted the Bozel cars and, invariably, something would happen to delay placement of their cars.

Mr. Bozel was not a particularly gentle person when his cars were late being placed; and, as a last resort, he complained bitterly to Mr. William Murphey, who, at that time, was Superintendent.

Mr. Murphey was not accustomed to being criticized in the way Mr. Bozel did it. Therefore, Superintendent Murphy made Dave Crawford, who was General Yardmaster at Camden, an offer he couldn't refuse; the Bozel cars would be spotted, on time, without fail!

On the next Sunday night, when I arrived at work, Mr. Crawford, who didn't normally work on Sunday night, met me and informed me that no matter what instructions I received, under no circumstances would I do anything until I set up Bozel, which was fine with me.

Our crew started work and proceeded to the lower end of the yard. Within less than an hour we had assembled the cars in the designated spotting order and proceeded to the Bozel plant. As we were passing the Yard Office, Mr. Crawford, again, gave instructions that if we had any problems we were to call him without fail. Even though we were less than two minutes away from the Bozel plant, he wasn't taking any chances.

On arrival at the Bozel plant, the procedure was to activate the roll-up door by pressing the "Open" button on the electric switch which started the door to roll up on a spool. As the door ascended, it got within a foot of clearing the top of the car and stopped. I again pressed the "Open" button with no results. I then tried to lower the door no results.

I went to the telephone and called Mr. Crawford, informing him I had a problem; and before I could explain what the problem was, his tires were screeching on the driveway. He got out of his car, very aggravated, stating; "I just knew you guys would mess this up!"

I explained to him what the problem was and that there was nothing I could do because the cars would not clear the door. At the top of the door was an electric motor which, when actuated, would wind up the door. Mr. Crawford was shining his flashlight up at the motor and noticed a piece of red rope coming out of the bell housing of the motor. He asked if I knew what the rope was for and I answered that I didn't know.

After finding a ladder, Mr. Crawford went up to investigate. After a careful examination, Mr. Crawford stated, "This rope has something to do with it", and exclaimed, "We got it made now," and pulled the rope quite hard. The door started to wind down but it didn't stop when it reached the bottom. The whole door unwound, like a spool of thread, and came crashing down across the tracks.

The rope was an emergency release to be used in case of fire and electrical failure to release the door, which it most certainly did!

It wasn't a particularly funny situation; but when I saw the look on Mr. Crawford's face, I couldn't control my laughter. Mr. Crawford descended the ladder, walked over to me and stated in a very serious tone, "Mr. Willis, I don't think this is so damn funny," to which I replied, "Mr. Crawford, if I had pulled that rope, I wouldn't think it was so damn funny either."

Needless to say, by the time we got a crane to get the door clear of the tracks, we missed the 3 AM set up time by about five hours.

I would have loved to have been a fly on the wall of the Superintendent's office when Mr. Crawford explained that delay to Mr. Murphey.

Quite a Railroad Trunk

By E. Ray Lichty
October 1995

When I was Assistant Trainmaster at Wilsmere Yard in 1962, the carnival came for its annual summer visit to Delaware. The James E. Strates Shows traveled by rail from their home in Florida. It was a grand time for the families of the area but a big headache for the railroad.

The circus train cars included coaches, box cars and flat cars with wagons. But the biggest problem was the elephants. They had their own car and they had to be spotted somewhere close to water. At Wilsmere, the elephant car was spotted near the engine ready track where a spigot was available for water.

Each night, after the show, the elephant trainer would bring the pachyderms back to the ready track for water and then put them to bed in their private railroad car.

The only problem was that the carnival grounds were at the

Circus trains were their own self-contained communities that traveled from venue to venue, with flat cars carrying wagons and carts, special cars for the animals, sleeping and dining cars for the performers and crews, and even their own cabooses. Here the James E. Strates Shows train is parked for performances somewhere in Minnesota during the 1970s. *Roger Bee photo.*

49

west end of the yard and the ready track was in the middle between the East and West Yards. There was no room to walk along the yard from the west end. To solve this problem, the trainer was instructed to call the Yardmaster on the phone, just two short rings, and he would be given instructions.

On this particular summer night, the trainer rang two shorts and was told, "#19, the second track from the North, is clear. Come through that track and water the elephants."

Shortly thereafter, Number 89 pulled in #3 running track, stopped opposite the ready track and called the Yardmaster. "This is Number 89. Where do you want me to set off?" The Yardmaster replied, "After the elephants come out of #19, you can set off there." After a long pause, the headman on Number 89 repeated, "This is Number 89, where do you want me to set off?" Before the Yardmaster could reply, the Headman said in a loud and excited voice, "Holy cow, there are elephants coming out of #19 track!" Out they came, trunk to tail, until the last one was in the clear. Then, as provided in the Operating Department Book of Rules, after the last elephant was in the clear, Number 89 lined the switches, gave the mandatory two toots on the whistle and set off in #19.

Memories of The Staten Island Rapid Transit Railway -- and of Staten Island

By Jim Sell
April 2001

I especially enjoyed the article Ken Roloson wrote about the Staten Island Rapid Transit Rwy. in the January edition of News & Notes. I worked for the SIRT, for several years, as Yardmaster at both St. George and Arlington Yards. As I remember, St. George Yard was a dead-end yard and served the piers that readied freight for lighterage to ships. There was also a Bay of New York coal dumping tipple and a float operation for cars to be interchanged with the LV, Erie, DL&W and other railroads. I don't remember the other interchanges. Another float operation from St. George Yard was the delivery of perishables to the B&O's 26th Street produce yard in Manhattan.

The one thing that particularly stands out in my mind about St. George Yard is that when the tide was high and the wind was blowing toward the yard and switching crews were working near the seawall, there was a mist that blew in from the ocean and you either had to wear rain gear or get wet.

Arlington Yard, much larger than St. George Yard, was principally a receiving, classification, and dispatching yard for trains to the CNJ and locals doing industrial switching for plants outside Yard Limits on the SIRT.

Arlington Yard had an unusual related condition also: ground fog. At times, the ground fog would cover the ground, the rails and the switches but only come waist high on a person. This made switching conditions very difficult. I can remember seeing the upper half of a switchman and when he bent down to throw a switch, after he located it, he disappeared under the fog.

The most memorable night I worked at Arlington was when Winston Churchill came from Washington, D. C., to New York by special train and laid up overnight on #3 track at Arlington Yard. We were instructed not to move an engine, or car, or make any noise that might disturb the Prime Minister's sleep. So all of us - Yardmaster, Clerk, switching crew, Carmen — spent the night just sitting around telling "Whopper" stories and eating our lunch.

As I remember, the only industry in the Arlington area was Procter and Gamble's Port Ivory Export Plant. It was, oh maybe, a quarter or half a mile from the yard office and from where the special train was laid up. P&G did their own switching for cars delivered and received between P&G and the SIRT on designated tracks. The P&G crew had delivered several cars to the SIRT just before they shut down for the night. Sometime during the night, a large truck (maybe more then one) was backed up to a load of boxed soap powder and emptied the carload into the truck(s). When Arlington Yard again commenced operations, the Yard Clerk checked the car as an empty but later found a waybill for the car. P&G was asked if the car was supposed to be a load or an empty. They confirmed the car was a load destined to Cincinnati. The carload of soap had been hijacked! There was an investigation that included the FBI. Each of us working that night was asked, by an FBI Agent, if we had heard anything at all. None of us did. I don't know if the case was ever solved or not.

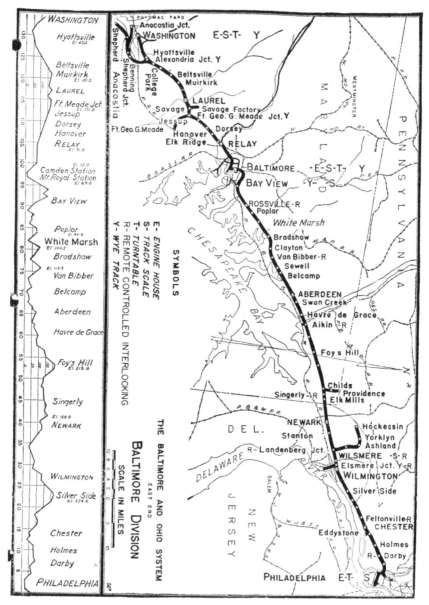

The 1963 Baltimore Division East End employee Timetable map
shows the mainline from Washington to Philadelphia. Shown in
lighter marked lines are the Metropolitan Sub Division going west
from Washington and the Old Main Line, which joins the
Metropolitan Sub Division at Point of Rocks, going off the mainline
at Relay. The Anacostia branch is showing which goes to Anacostia
Jct. where is connects to the PRR enroute to Potomac Yard and
connections to the southern roads. The division headquarters, like
the division's west end, was on the 2nd floor of Camden Station in
Baltimore.

Ray Lichty Collection.

Now, that was the most memorable railroad experience I had on the SIRT. However, the very most memorable happening for me was that I met my wife on Staten Island. During the time we were dating, she was attending Catherine Gibbs Secretarial College on Madison Avenue in Manhattan. I was working at night; and when I was relieved, I would ride the Rapid Transit to the St. George Ferry Terminal, meet her and ride the ferry, with her, to the Battery in Lower Manhattan, take the IRT Subway to Penn Station and walk to Catherine Gibbs College. After she went to school, I reversed the trip – walked to Penn Station, took the subway to the Battery, the ferry to Staten Island and a bus to where I lived. I would go to bed and then get up in time to take the bus to the ferry, the ferry to the Battery, the subway to Penn Station, and walk to the school to meet her and take her home. Then, I would go home until evening when I would take the bus to her house (actually her parents' house) go back to where I lived, and go to work. The next day - do it all over again.

After about a year of this, I said, this routine is killing me. If we would get married, we could be together and I could live a more normal life. She said, "When I graduate, we will get married." We were married, on my birthday, in 1946, 54 years ago. It was a strenuous courtship but well worth it.

I have been back to Staten Island several times to visit with her relatives but I have not ridden a bus, train or ferry since leaving in 1950 to become Night General Yardmaster at Parkersburg, West Virginia. (I had already contributed to them being solvent for about a year.)

The Staten Island Rapid Transit Railway and WW II

By Jim Sell
April 2008

I learned from Bud Fischer that there were going to be some World War II stories in this issue of the newsletter and he suggested that I write something about my time as Yardmaster on The Staten Island Rapid Transit Railway during that period of history. That has been a long time ago and I am sure I have forgotten much of what I experienced. Anyway...........Here goes:

St. George, Staten Island yard. B&O maintained a compact complex of piers, warehouses, and rail-water transfer facilities at St. George, Staten Island, to serve New York Harbor. (The company's Staten Island properties were owned and operated by a subsidiary, the Staten Island Rapid Transit Company.) This rather bleak view of St. George yard from the 1960s foretells the fate of virtually all the once-crowded railroad freight terminals in the harbor, doomed by high operating costs, truck competition, and the switch to containerized export-import traffic.   Tom Griffiths photo.

I was a Yardmaster on the B&O-owned SIRT in early January, 1945. I had very recently been discharged from the U.S. Navy after over three and a half years of military service. The reason I was able to begin as a Yardmaster so soon following my discharge from the Navy was, in part, because I had previous railroad experience dating from January 1, 1937, and more because the SIRT was having a serious manpower problem. They were woefully short of Yardmasters, Yard Clerks and, particularly, Yard Brakemen. Some recently hired brakemen would work until pay day and then they were gone. I think some

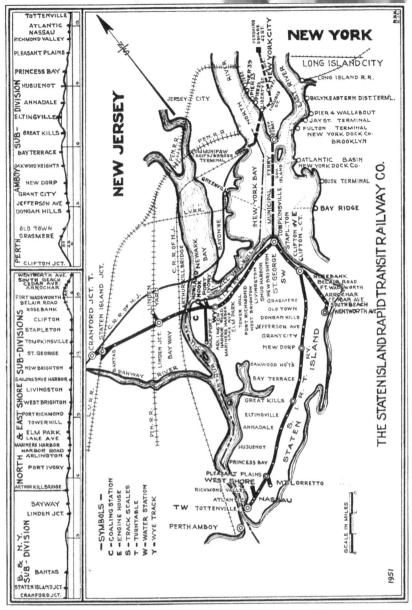

The 1960 employee timetable map of the Staten Island Railway shows in a bold line the routes of the railroad on Staten Island and across the Arthur Kill Bridge into New Jersey. Major foreign (non-B&O) are shown as well as the destinations in Manhattan and Brooklyn that are reached by carferry. The CRR of NJ is shown in a light bold line as this is the route over which the B&O passenger trains operated to Jersey City and also shown is the carferry for the buses to Manhattan carrying passengers to and from the B&O passenger trains. The division headquarters was next to the passenger station for the computer trains and ferries at St George. *Ray Lichty Collection.*

were "boomers" and they knew they could get jobs on other railroads most any place in the country.

I particularly remember one Yard Brakeman. He had been an acrobat clown with the Barnum & Bailey Circus. I remember him because of the way he got on and off box cars. He never used the car ladder. He would shimmy up the brake staff like a monkey; do what he had to do; and, if the box car door were open, he would lean down, grab the door rail and swing out and into the car and tumble out to the ground. He did that very fast. He was constantly being warned by the Assistant Trainmaster about safety but he didn't change his ways. He said: "Most of the guys you have climbing up and down ladders are more prone to be injured than I am. I made my living as an acrobat for years!"

Several trainmen worked double shifts for 30 consecutive days. The Assistant Trainmaster finally told them to take a day off and rest up.

As a Yardmaster, I often worked double shifts and always six days and often seven days a week. I worked at both Arlington and St. George Yards.

Arlington Yard was at the west end of Staten Island near the Arthur Kill River that separates Staten Island and New Jersey. It was principally a receiving, classifying and dispatching yard. There was a second yard at Arlington. It was called the "Hospital Yard". It was built during the war for the purpose of dispatching and receiving hospital trains for the sick and wounded service personnel. The hospital trains were made up of specially-designed cars to accommodate the military patients. For the trains we originated, the sick and wounded were mostly from Staten Island's own Holloran-General Hospital. They were being transferred to other hospitals for further and specialized treatment.

During "Transfer Day", the Hospital Yard was restricted to the sick and wounded, doctors and nurses and other military and medical personnel. When the train was ready to move, someone (doctor or military) so advised the Trainmaster or Assistant Trainmaster who was always on hand to see to it that the train was properly and promptly handled.

A yard engine would couple to the train and pull it out of the Hospital Yard and shove it westward up the main track where the road engine was coupled to it. The yard engine stayed coupled to the train as it had to help the train over the grade to Arthur Kill Bridge; but before the train could be moved, it was necessary to phone the bridge operator to make sure the bridge was lined for the railroad and not the river. The river traffic had priority.

As I remember, Arthur Kill Bridge was a swing bridge. There was, I think, a concrete pier in the middle of the river and the bridge sat on it; and when the bridge was lined for river traffic, it was parallel to the river; and, as necessary, it was revolved around to connect with the railroad. When all was ready, the train departed with the yard engine assisting until the yard engine cut off on the fly.

There was a lot of switching and classifying at Arlington Yard for the Staten Island army base. When the army officer at the base wanted a train to come to the base, he would notify the Superintendent of the SIRT, in writing, as to what time he wanted the train; what cars were to make the train; and how the train was to line up. Trains were made up, in order, by car number. The bills of lading simply said the car was to go the "army base". You never knew what was in the box cars. Flat cars with tanks, trucks and such were obvious.

There was one commodity that everyone knew its identity. (We called them the "headache cars".) They were gondolas loaded with large, heavy-webbed steel plates that were to be used as landing strips for planes. I suppose they were best used where the ground was not conducive for planes to land or take off or maybe to build a quick air strip or perhaps just a temporary runway. Anyway, those gondolas had to be lined up by number along with other cars that went with the gons. That was fine except, more often than not, before the train was dispatched there were numerous changes in either the specific cars or the line-up of cars or whatever. I remember we switched one train three times. When the train arrived at its destination (the Base) the cars were unloaded as they stood into the hold of the ship so that when the ship got to its destination, they knew where everything was located. Sometimes they had to use another ship or the destination (s) of the ship was changed--hence the changes in the make-up of the train.

St. George Yard was located on the shore of the Atlantic Ocean adjacent to the Staten Island-Manhattan Ferry Terminal. It was principally an Import-Export yard with an open-end dock for lighter and railroad car service. It also had float bridges for carfloat service. Some military materials went through the dock and some through the carfloats.

I remember once the yard crew was loading a locomotive on a carfloat. I don't remember what happened but the locomotive broke away from the yard engine as it was being shoved onto a float and the locomotive went over the end of the float into the ocean. It was necessary to hire divers and a large crane to retrieve it.

Of all the "Imports" arriving at St. George, the most interesting were the Prisoners-Of-War. They arrived at Manhattan by ship, were unloaded and put through a "delouse" there, just as they were--clothes and all. They were then put on a ferry, under heavy guard, and sent to St. George, Staten Island, where they were to be put on a train and sent to wherever the military wanted them. I always thought they looked kind of comical because, after being "deloused", their hair was all frizzy and standing on end and sort of gray.

Their uniforms had a washed-out look and I thought even their skin looked different. The train cars for them were the old "knee-knocker" type. If you remember, the seats were straight across and you could flip the back of the set forward or backward depending on which way the train was headed. Of course, if four people wanted to sit facing each other they could do that by adjusting the seat backs accordingly. If the four people were of any size, their knees touched—hence, the expression "knee-knocker".

I personally never knew of any of the prisoners trying to escape from St. George; but I was told that before I came there, one of the prisoners broke ranks and crawled under the train and out the other side only to come face to face with a two-story concrete wall with a street above. Two security people hustled through the train doors and found him against the wall looking up with no place to go. They took him back to ranks and cuffed him.

All people, except those who had business there, were kept away from the prisoner arrival, positioning and loading process. I had to be in the area on one occasion and one of the prisoners noticed a large Coca-Cola sign over a storefront at St. George and he said to me, "Do you have Coca Cola over here also?" I told him, "Yes, we have had it for some time." He then asked me for a cigarette and a security guard yelled at me, "Don't give him anything."

I think many of the prison trains went to Camp Kilmer in New Jersey for further disbursement. I do know that they were fanned out. I have a good friend whose father had a farm in Wyoming then and he told me they had twelve German prisoners working on their farm. He said he never knew of any of them trying to escape and that several of them would have liked to have stayed in the United States after the war ended.

I was not on Staten Island when military equipment began to come back to the States or prisoners were sent home. But I can imagine it was a busy time at both St. George and Arlington Yards as it was when the fighting was still going on.

As for me, it was an experience. It was long ago but I have some memories of that time--the same as I have memories of all the other places I worked during my 42 years on the B&O and Chessie System. As a matter of fact, even my last assignment is getting to be "long ago" also as come August 1st, 2008, I will be retired 30 years.

Is this a great country or what?

Chapter 4   A Solid Foundation

Bring in the Experts

By Bob White
April 1997

Sometime early in 1972, I don't remember the exact date, a gasoline barge exploded under the B&O railroad bridge over the Ohio River connecting Parkersburg, West Virginia, and Belpre, Ohio.

There was a tremendous explosion which totaled one main span of the bridge and damaged two spans. Two crewmen on the barge were killed. An adjacent highway bridge was damaged, as were homes along the river on the Belpre side. The barge was blown to smithereens. I believe one of the crewmen was smoking, not realizing that an almost empty gasoline barge is much more susceptible to ignition than a loaded barge. (I don't think I would light a match on either.)

At any rate, the B&O bridge sustained considerable damage; and although we intended to hold the barge owner responsible, we had to report the loss to B&O's property insurance underwriters. The underwriters assigned the loss to Everitt Hlavin, a General Adjustment Bureau, Inc., adjuster. Several months after the occurrence, Mr. Hlavin obtained the services of a bridge expert from St. Louis, Mr. Carl Shenk, who was to meet with myself, Gus Spangler of A&A (Alexander & Alexander, Inc.) and representatives of our Engineering Department in Huntington, West Virginia.

When we arrived at the OH Building in Huntington, there were about ten Engineering Department representatives assembled including, among others, E. Q. Johnson, Dulaney Wood and Bob Kendall. A male secretary from the Engineering Department had gone to the Huntington airport to pick up GAB's bridge expert, Carl Shenk. When Mr. Shenk arrived, he appeared a little bewildered at the number of people present. I remember him saying to E. Q. Johnson, "I think I know you." E. Q. shook his head, because he had never met Mr. Shenk and neither had we. Memory may serve me badly, but I'm sure I said, "This is Mr. Carl Shenk who was asked by Mr. Hlavin to represent our insurance underwriters in connection

When completed in 1871, the B&O's 7140 foot long Ohio River Bridge, linking Parkersburg, West Virginia, and Belpre, Ohio, was the longest bridge in the world. It consisted of 46 spans: 25 deck plate girders, 14 deck trusses, 6 through trusses, and 1 through plate girder, all resting on 53 piers.

Four B&O divisions are in the vicinity of the Parkersburg bridge. The single track bridge is part of the Monongah division which connects to the Ohio Division on the west end of the bridge at Belpre, Ohio. On the West Virginia side, the Wheeling division's Ohio River Branch runs under the bridge and on the Ohio side of the river the Newark division's Marietta Branch connects with the Ohio division at the west end of the bridge.

The Parkersburg bridge and the bridge south of Wheeling at Benwood, West Virginia, were the B&O's only bridges over the Ohio River. (The B&O crossed the Ohio River at Pittsburgh, Cincinnati and Louisville on bridges owned by other railroads.) The Parkersburg bridge was a critical link in the B&O's line from Baltimore to Cincinnati and St. Louis. That became very obvious in 1972 when a pier was struck by a gasoline barge which exploded and did considerable damage closing the bridge. Most of the traffic was rerouted over B&O lines to Fostoria, Ohio, on the Chicago mainline and then over the Toledo Division to Cincinnati where it resumed its original route. Intermediate traffic was rerouted over the bridge at Benwood. The bridge was repaired by replacing the span over the main river channel.

Barnard photo, B&O Railroad Historical Society collection.

with this bridge loss." Mr. Shenk was still looking around the room with a puzzled look on his face as if searching for someone to recognize.

One of the bridge engineers went into a detailed report about the damaged bridge, outlining alternatives for repairs and then advising why B&O had decided to proceed in a certain manner He then said that the bridge repair would cost about $1,000,000. Mr. Shenk allowed that was a lot of money but maybe something could be done about it. He mentioned the name of someone to whom we might want to talk. During a period of discussion about the repair proposals, Mr. Shenk had very little to say, except for a few innocuous remarks, and continued to have a puzzled look on his face. This went on for about 20 minutes.

Finally, Mr. Hlavin, visibly embarrassed by the evasive responses or lack of response by his high-priced bridge expert, said, "Aren't you going to say anything about the repair proposals?" To which Mr. Shenk replied, "Well, I don't really know anything about that." Realizing that something was terribly wrong, I asked, "Who the hell are you?"

The man who we thought was bridge engineer Carl Shenk, said, "I'm Carl Perkins, Congressman from East Kentucky."

Well, I almost fell off of my chair and the whole room broke down in laughter and disbelief. I went into the other room and called my boss, Gene Gibson, to tell him. It was one of those situations where you had to be there to get the full impact.

It developed that Congressman Carl Perkins was on his way to speak to a Garden Club in Ashland, Kentucky. He heard nothing beyond "Carl" when our man approached him at the airport and, apparently, during my introduction. He knew he was going to the Garden Club but he was trying to figure who had sidetracked him, and for what purpose, and perhaps to see if it had any political implication. I'll say this for the congressman. He laughed along with us and showed no animosity. You could almost perceive his thoughts; "How am I going to explain my tardiness, with political correctness, to the Garden Club?"

I understand Carl Perkins was Chairman of the House Appropriations Committee at the time this occurred. Perhaps we could have gotten Congress to pay for the bridge repairs.

Mr. Carl Shenk eventually made his way to the OH Building from the airport by cab, and we had a very good meeting. However, it would have been tough to top the preliminaries. The barge owner ultimately paid B&O for the bridge repairs.

N&N Editor's note; I was Superintendent of Transportation when this accident occurred. I got a call from someone at Parkersburg who advised there was a piece of the barge on top of the bridge. In disbelief I asked, "How could that be? The bridge is so high!" He replied, "That's nothing. There is, also, a piece on the roundhouse and that's half a mile away!"

On the Preservation of
Historic Railroad Landmarks

By Stan Gearhart
July 2001

While gassing up in Winchester, Virginia, on the 12th of June, my eyes were directed to the current edition of the *Winchester Star* which featured a story on the renovation of the B&O passenger depot. It was reported that, after considerable delay, the restoration-renovation was about to begin and it appeared that the guidelines worked out point toward a historically correct renovation and not something to be done "on the cheap". A lot of money found its way to assure a first-class effort. Although the city will pay the costs of the rehabilitation, Winchester has been approved to receive $325,000 in federal funds to reimburse the city's outlay. The city agreed to pay 20 percent in matching costs for the project. Additional funds were also being sought from the Virginia Department of Transportation. Civic pride, no doubt, carried a lot of weight pushing through a project such at this to save an old train station. We have heard, first hand, how difficult it is to pull off such things those days, like the Martinsburg roundhouse project as well as the Grafton passenger depot and the Willard Hotel efforts. And we could only shake our heads when we lamented the free pass that was issued to clear out all memories of the Queen City Station in Cumberland. The list continues to grow when we add to it the roundhouse facility in Brunswick and more recently the Western Maryland treasure that was buried in Hagerstown. Roadblocks continue to thwart similar efforts to preserve these historic railroad landmarks--the most recent being the delivery of "R" Tower (formerly at Cherry Run) in three sections right ahead of the wrecking ball only to stumble just in time to find a temporary resting place set aside for it in the Martinsburg roundhouse complex.

Combined railroad station-hotels were once common in Europe, but the concept never caught on in the U. S. But John W. Garrett, the B&O's legendary 19th century president, built at least five of varying sizes on his railroad. Garrett's largest and most elaborate was the grandiose three-story Queen City Hotel and station at Cumberland, Maryland, located at the base of the Alleghenies and the junction of two B&O principal main lines. Never wholly successful as a hotel, in its later years the building primarily housed B&O offices and overnight quarters for train employees. Sadly, it was demolished in 1972 after an intense preservation battle.
Elmer Treloar photo, 1970. H. H. Harwood, Jr., collection.

It was interesting to note that early on into the article in the *Star*, people were promptly reminded of Admiral Richard Byrd and his return to his home town via the historic station from the Antarctic Expedition. Of course, the Byrd family "owned" Virginia politically and perhaps economically, at one time and political capital seems to drag along with it some long coattails that influence decisions of a later day.

And, of course, the B&O bears its share of historical markers along the way to remind one of previous connections. Even I can remember, when first venturing into the "Valley" for the company almost 50 years ago, being reminded by old timers of solid trainloads of apples from the Byrd interests in Winchester for export to various countries in Europe. Arguably, the apple

The B&O's handsome Winchester, Virginia, station was completed in 1892 and designed by E. Francis Baldwin, the notable Baltimore architect responsible for numerous distinctive late 19th century B&O buildings. The third and last B&O station to serve the city, it remains well-preserved today.

H. H. Harwood, Jr., photo, 1972.

trains were a forerunner of the unit trains to come in later years.

One wonders how much tradition eventually finds its way into "hard dollars" supporting efforts to preserve historic landmarks elsewhere.

The depot of sandstone was built in 1892. We are told that phase one includes the dismantling of the roof canopy and its replacement with historically accurate materials as well as some replacement of slate on the depot roof. Since federal funding is involved in the project, certain preservation standards must be met. The architectural firm employed specializes in historically sensitive sites and has worked on two other railroad depots in Virginia in recent years, namely at Orange and Culpepper.

Phase two of the rehabilitation project, primarily dealing with foundation problems, will not begin until CSX employees currently housed in the B&O station are moved into a building to be constructed nearby. I haven't been around the building for about ten years; but the last time I looked, an office of the Winchester & Western Railroad was located on the second floor but no doubt that has been moved in keeping up with the new-found wealth for the rail industry continuing to serve Winchester in recent years.

In December, 1999, the City of Winchester entered into a 99-year easement agreement with CSX which allowed the city to renovate the historic depot. Shades of the old days when 100 year leases and agreements were the norm. Perhaps there is hope yet!!

At the RABO meeting last week, Maurice Good was telling me that during his carefree early days when near the bottom rung of the "ladder" with the company, he and some of his associates buried some artifacts and mementos in a glass jar at this site near the depot. We should keep an eye on this project to see what turns up that marks another special occasion in the B&O's history.

A Personal Memoir of Tunnel #21
Eaton, West Virginia

By Earl Scharper
July 2002

When I began working for the B&O Railroad in 1936, its Parkersburg Branch was known as the bottleneck for high and wide shipments on the route between Cumberland and Cincinnati.

The main impediments were the 23 tunnels on the Parkersburg Branch. Over the years, clearance improvements were made from time to time but freight cars were also becoming larger and the Parkersburg Branch was still THE BOTTLENECK.

In the early 1960s, a comprehensive clearance project was begun to remove THE BOTTLENECK. Some tunnels would be open cut and others would be enlarged by setting walls back and/or raising the tunnel roof. This was a combination project utilizing the B&O's tunnel repair gangs but principally outside contractors. Railroad traffic was maintained but most of the rail traffic was scheduled at night to provide maximum working intervals for the clearance work while maintaining reasonable schedules for railroad traffic.

Work progressed smoothly and, in due course, work was begun at Tunnel #21 to widen some portions of the walls and to raise some portions of the roof by the railroad's tunnel repair forces. Work was on schedule until that fateful day when there was a roof failure which closed the tunnel and trapped three men inside.

Work was immediately started to rescue the trapped men but

This 1963 B&O publicity photo illustrates the ability of the newly completed Tunnel 21 to handle high-profile equipment such as these trailer-on-flatcar shipments.

B&O photo, H. H. Harwood, Jr., collection.

progress was agonizingly slow. As soon as some of the debris was removed, there would be additional failures and the cleared area would be filled with newly fallen rubble. After a week or two of this impasse, it was obvious the old tunnel could never be repaired because of the extensive roof failures and the decision was made to drive a new tunnel about 300 feet north of the old one. A survey was quickly made, a new alignment established, plans for the new tunnel prepared and a contract let for the new structure. Since the Parkersburg Branch was completely closed and all through traffic was necessarily rerouted over other lines at much greater cost, the new tunnel contract specified construction was to be carried out 24 hours a day and seven days a week until completion, with a construction gang to start at each end of the tunnel and work towards the center.

In the meantime, rescue work at the old tunnel was being pushed as hard as possible; but the roof falls were also becoming more extensive and working conditions were becoming exceedingly dangerous. When it was apparent that all rescue work which could be done had been performed, it was decided, with the concurrence of the trapped workers' families, that all hope for their recovery was gone and it felt it was foolhardy to expose the

For a variety of reasons, including rock structure and alternative cost comparisons, some of the tunnel clearance improvements were best achieved by completely eliminating the tunnel, a technique called "open cutting." That alternative involved substantial grading to remove all of the material above the former tunnel and to provide proper slopes for the sides along the new open cut. In some cases the line of railroad was moved a short distance to minimize the amount of grading and also to provide a work location which minimized the disruption to the ongoing rail operations.

B&O photo, H. H. Harwood, Jr., collection.

rescue workers to more and more dangerous conditions in the rescue procedures. So the old tunnel was sealed at each end and it remains the tomb for the trapped tunnel workers.

The work at new Tunnel #21 presented a problem for the construction engineers. With work progressing at each end of the tunnel and continuing around the clock, it was increasingly difficult for the engineers to provide alignment and elevation controls when needed by the contractor without delaying his progress. It quickly became apparent that the new Tunnel #21 project needed to have its own engineering crew supervised by an experienced tunnel construction engineer.

John Packman, who was in charge of the outside contractor projects, had good crews assigned to him; but he had no one with experience in driving new tunnels. So Packy asked his boss, Les Kroll, to obtain a qualified person to take charge of the Tunnel #21 project while Packy would retain supervision of the ongoing clearance improvement projects. As I was one of the few men in the Construction Engineering Department who had supervised new tunnel construction, Les Kroll asked me if I would take the assignment at Tunnel #21. Of course, I said yes.

At the time, I was Assistant Office Engineer with a salary larger than John Packman's. When this was discussed, Packy said that was OK with him as long it was understood I was to be in charge only for Tunnel #21, while Packy continued on with the other contract work. That was a happy solution to a potentially contentious situation since Packy and I had worked together very well on other projects and surveys and we saw no reason why there should be any conflict about our separate responsibilities at Tunnel #21. 1 did not realize it at that moment but I was going to be much too busy at Tunnel #21 to ever try, or even want, to nibble into Packy's other projects. We did work together smoothly in sharing engineering crews, when necessary, and in supporting each other with advice and suggestions when asked. There were no incidents of authority clashes during our tenure together.

One thing was made clear to me from the beginning — the first priority was that the contractor at Tunnel #21, C. J. Langenfelder & Son, was not to be held up or delayed for any reason. We had to work around that condition and we engineers had to provide the center line controls and elevation checks in the periods of natural pauses in construction activity, such as shift changes, moving drilling jumbos into and out from the drilling face and during safety checks. We could not even count on lunch periods (there were no coffee breaks) because the crews ate when, and as they could, as the work progressed. This unceasing progress also meant that the engineering crews had to be available on very short notice and ready around the clock. Long workdays became the norm and we quickly acquired the ability to tolerate interruptions to our routine duties in order to set line and grade controls for the construction gangs at both ends of the tunnel.

I went to Tunnel #21 immediately after the 4th of July to find work was well underway at each end. Unremitting pressure was on for progress and there were no times off, no breaks, no holidays and no overtime pay for the engineering crews. We worked for two weeks straight and then had two days off. Also, the days were long and we didn't have enough hours away from the job to have the opportunity to get into mischief. When we left the site, our only interest was to get a decent meal, get a shower, get to bed and get some sleep and then start all over again.

That was our schedule through July and August. Around the end of August, the contractor's forces said they would not work over Labor Day and they wanted that Sunday and Monday off. After some consideration by the railroad and the contractor, their request (read that "demand") was granted. For the engineering crews, though, it was the first opportunity we had to run a thorough check of our alignment controls and profile elevations and we spent the Labor Day holiday in that fashion. The check of our controls was good and we breathed a sigh of relief and rejoiced.

After that two-day shutdown, work began once more and the pressure was still on. Around the end of September, as I recall , the tunnel construction gangs from each end met, the barrier wall was blasted and excavated. Work could now continue on construction of the concrete sidewalls and arch roof.

With the Parkersburg Branch closed while the new tunnel was being driven, it was possible for the railroad's tunnel forces and the outside contractor's to intensify and speed up their work so they were finished before track was laid through the new tunnel. Soon after the tunnel sidewalls and arch roof were being constructed, Packy was able to retake control of Tunnel #21 and I returned to Baltimore.

I must make mention of the fine men I worked with at Tunnel #21 and acknowledge the outstanding engineering control work they performed. They were a joy to be with. They included Bill Barker, Al Bogdon, Tony Braden, Herb Dankert, Ron Fitrow and many others as well.

Addendum to a Personal Memoir of Tunnel #21 Eaton, West Virginia

Now, outside the realm of our workaday world and to show that fact is stranger than fiction, I will mention Tom Swann. He was one of John Packman's men who happened to be in the wrong place at the wrong time. This event happened before I came out to Tunnel #21 and it happened near West Union, which is quite distant from Tunnel #21. This is my recollection of it.

Tom and some of his peers were having a beer or two after work when a man came into the bar, headed for Tom and after saying something to the effect of "Keep away from my wife," shot him. Tom died shortly thereafter and the man was arrested. He was convicted of homicide and sentenced to prison.

Of course, this was a big item at the time and feelings ran high, pro and con, as to Tom's involvement. As I recall the situation, it was generally felt, at least by the engineering crews, that the shooter was mentally unbalanced and that Tom was a victim of mistaken identity. Obviously, this incident was especially traumatic to Tom's widow and small child.

Memories Of Tunnel 21

By Tony Braden
April 2000

Tunnel 21 was in Eaton, West Virginia, on the Parkersburg Branch, Monongah Division of The Baltimore and Ohio Railroad. It was one of 23 tunnels between Clarksburg and Parkersburg. In 1961, several large joint venture contracts were to be awarded, simultaneously, by the Engineering Department to improve the clearances in all 23 tunnels. These improvements would allow piggyback trailers to be transported along the Parkersburg Branch for the first time. The scope of such a large undertaking was as follows: Some of the 23 tunnels were to be completely eliminated, a process called open-cut; others were scheduled to be bypassed by excavating the hillside and realigning the track around the old tunnel; and still others were to be enlarged by constructing new arches and sidewalls.

Tunnel 21 was one of several that were to have the "floor" lowered to improve the overhead clearance. This design concept consisted of removing the track and roadbed, excavating 50 to 100 foot segments of the tunnel floor for a depth of three feet and installing concrete struts, on 25 foot centers, perpendicular to the track centerline. The purpose of these struts was to support the tunnel sidewalls, since they would be undercut. The tunnel was 1,840 feet in length and the single track had an alignment of a 1,000-foot tangent in the center with a 420-foot spiral curve at each end. Operationally, the contract work was to progress through the first several stages "under traffic", meaning trains would be allowed to run as scheduled. Therefore, any debris or equipment on or near the track would have to be removed before the next train was due. Then, during the final stages of work, the Parkersburg Branch would be shut down for 90 days and all train traffic would be rerouted to Moundsville, West Virginia, and down the Ohio River Branch to Parkersburg.

During this period of time in my railroad career, I worked for Harry Roebuck and Urban Holden in the Office Engineer's office on the 13th floor of the B&O Central Building in Baltimore. The Chief Engineer was C. R. Riley and Les Kroll and Jim Caywood were Assistant Chief Engineers of Design and Construction. I was one of several junior engineers sent out to perform survey work on the Parkersburg Branch in preparation for awarding the joint venture contracts. Bill Barker, Rex Sumner and, later, Al Bogdon were part of this survey crew. John Packman from Grafton, West Virginia, was in charge of the group.

At Eaton, West Virginia, the survey crew began work by establishing top of rail elevations through the tunnel. Next, we set large reference pins (known as PK nails) into the sidewalls, so that when the lowered track and roadbed were re-installed, measurements could be taken from these pins to determine new top of rail elevations. Every 100 feet along these sidewalls were openings, about six feet high, known as "manholes," where someone could get in the clear if a train approached while working inside the tunnel. Even though we called the Train Dispatcher several times a day to get a "line up," on more than one occasion, a train would arrive unexpectedly. Before you could hear or see the approaching train, you could always feel a strong current of air being sucked through the tunnel as the train entered at either end. When I was operating the transit for the survey crew, I had to quickly get in the nearest manhole with the transit and tripod in my arms as the train rumbled through at what seemed like 50 miles per hour just two or three feet away. Thanks goodness none of these trains ever derailed inside the tunnel. It was one experience I've never forgotten.

The contractor for Tunnel 21 was C. J. Langenfelder from Baltimore. As they began the work to excavate the floor, before the support struts could be installed, a huge portion of the 100-year-old tunnel collapsed and trapped three of Langenfelder's employees. Within a few hours, nearly everyone from the Chief Engineer's office had flown out to the accident scene. Despite all of our efforts to locate and recover the victims, none of the bodies was ever found. Part of the reason was that digging had to be performed by hand because it was believed that use of heavy machinery could cause further harm to those buried in the debris.

After several days, when it was obvious no one could still be alive, the decision was made to abandon the old tunnel and "drive" a new tunnel through the mountain, 100 feet north of, and parallel to, the alignment of the old tunnel. Work was to begin at both ends of the proposed new tunnel at the same time to expedite the project. Once new design drawings were finalized in Baltimore and revised contracts were awarded, the hillside approaches to both sides of the mountain were excavated so the actual drilling of the bore hole could begin as soon as possible. Work would continue on a 24-hour, 7-day a week basis until completed. Time was of the essence because the Parkersburg Branch was now shut down indefinitely and rerouting traffic beyond the planned 90-day period could result in increased costs as well as lost customers.

Austin Powder Co. was commissioned to design a shot pattern of explosives. About 70 holes were drilled into the raw rock face. Each hole was then filled with millisecond delay caps that, when detonated, would result in the raw rock landing in a pile that could be quickly removed. Next, steel posts and steel arch were bolted together and placed on 25-foot centers as the tunnel was driven through the mountain.

Our engineering job was to give the tunnel crews proper alignment and grade as the hole was bored through the rock. Once line and grade were given to one tunnel crew, we had to drive over the mountain along a narrow road to give line and grade to the crew on the opposite side.

In less than 120 days, both crews broke through the rock to see each other for the first time. Our tunnel centerline met within two inches of exact alignment. In the final phases, concrete was pumped in and around the steel posts and arch to create a smooth tunnel wall. Then, new track and roadbed were installed. The Parkersburg Branch reopened to piggyback traffic within 180 days of the collapse of old Tunnel 21.

"Willow Valley"
B&O MP 141 St. Louis Division

By Bill Lakel
January 2004

Willow Valley, a small marshalling yard for U.S. Gypsum, sits nestled between several of the few hills in southern Indiana. Most of the area is very flat, heavily wooded with lots of wildlife and almost completely isolated, with the exception of US Highway 50 which is never too far from the B&O Mainline running from Cincinnati to "Shops" at Washington, Indiana. One would not think there would be a story here but one could be wrong for there are several chiseled in my mind.

The first one started on a very cold, snowy December day when my very capable boss, General Manager A. W. Johnston, called and said the undercutter unit was coming to lower the single main track through Willow Valley tunnel. It seems the

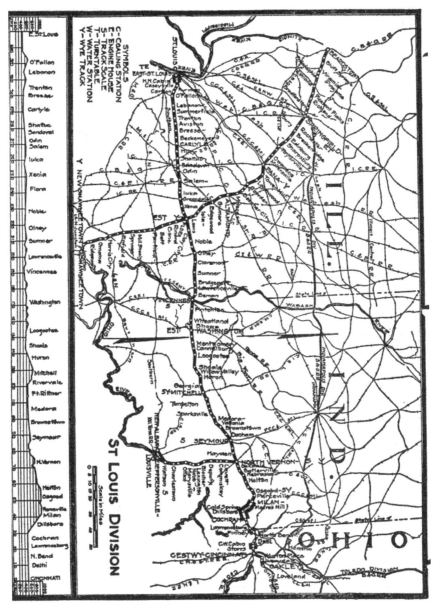

The 1964 employee timetable map of the St Louis Division shows the mainline from Cincinnati, on the Ohio River to St Louis on the Mississippi River and the branch lines from Beardstown on the Illinois River to Shawneetown on the Ohio River and the Louisville Sub Division from North Vernon to Louisville, also on the Ohio River. At Cincinnati, the light lines show the Toledo Division and Ohio Division connections and at Springfield the Indianapolis Division connects with the St Louis Division. Nearly the entire division was single track. The Division headquarters was at Washington, Indiana. *Ray Lichty Collection.*

track needed to be lowered to accommodate the new covered tri-level auto racks. The unit would be set off in Willow Valley Yard along with several "AD" air dump cars needed to handle the dirt. As usual, I got the job along with "Russ" Widdows, the Track Supervisor from Shops. I was no stranger to the undercutter for A. W. Johnston gave me the job of undercutting the westbound main track from east of Rockville, Maryland, to the top of Barnesville Hill, several years earlier when he was Division Superintendent in Baltimore and I was Division Operator-Rules Examiner. G. W. "George" Shelleman, Road Foreman of Engines, was my "partner in crime" for that massive project but that is another story.

The day we started it was below zero and the roadway was frozen like a rock. We had to start several rail lengths from the west portal to have a "run off." To get the undercutter chain in position under the ties required a trench to be dug between the ties across the roadbed. It didn't take long to realize picks were useless and jackhammers would be needed to dig the trench. Using the brakepipe air, we got the chain installed and started the machinery. The chain would not cut the frozen roadbed and we were shaving the ties in half. It was obvious we would have to loosen the roadbed to the tunnel—day one, and maybe two, shot to hell!

When the unit entered the tunnel, the roadbed was not frozen and the project went well for a short distance until the unit foreman stopped the machinery. It seems we had hit an underground spring. The cutter chain went down in the mud digging a large deep hole and filling the "AD" car with soft wet mud. We had to remove the cutter chain and reinstall it east of the spring. We got a load of ballast to fill the hole and finished the job with no further problems except the hard work to establish a "run off" at the east portal. We set the unit off in Willow Valley Yard, dumped our new ballast and gave the railroad back to the Chief Dispatcher at Shops at 10 mph until the track was stabilized.

The next morning, we had resurfaced the track through the tunnel and dumped the two "AD" cars. The first car dumped fine. We set the empty car off and started to dump the second car—the one with the mud. We had one problem! The mud had frozen to the car and the whole damned thing, car and all, rolled down the bank. The trucks on the "AD" cars were secured to the car so it went in one piece. We were dumping just outside the east portal. The ditch was deep and the car was not too obvious. Russ Widdows said "Oh s__t. What are we going to do now?" I said, "Nothing, it's in a good spot 'til Spring." I called Chief Dispatcher L. J. Bies at Shops and told him of the mishap. When he stopped laughing, he said, "Next time Jack Harmeling comes by with the Cincinnati 'hook' we will stop and get it." That's exactly what we did the next summer. I don't think anyone ever missed AD #15. I don't think I ever told GM Bill Johnston, (Editor's note: He knows now!) but knowing the kind of railroader Bill was, he would have agreed with my decision.

Another story that comes to mind at Willow Valley was during the summer of 1972 when General Track Supervisor Dave Ledford and I were involved with laying welded rail from about MP 131 at Georgia to MP 147 at Shoals, Indiana. I had unloaded 15 miles (3 trains) of CWR (Continuous Welded Rail) the previous winter at this location. Willow Valley, located at MP 141, was close to the middle of the work area and a good place to tie up the equipment. To unload from the main track, the machinery needed to install the rail required running the machines up to the Pettibone crane which set them off in sequence to the side of the right-of-way. The time it took to unload this equipment and then put it back on the rail would be at least an hour or more lost. This amount of time could mean the difference between installing four, five or even six strings of rail in a working day. Installing only three strings of rail, each being 1,440 feet long, was a poor performance day. Four strings was a good day; five strings was excellent and to install six strings was a very outstanding day.

There was one problem in this area. No 1--the National Limited Washington, DC, to St. Louis—was due at Willow Valley at 9:54 AM, right in the middle of the workday. This required the rail unit to clear up and lose an hour or more and at least one string of rail. At that time, No. 1 consisted of one F-7 locomotive and usually two or three coaches--having downsized considerably with few passengers west of Cincinnati.

Dave Ledford and I talked to Chief Dispatcher Bies at Shops about holding the main track at Willow Valley and running train No. 1 through No. 1 track at Willow Valley. We instructed No. 1 at North Vernon to use No. 1 yard track at Willow Valley and we would handle the switches. No. 1 track at Willow Valley had good 100 lb. rail and handled road locomotives, so we saw no problems. No. 1 kept moving slowly and we went right back to work and installed five strings of rail -- Atta boy!! Good job.

The next day, making the same move, we installed six strings of rail on tangent track just west of Willow Valley Tunnel— Outstanding!! Next came a radio call for "yours truly" to call General Manager A. W. Johnston in Cincinnati who said, "The Vice President said to tell me if No. 1 ever went in Willow Valley Yard again to consider myself dismissed." Somebody blabbed! I said, "Bill would I do that?" and he answered "Damn right you would. No wonder you got six strings."

No need to worry about it happening again for we were closer to Shoals Yard and no one said anything about Shoals Yard.

Speaking of Shoals, Indiana, another incident comes to mind. Like Willow Valley serving as a yard for U.S. Gypsum, Shoals was the same for National Gypsum. There was a very steep winding lead from Shoals Yard to a huge gypsum plant producing wallboard, gypsum rock, ground gypsum and other gypsum products. It was not unusual to pull 20 or more heavy loads from this facility.

National Gypsum went on strike for months. Our crews would not cross their picket lines, so the job of switching this plant was given to me and Road Foreman E. H. Coulson. "Gene" and I would drive to Shoals, arriving at 6:00 AM. The yard crew would have the train ready to go up the hill.

One day, Gene was shoving 17 empties up the lead. I was riding on the head hopper car on the center sill under the slope sheet. We had radio contact and I was to relay instructions to Gene. At the plant entrance, there was a locked gate with a derail just outside the gate to stop any runaways from going down the lead. As we approached the gate, I told Gene "5 cars". No response. "3 cars"; still no response. "Gene, that will do!" Still no response. The lead car, with me aboard, went over the "one-way derail", through the locked gate, followed by several more cars before the train stopped. Gene walked up stating he heard no radio calls and knew we were close. He asked if I were hurt and I told him I probably needed clean underwear.

Several days later, it was my turn to be Engineer. We were coming down the hill with 21 heavy loads and we kept picking up speed even though I had increased the brake enough to stop the train. I asked Gene, "How many cars have air? He said, "About 8. Why?" I said, "Not enough" and put the train in emergency. We slid the rest of the way down the hill, finally stopping in front of the Yard Office and a laughing yard crew. They stopped laughing when they had to use that engine to set up the pickups. The considerable flat spots on the locomotive must have shook the daylights out of them.

Not too long after that, a crew coming out of National Gypsum lost their air and the engine overturned just by the Yard Office. The engine slid down the bank, coming to rest against a large tree. When the Cincinnati hook was re-railing the engine, a cable broke and the 250-ton Brownhoist turned over. "Hobie", the crane operator, suffered two broken legs in the accident. This was the first time this crane had turned over. Of the four cranes the B&O had in service, the other three had turned over, some with disastrous results.

You Needed to Be Connected

By Jack Reed
April 2009

Back in the early 60s when Jervis Langdon, Jr., was President and the B&O was moving into the operation of coal unit trains, there was a hot project to install a coupled weigh-in-motion scale at Green Spring, West Virginia. Green Spring was picked as the location for the scale as it would catch unit trains coming from the Cumberland and Monongah Divisions, including what was made up at Keyser, West Virginia, and moved over the Patterson Creek Cut-Off, and from the Pittsburgh Division.

The scale was automatic and unattended. The scheme was that an eastbound unit train at Patterson Creek Tower would activate the scale and the Operator at Patterson Creek got an indication that the scale was ready for weighing. Based on instructions from the Dispatcher in Cumberland, the Operator would permit the unit train to move over the scale and a readout of the weights was sent to Cumberland. The unit train's Engineer had to maintain a speed of between 5 mph and 6.5 mph over the scale in order to get accurate readings. The success of that first such scale on the B&O and C&O was important to the success of the unit train's money-saving concept.

Vance Freygang, Transportation Engineer, was the Project Manager (or some such title) and he led the team assigned to get this scale installed and working. He reported directly to Ted Klauenberg in Baltimore and was his representative in this matter. John Collinson, Sr., was Chief Engineer at the time. Vance was totally committed and, you might say, had a one-track mind in getting the scale operational, plus the handling of coal waybilling, etc. As such, he probably ruffled a lot of feathers, including the Cumberland Division "power structure". Dick Priddy was Superintendent at Cumberland at that time. I was the Freight and Coal Billing Agent at Cumberland. Bob Patterson was also part of the team working on this project.

Sometime soon after the scale was put into operation, Vance told me that he had not been to his home in Baltimore for several weeks and needed a couple of days to recuperate. He asked me if I would "look out for him" for a few days as he got a little "R&R".

Sure enough, just after he was out of sight, the Cumberland Chief Dispatcher called to advise me that the scale would not activate itself when a train was standing at Patterson Creek, waiting to be weighed. I told the Chief I would look into it; and on my way down to the scale house, I was thinking both Vance and I were in trouble because there wasn't the smallest chance I would know what was wrong or that I could actually "fix" something.

However, on arriving at scale house, I quickly discerned the problem. Vance had left the equipment unattached to the electric supply. Said another way, "It was unplugged!" I quickly corrected the condition and advised Chief it was ok to start the train.

Of course, the Chief wanted to know the cause of the malfunction. Since I considered Vance a good friend and not wanting to see him embarrassed, I quickly told the Chief, "The male projection was not properly introduced into the female

A weigh-in-motion scale was a wonderful railroad tool which came into existence in the early 1960s, about the time that unit trains were coming into vogue. Unit trains were solid trains of one bulk commodity, mostly frequently coal. Essentially, they were trains from one shipper to one customer. While some coal load-out facilities could weigh the cars' contents, the railroad still wanted to weigh the cars in the train to be sure they were getting accurate weights.

The weigh-in-motion scale had the capability to weigh the individual cars in a train as the train passed slowly over the scale. B&O's earliest installations included a scale house building but were not attended by an operator. Later installations eliminated the scale house altogether. The scales were controlled from a remote location and data collected was reported electronically to a billing location. The scales were installed at strategic locations on key lines away from classification yards as determined by traffic flows.

receptor." The Chief said, "Aw---OK." I must have given an acceptable answer as I never heard about it from the "big tent" and Vance told me afterward that he never heard any complaint.

Bob Patterson has some more amusing stories related to this scale prior to its becoming certified. With a little prodding, I am sure he will relate them.

Chapter 5   Engines and Cars

Sandhouse Gossip

By Ken Roloson
October 1999

In 1937-38, I was a member of the Baltimore Society of Model Engineers, which operated an extensive O gauge model railroad layout on the second floor of a building at 1613 N. Chester St. The members met once a week to build and operate the layout and discuss railroading in general, mostly "sandhouse" (gossip) in nature. Tom Arnold, a volunteer at the B&O Museum, who recently passed away, and Edward G. Hooper, Assistant Secretary of the B&O, were among the members. A considerable amount of "sandhouse" gossip was thrown about at these meetings and I recall one in particular.

An unusual locomotive was built at B&O's Mt. Clare shops in Baltimore in 1937, the brainchild of Col. George Emerson, General Superintendent of Motive Power and Equipment and his Master Mechanic. The "Emerson" (photo on following page) engine was being tested on the Washington Branch, and in negotiating the westbound curve at the Thomas Viaduct, the engine cab came in contact with the canopy at the Relay station. It demolished a portion of the canopy and caused considerable damage to the cab of the locomotive.

This was extremely embarrassing to Colonel Emerson and the matter was immediately "hushed up," and we heard no further word about it. No. 5600 continued to operate during the war years but spent much of its time in the shop at Mt. Clare, as maintenance costs for the engine skyrocketed.

Col. Emerson retired on January 1, 1942, and was succeeded by, former RABO member, Mr. A. K. Galloway, as General Superintendent Motive Power and Equipment. The locomotive was scrapped in 1950, long before the actual end of steam on the B&O Railroad. A short life but an interesting story.

Editor's note; When Col. Emerson died, "sandhouse" has it that A. K Galloway called Mt. Clare and said scrap the SOB.

Starting in the late 1920s, B&O Chief Mechanical Officer George H. Emerson indulged in a succession of experimental steam designs in a futile effort to match the economics of diesel power. The culmination of his efforts was this impressive four-cylinder rigid-frame duplex 4-4-4-4 turned out by Mt. Clare Shop in 1937 and modestly christened the "George H. Emerson." It was tested for a while on the Washington-New York, and is seen here demonstrating its speed and weight-hauling capabilities with a heavyweight train on Central Railroad of New Jersey trackage. In the same year it was completed, however, the B&O bought its first streamlined Electro-Motive passenger diesels, and the unfortunate "Emerson" never had a chance.

C. B. Chaney photo, Smithsonian Institution Collection.

My Two and a Half Year Ordeal
at DuBois, Pennsylvania

By John S. Ketzner
April 2002

In the late 50s, I was ensconced in the cushy position of B&O Storekeeper at Keyser, West Virginia. There, at that time, a highly efficient program was underway, building and repairing hopper cars, with most of the car parts being manufactured at the Cumberland Bolt and Forge Shop. My only concern was not knowing when my boss in Cumberland, Bill Dillion, would be promoted so I could inherit his job.

My tranquility was crushed when the powers to be asked (told) me to assume the position of Division Storekeeper at DuBois, Pennsylvania. My first reaction was, as Charlie Eckman would say, "Ain't No Way". I had seen DuBois. It was the pits! It was a disaster! It was chaos! No one in their right mind would even consider taking that job.

DuBois Shops was a large steam locomotive repair facility, inherited from the BR&P Railroad upon their takeover by the B&O RR in the thirties. With the elimination of steam locomotives in the fifties, the shops became idle.

Frank Rykoski, located in Pittsburgh at that time, headed up the Mechanical Department on the Central Region, which included DuBois. He and his advisors apparently decided that the idle shops at DuBois could be converted into a first class new freight car building facility. They apparently convinced their bosses, A. K. Galloway and W. C. Baker, that this was a great idea. So, after a couple million dollars spent on upgrading the shop facilities, DuBois was in the new freight car building business. While this certainly was a noble plan, that would give work to several hundred furloughed B&O shop workers, there were serious drawbacks.

The ancient facilities at DuBois consisted of a large back shop, a tender shop, a roundhouse and an ash pit. A transfer table, a turntable, plus various and sundry overhead cranes, became part of the so-called assembly line. The ash pit was filled in and its gantry crane was utilized to hang box car sides. With these facilities, the shops were trying to turn out each day ten new hoppers, ten new boxcars complete with DF equipment and six new gondolas with coil steel covers. Thirty condemned cars per day were being dismantled in the dismantling yard, with some of the parts being trucked for use on the new car assembly line. Across town, in the old car shop, a few hundred men worked on hopper car running repairs. Much of the work was performed outside. In the winter, 15 below zero Fahrenheit temperatures were not uncommon; and at worst, I have seen 28 below Fahrenheit readings. At DuBois, diesel cranes, the backbone of the stores operation, simply would not operate at 28 below zero, even when blowtorches were constantly run up and down the fuel lines.

To compound the problems, stores and purchasing management, having no previous experience in the assembly line car building business, simply ordered all needed materials for immediate shipment. The shops were consuming 35 to 40 carloads of car parts a day, plus a large number of highway truck shipments.

Some days, the daily local freight train (the BR-4) contained up to 120 carloads of material consigned to the storekeeper at DuBois. The result: DuBois yards were filled to capacity, with the overflow being held in Riker (Punxsutawney) Yard, which soon, also, filled to capacity. At times, more than 400 carloads of materials were backed up awaiting unloading. Per diem costs soared. In this mess, sometimes carloads of vital car parts, desperately needed on the shop assembly lines, simply could not be found.

To further complicate the situation, top management had hired the Proudfoot Organization to study the operation at DuBois (and elsewhere) and make recommendations. Their recommendation was to cut stores forces from 120 to 60 and assign one man out of every six to schedule the work of the other five. In other words, one sixth of the force was non-productive.

In this frightening situation, I was being pressured into leaving my "cushy" position at Keyser, my nice home in Cumberland and moving my lovely wife and four small children to DuBois.

With nothing better available, we would have to move into a 100-year-old mining company house with a steam furnace that

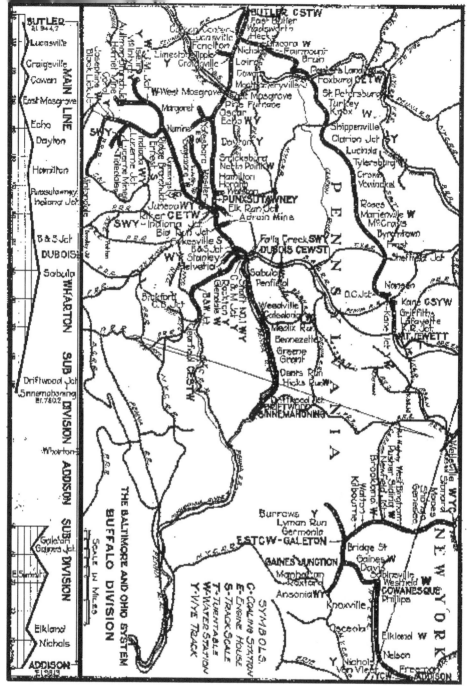

Buffalo Division West End April 28, 1946, employee timetable map showing the main line from Butler to DuBois, Pennsylvania not long after the B&O acquired the BR&P and B&S in 1932. This map still includes lines to Wellsville, Addison and Galeton which washed out in the 1942 flood.

Ron Stafford Collection, Courtesy of Brian DeVries.

banged all night and provided very little heat.

If I would accept this wonderful promotion, I was promised a $90 per month pay raise, up to $690 per month. And, I would remain first in line for promotion to the Division Storekeeper position at Cumberland when it came open. That was the "carrot". The "stick" was the assurance that if I refused to move, I would be stuck in Keyser, West Virginia, for the balance of my railroad career.

So, in a lapse of good judgment, I gave in and moved to DuBois. While there, the company awarded all management people a 10% pay cut, wiping out most of my increase. The Division Storekeeper's job came open at Cumberland; and when I reminded all concerned, loud and clear, that I had been promised that job as an incentive to get me to move to DuBois, the top brass told me in no uncertain terms, "We don't move people around, just to move them around."

So, here I was, in the spring of 1959, condemned to the Storekeeper's job at DuBois. My predecessor, a kindly old gentleman, and a lifetime native of DuBois, had been the top purchasing and stores manager on the BR&P RR when it was acquired by the B&O in 1932. He was allowed to stay on with full salary as Buffalo Division Storekeeper until age 65, which would come six months after my arrival at DuBois. He was told that he could stay on, mark time and enjoy life for the next six months but that I would be the boss.

It was here that I first met Arch McElvany. He had some fancy title, worked for shop superintendent Larry Schalk and had the awesome responsibility of assuring that all materials were on the three-car building assembly lines as needed. Arch was the jewel in the crown at DuBois. Without him, we couldn't have made it. In my 44 years on the B&O/C&O/Chessie, I never met a more intelligent, hard working and dedicated company man. To this day, I consider him a best friend.

So, now to the task at hand. You didn't have to be a rocket scientist to figure that the problem was material scheduling, or lack thereof. Old line freight car builders knew all about it, and the Japanese were busy polishing their "almost out" systems which would help propel them ahead of GM, et al. So Arch McElvany and I spent untold hours each night, for weeks,

When the B&O acquired the Buffalo Rochester and Pittsburgh Railroad in 1932 that company's major locomotive shops were at DuBois, Pennsylvania. It was an antiquated steam locomotive facility whose usefulness gradually diminished as it was integrated into the much larger B&O system.

In the late 50s, the B&O was experiencing some very difficult economic times. Nearly all of the physical plant was in serious need of extensive maintenance. The locomotive and revenue car fleet were no exception. This was a particular problem for the hopper car fleet that was inadequate to meet the needs for loading coal and stone and other bulk products. In an effort to meet the demands, a program was initiated to build new hopper cars in the revamped DuBois facility. The shop became an assembly line building cars from "kits" made up of the many parts needed for the finished product.

The DuBois operation was a good example of the type of measures undertaken by the B&O to keep the railroad running in very difficult times.

scheduling deliveries on every piece of material needed to manufacture a mixture of 26 new cars per day on three assembly lines. Arch would give to me the exact date on which an item would be required on the assembly line and I would schedule it for shipment, accordingly, usually one to three weeks before the need, depending on supplier distance and reliability. This meant following and tracing shipments very closely, with a lot of expediting. The suppliers howled. They were used to shipping an order at their convenience and they had no desire to change their practices. We told them that if they shipped early, the load would be sent back to them for later return shipment, all at their expense. We carried out this threat on more than one occasion. The suppliers complained bitterly to Baltimore but the brass backed us up, not wishing to be blamed for any part of the mess at DuBois.

After three or four months, we began to see a light at the end of the tunnel. Our efforts began to pay off. The situation eased. Inbound cars held under load decreased dramatically. The brass from Baltimore and Pittsburgh, who had been avoiding DuBois like the plague, began to show up for a look-see. The big day came when Central Regional Manager, Chester Williams, showed up with his entire entourage. He arrived in his office car, on the back end of a freight train (BR-4) to inspect DuBois. I was called on the carpet. How many inbound material cars do you have under load? How many foreign cars? How many did you release yesterday? How many today? What is the average holding time? I knew what the questions were going to be so I had rehearsed the answers. Things were going well. Chester looked deflated and downhearted because he could find very little to complain about. That's when I made my fatal mistake. Fishing for a little pat on the back I foolishly said: "Don't worry Mr. Williams, you will never see conditions here return to their previous state." To which Mr. Williams replied: "You're God Damn right I won't, or YOU won't be around here!" That's the nearest I ever came to getting a compliment from Mr. Williams.

Epilogue: After two and a half years, my sentence to DuBois was commuted and I was allowed to move to Pittsburgh. Soon after, the C&O took over and forever ended new car building at DuBois, Pennsylvania.

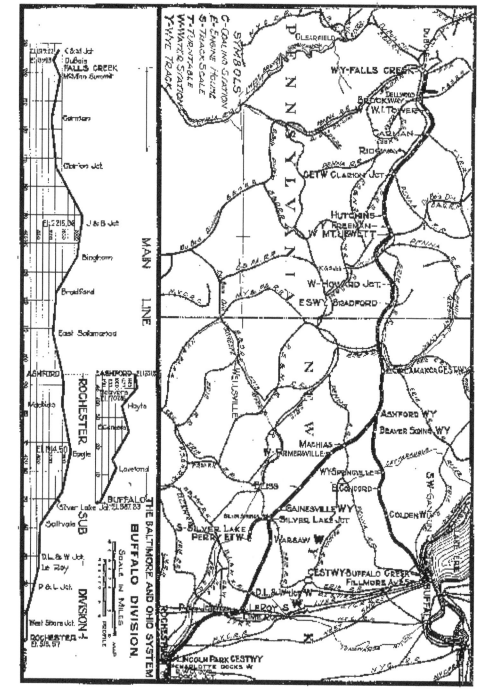

Buffalo Division East End April 28, 1946, employee timetable map showing the main line from DuBois, Pennsylvania, to Buffalo and the branch to Rochester, New York., not long after the B&O acquired the BR&P and the B&S in 1932.

Ron Stafford Collection, Courtesy of Brian DeVries.

The DuBois Mystique

By Ray Lichty
April 2002

John's story about DuBois brings back my memories about that period of B&O history. The early 60s were hard times on the B&O. That's when there were derailments everywhere. The Cumberland Division West End was legendary for its derailment problems, about which much has been previously written in these newsletter's pages. The physical plant was falling apart right before our eyes—the result of years of no money and no maintenance. The rolling stock was no different.

As John's story describes, the B&O took some extraordinary measures to try to correct the equipment problems. The ancient DuBois shop, along with similar facilities at Cumberland Bolt and Forge and the Brunswick Car Shop, just to name a few, were called upon to rescue a situation which less industrious people would have simply considered unsolvable.

It was at this time that I was in the first year of the Management Training Program. I traveled with Stu Burgess and Pete Pacheco. While with the Mechanical Department, we were sent to DuBois for a week to see what the car building effort was all about. Arch was our "host".

Arch was a bit of a folk hero at that time. Young and hard working. Indefatigable! Someone the trainees and many others, as John related, looked up to and admired. It didn't hurt that he was a little eccentric and not like many of the other railroad managers we had encountered.

It was bitter cold and nasty in western Pennsylvania during our stay. I recall walking from one of the shop buildings to another with the wind whipping the snow all around the place. Pete, Stu and I were dressed appropriately and still cold. Arch was in shirt sleeves. We told him he would catch a cold running around like that. He replied, "You don't get a cold from the cold; you get it from people with germs." In talking to Stu Burgess about this story, he recalls the following. "My memories of our time at DuBois include Arch requiring us to memorize and undergo a verbal exam on the diagram for operation of the air brake system for freight cars which, believe it or not, led to a pretty good understanding of train air."

Oftentimes, those early impressions are lasting ones. They were in the case of Arch.

Chapter 6   A Little Off the Beaten Track

Derailments

By James E. Sell
April 1999

Derailments are the bane of everyone involved and major derailments involve almost every department of the railroad. Not only Transportation, Mechanical and Engineering but also Claims, Sales, Public Relations, sometimes Law, Signal and Communications--just about every department. Occasionally, they also involve other railroads when detouring of traffic is necessary.

From the time I was a Yardmaster (1946) until I retired as Division Manager in 1978, I was involved, in some capacity, in all too many derailments--both major and minor.

I can't remember many of them but one, however, sticks in my memory and with good reason. For various reasons, there had been a series of derailments within the corporation limits of the small town of Ellenboro on the former Parkersburg Sub-Division. Since the roadbed was a good deal higher than part of the town site, the Mayor and Council became worried that cars involved in a derailment in their town might roll down the embankment and hit a home or place of business. The Town Hall was located in such a position. So, they voted to put a 10 MPH slow order on all trains through the town. This, of course, interfered with schedules and meets on the single-track subdivision.

After a period of many months and no derailments in the town, or even in the vicinity of Ellenboro, I wrote to the Mayor to ask if I could address the Mayor and Town Council at their next scheduled meeting. The purpose, of course, was to ask them to lift the speed restriction or at least to raise the speed of the slow order. The Mayor wrote to me and agreed that I could address them and he gave the time and date of the meeting.

On the date of the meeting, I was introduced to the members of the Council by the Mayor. I proceeded to tell them that the railroad had not had a derailment in the town, and indeed, not in the vicinity, for many, many months. Considering schedules and trains meeting on the single-track sub division, I told them it would be appreciated if they would agree to lift the slow order or at least to consider raising the speed of the slow order. I thought I had their sympathetic attention and was still giving my pitch when No. 94 came rumbling through the town limits, on the track above the city. Believe it or not, No. 94 derailed five cars! I'll never forget it. To make it even more exciting, an MP box car rolled down the embankment. Fortunately it did not hit anything.

Needless to say, that ended my appeal and the 10 MPH speed limit remained in effect and was still in effect when I retired years later.

As I remember, the MP car was donated to the town and was used as storage and was still there when I retired.

N&N Editor's note; Jim's telling a derailment story reminds me of my favorite railroad story which is, also, told by Jim and appeared in an earlier issue of *News & Notes*. One night at Fairmont, West Virginia, Jim got a call at home from the Yardmaster, "I just put a car in the roundhouse off #5 track" Jim replied, "#5 doesn't go in the roundhouse." The Yardmaster replied, "That's why I called."

The Skipper
By Nelson Blankenship
April 2002

I notice that April is newsletter's "information month" about derailments, so I might as well include this one story out of about 1,000 that I was on as a Trainmaster on the Monongah Division, hoping that it brings a few laughs. I remember this one due to the fine article that Mr. Johnston had in January's issue about James E. Sell who was my Superintendent and Division Manager for some 10 years. Jim, "The Skipper," was one of the finest bosses to work for because he was strong and dedicated to his job. Also in my case, I was one of the officers he inherited when he came back to the Division, I believe in 1969.

First of all the, "Skipper" believed that a Trainmaster's assigned territory was the entire Division so when my telephone would ring, as it did on this night at around 8 PM, it came as no surprise to hear the Chief Dispatcher instruct me that Mr. Sell wanted me to go and relieve Trainmaster C. N. Jaco down on the Elk Sub-Division close to Falling Rock, West Virginia, and to be there by 12 midnight. So being about a two-hour drive, I left soon thereafter. On arriving at Falling Rock, I called on the radio for Trainmaster Jaco, wondering how I was going to get across the river that separated the main highway from our right-of-way for miles between Gassaway and Charleston. Jaco answered me and told me to stay right where I was, that he would come after me. I could see Donahue Bros working with their off track equipment and knew I was right on top of the problem. Then, I happened to notice what looked like a row boat with a light sitting in the bottom and someone rowing with oars. As it approached, I hollered, "Jake is that you." Lo and behold, he answered, "YES". He threw a rope to me and I tied him off and he got out and told me to get in and he would take me back to the other side. I said, "Jake, you are not going to take me back to the other side and leave me without the boat." He said, "No. No. No. Mr. Sell gave me specific instructions not to leave you the boat because he was afraid you would leave the derailment and spend the night in the company car and have someone else do your work."

This is a true story. You see the "Skipper" got to know me pretty well. It is good to know he and Vigdis are doing well. I wish I could see them again.

Chasing Derailments

By Ray Lichty
April 1999

All of this talk about derailments brings a lot to mind. For me, derailments were a big part of my early fascination with this railroad business.

When I was working as a Telegrapher/Train Dispatcher, 1955-1959, I started to chase derailments.

Once on third trick, the operator at Greenwich, Ohio, come on the dispatcher's line and said, "I think I have a derailment. Better detour #5 and #25." He had a derailment alright. Turned out to be 50+ cars of an NYC train piled up on the two railroad's double track crossing diamonds. This is the location of the new Conrail/CSX connection for trains to and from Chicago.

When I got off duty I drove to Greenwich. The local police were keeping spectators from the site. As I walked down the right-of-way the officer stopped me. I told him, "It's ok. I am from Willard working the New Castle hook." "OK" he said and let me pass.

It was the biggest wreck I have ever seen. All of those cars piled up in a big heap. The entire pile wasn't more than three cars from the diamonds. There were eight tracks coming to the diamonds (two double track mains; two directions) and there were wrecker cranes working on seven of the eight.

In this time period, I was dating Judy, the gal who later became and still is my wife. (That's another story for another time.) One Friday evening, we went out somewhere and when I took her home, I told her I would pick her up at noon after work on Saturday. I then went to XN Tower in Cuyahoga Falls. The operator on duty told me there had been a big derailment out west and #5 and #25 were going to detour by way of Toledo and the NYC to Chicago. I quickly drove to Akron, boarded the engine of #5 and headed off for Chicago.

When I arrived in Chicago, I called Judy at work and told her I couldn't pick her up as promised. When she inquired why not, I told her I was in Chicago. She hung up on me. I never understood that.

Another big derailment was #5 at Lodi, Ohio. The second engine was hit by a coal truck with a trailer and derailed. The train was reported by the operator as "By". In a few minutes, the Conductor came walking up the steps of the tower. "What are you doing here?" asked the Operator. The Conductor then explained that nearly his entire train was derailed just west of the tower.

"Fran" of "Kukla, Fran and Ollie" was on board. Most of the passengers were bused to Chicago. I recall a piece of broken rail came up through the porter's berth and out the roof. Good thing he wasn't in the berth at the time.

As I said, I was fascinated by the wrecks. When I became an Assistant Trainmaster and had some responsibility for cleaning them up and getting the railroad open, my fascination quickly turned to personal dread.

I have only witnessed one derailment of any significance actually take place. #94 was pulling through the yard at Wilsmere, Delaware, to set off. The headman ran for the switch but the Engineer "big holed" it (emergency brake application). Cars, in slow motion just stood up on end and went every which

Trains #5 and #6, *The Capitol Limited*, were the pride of the B&O passenger fleet. Operating between Jersey City, New Jersey, and Chicago, The overnight trains were all first class sleeper accommodations. They provided the best services, including stewardess/nurses and in the dining car the B&O famous help-yourself salad bowl.

On April 3, 1958, the westbound #5's entire train, except the last car, the observation/lounge, was derailed when the second diesel locomotive of the train was struck by a coal truck at a highway crossing. The driver of the truck, which was pulling a trailer, said his brakes failed, a claim disputed by many. The locomotive derailed and when it encountered the facing point crossover at the Lodi, Ohio, interlocking, just west of the highway crossing, derailed the train as it was pulled towards the eastbound main track.

Even such a spectacular derailment resulted in no serious injuries to the passengers or crew.....or the truck driver.

Baltimore & Ohio Railroad Historical Society collection.

way. I was walking alongside, a few tracks away, and started to holler at the train. As the last of the derailed cars crashed down, I ran to the yard office and called Bill Johnston, the Superintendent. I was rather excited. "The boss" told me to calm down and call the tool cars. I don't think he realized the fact that I had just seen the train derail!

Finding the cause of derailments is another significant chapter in railroad lore. In this case, it was no big secret. As we inspected the wrecked cars, on one center sill, in chalk, were these words, "Bad Sill" right next to where the center sill had failed.

School Bus Accident
Bancroft Ave.
Staten Island, New York
November 7, 1960

By Bud Fischer
January 2008

The photograph on the next pageof the school bus lying on its side represents one of the more memorable incidents in which I was involved during my 13-year career in General Claims as District Claim Agent for the B&O and SIRT Rwy. at St. George, Staten Island, New York. I was assigned to this location in August, 1952, and remained there until transferred to Toledo, Ohio, in February, 1965.

It was about 4 PM, November 7, 1960, while in my office at Pier 6, St. George, that I received a call from the Train Dispatcher that one of our trains, a four-car consist deadheading from Tottenville to St. George, had struck a school bus at the Bancroft Ave. crossing in Grant City.

At that crossing, we had two mainline tracks which ran northeast to southwest (by compass) from St. George to Tottenville. The tracks, at that time, were at grade level from Bay Terrace on the south to Jefferson Ave. on the north. Running parallel with our tracks on each side of the right-of-way at a distance of about 25-30 feet were two, two-lane streets, North Railroad Ave. on the east side and South Railroad Ave. on the west. (Confusing, but those were the names of the streets.) Bancroft Ave. crossing was about midway and the only east-west crossing between New Dorp station on the south and Grant City station to the north. Our tracks at that location were about four feet higher than street level. In order to traverse this crossing, it was necessary to make a sharp left turn from Bancroft Ave. onto North Railroad Ave., travel about 50-75 feet, then turn hard right and move up a grade to reach the near rail of our westbound main (railroad directions). While Bancroft Ave. was an east-west street and, normally, one would think that it would be a straight line over our tracks, that was not the case.

The crossing surface was smooth asphalt, in good condition, and about 20 feet wide. For crossing protection, there were cross-arm warning signs on the NE and SW corners of the crossing (compass directions) and on each mast was a warning bell which operated in conjunction with flashing lights. There was one unusual thing about the flashlights, however, in that one flashlight lens on the NE mast pointed NE while the other lens pointed SE. The same was true on the west side warning sign. (It did have the approval of the Public Service Commission and was not a factor in the lawsuit which arose out of this incident.)

My memory fails me as to the train number involved in this accident, however, as it approached the Grant City area, traveling at approximately 30 MPH, well within the timetable speed limit. Bill Allen, the engineer, stated that he observed the school bus turn from Bancroft Ave. onto North Railroad Ave. and approach the crossing at a speed of about 5-10 MPH. It did not halt but moved in one continuous motion toward the crossing and up the incline toward the tracks when his train was about 300 to 350 feet away. At this time, Allen was giving the proper whistle warning signals for the crossing; and when it was apparent the bus driver was not going to halt his vehicle, the engineer applied the train brakes in emergency and, at the same time, released his hand from the controller which triggered the "dead man" control. After this, there was nothing Bill Allen could do except continue short blasts of the whistle in an attempt to get the bus driver's attention. This failed and our train struck the bus just to the rear of center, spun it around and tipped it over as shown in the photo. Our train halted with the rear car of the four-unit consist approximately 50 feet beyond the crossing.

I had brought my secretary, Marge Barnett, with me to the scene and she went to the location where the New York City police had set up a command center in order to try to obtain names of the children on the bus. At the same time, I started to scout for possible eyewitnesses. As luck would have it, I located two excellent eyewitnesses. One was an off-duty NYC motorcycle police officer who was on the west side of our tracks waiting for the bus to clear the crossing and observed the entire incident. He confirmed the speed of our train, the lighted headlight, the whistle warnings and the flashlight and bell warning system, as well as the action of the bus driver. On the opposite side of our tracks, an off-duty New York State Thruway police officer was about to follow the bus over the crossing and he too observed all that the NYC police officer had reported. Later, I was able to locate several people who, while not eyewitnesses to the incident, did confirm that they heard our approaching train and the unusual whistle warnings for the crossing. At that time, we determined that there were approximately 12 children on the bus, several with minor injuries and one who was hospitalized.

As expected, a number of governmental agencies wanted to get in the act; but we were able to control the investigation to some extent. We provided our train crew for testimony at a meeting to which we invited the FRA, the NY Public Utility

District Claim Agent Bud Fischer examines the school bus after a grade crossing accident on the SIRT in Grant City, New York, on November 7, 1960. The railway was found to not be negligent in the accident but that doesn't mean that justice was served.

Bud Fischer collection.

Commission and the local District Attorney to send representatives and gave them copies of statements obtained at that hearing. In charge of this meeting was Mr. Donald Dunn, our Defense Attorney. He did most of the interrogation but the others were permitted to question our crew about the incident. As a result, there was no action taken by any of those agencies as it was very apparent that the SIRT crew was not at fault.

As expected, a number of lawsuits were filed in Supreme Court, Richmond County, New York, by the parents of the children who were on the bus at the time of the accident for injuries claimed. They alleged negligence on the part of the SIRT as well as the bus company. In the proceedings, prior to trial before Judge Henry Crane, (the only Republican judge in Richmond County and Kings County Brooklyn where he sat) it was decided to combine all the suits into one action. Also, the trial was to be bifurcated. That meant the first part of the trial was to determine negligence, if it existed. Thereafter, a second trial was to be continued with the same jury to determine the extent of injuries and the dollar amount of damages, if warranted.

My memory is not clear as to the trial date. However, I think it was in early fall of 1963 or spring of 1964 that the trial commenced before Judge Crane and a jury of 12 (tried & true). After approximately five to six days of testimony, the jury returned a verdict in favor of the SIRT but against the bus company. Thereafter, Liberty Mutual Insurance Company, the insurers of the bus company, immediately proceeded to attempt settlement on all of the claims.

This, I thought, ended the matter; but I learned later, after I was transferred to Toledo, Ohio, in 1965, that one or two additional lawsuits were filed by the parents of children who claimed injury whom we did not even know were on the bus. (They came out of the woodwork, so to speak after the incident which was not unusual for some New York City claimants. It occurs all the time.) The evidence at the trial was not preserved and, at that time, the statute of limitations for minor children in the State of New York had one year beyond the time they reached their majority. Therefore, even though we were found not guilty in our trial, the expenses for a new trial far outweighed the cost of

A two-car train of the type that hit the school bus.

settlement. So, we capitulated and settled their claims for a reasonable amount. However, I do not know the amount of the settlements.

An Afterthought

We were extremely fortunate in having Mr. Dunn as our Defense Counsel. One day in open court, (U.S. District Court for the Southern District of New York) Judge Irving Kaufman, the judge who sentenced the Rosenbergs to death for spying for Russia, stated that, in his opinion, Donald Dunn was the most dangerous defense trial lawyer in New York City. Obviously, we were exceedingly proud that he was our attorney.

In the 13 years that I was assigned to the New York area, we settled those cases where we felt we had responsibility for injuries or property damages claimed, for reasonable amounts. But, if a case had to be tried because of untrue allegations claimed, or excessive monetary demands made by plaintiffs, we never, ever, lost a case. THAT'S SOME RECORD!!

Collision at Leith

By Bill Drumm
January 2006

In 1948, there was a collision of a B&O westward coal train (towards Connellsville, Pennsylvania) and an eastward Western Maryland train of empties at Leith, Pennsylvania.

Leith is located 14 miles east of Connellsville, Pennsylvania, on the Fairmont, Morgantown and Pittsburgh (FM&P) subdivision. This subdivision ran from Connellsville to Fairmont, West Virginia, and was known locally as the "Sheepskin." There are many stories as to the origin of this nickname but that's the problem. There are many stories! The Western Maryland had trackage rights over this part of the B&O to reach their branch lines at Chieftian, West Virginia, that served local coal mines.

In 1948, there was a passing siding located on the south side of the single main track at Leith. There was an open train order office located at the east end of the passing siding. Manual block rules were in effect on the main track.

The operator at Leith controlled a hand-operated switch at the east end of the siding just outside of the office and a semaphore signal that was controlled from inside the office. Trains approaching Leith were given the semaphore signal to proceed when the block was clear of opposing trains.

Oliver, Pennsylvania, was the next train order office located three miles west of Leith.

If an eastward train was to take the siding at Leith, the Train Dispatcher in Pittsburgh, Pennsylvania, would authorize the Operator at Oliver to give the crew a message to take siding at Leith. If this message was not given, the eastward train would proceed up the main track to the Leith train order office.

On the day of the collision, there was an eastward Western Maryland train approaching Oliver and a westward B&O train was near Leith. At first, the Train Dispatcher wanted the eastward Western Maryland train to go up the main track to the Leith train order office and the B&O train was to take siding at Leith. The operator at Leith, upon hearing this, lined the switch to the siding for the westward train. However, at the last minute the Dispatcher decided to have the eastward Western Maryland train take the siding at Leith. The Operator at Leith forgot that he had the siding switch lined for the siding. He then gave the westward B&O train the signal to proceed. The crew on the B&O train was approaching Leith at 30 mph. They did not notice the switch was lined for the siding. They entered the siding and struck the Western Maryland train head on approximately ten car lengths west of the office. However, before this happened, both crews jumped from their engines

The result of this accident caused at least 60 cars to derail and both engines were destroyed. Both were steam engines.

The Leith train order office sat at ground level and the derailed cars surrounded the office but the office was not damaged. Fortunately, no one was killed or injured.

The Operator at Leith that caused the accident was a man by the name of Aggie Blosser. He was in his early 60s and had worked as an Operator for about 40 years. His service record was clear.

This accident happened on a Sunday and, at that time, I was a Telegraph Operator and was scheduled to work the first trick at Leith on Monday, the following day. When I arrived at Leith, I had to climb over derailed cars to get into the office. The single main track was blocked for three days, and the cleanup took about two months. There was a streetcar line that ran next to the B&O main and it was also blocked.

Everyone thought Aggie Blosser would be dismissed for causing this accident but he was not. All he got was a reprimand. Aggie Blosser continued to work at Leith until he reached 65 years of age and then retired.

I knew Aggie Blosser from working at Leith and I found him to be a no-nonsense person, who I considered very reliable. I left the area shortly after the accident to work in Pittsburgh and never saw Aggie Blosser again.

Very Hazardous Duty

By Bill Lakel
October 2007

It was August, 1969, and hot and dry in Indiana. I was Trainmaster at North Vernon. I had just returned from Seymour, Indiana, and the handling of a Milwaukee Railroad interchange. These interchange moves always included a cut of cars from the Crane Army Ordinance Depot located just north of Seymour. To save time for both crews and to keep from blocking all roads in the city, I had made arrangements with both crews to expedite the move. The B&O crew would make a cut including the required idlers and pull ahead. The Milwaukee crew would then pull ahead on our tracks and back the pick-up out on our main and then leave

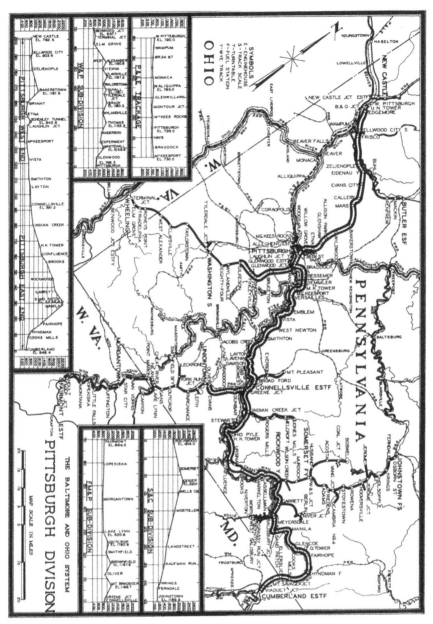

Pittsburgh Division April 26, 1964, employee timetable map. It shows the main line from Cumberland, connecting to the Cumberland Division, to New Castle, Pennsylvania where it joins the Akron-Chicago Division enroute to Chicago.

Ray Lichty collection.

town. Our B&O crew would then only have to make train solid, do the air test and leave town. While not "kosher" with some rules and labor agreements, this move saved time and lots of problems with the city of Seymour which was divided completely in half by our main line.

When the Chief Dispatcher at Shops (Washington, Indiana) called me at home and said that the eastbound was derailed at East Osgood, Indiana, I immediately thought that maybe we would be lucky and those cars we picked up at Seymour would not be involved in the derailment. No such luck! The derailment was between the high bridge and the Milan train order office and was close to some road crossings.

I had ordered the wreck train from Cincinnati and had the head end of the derailed train inspected and they continued to Storrs Yard, leaving the waybills at Milan for the balance of the train, including the derailed cars. When I picked up the bills, I found four cars placarded "Dangerous" and on military waybills. I called the Depot at Crane and found that I had one boxcar of M-10 bombs, one car of 20 mm cannon shells, one car of small arms ammunition and a 50-ft double-door boxcar of smokeless powder in 50-lb boxes. I called our hazmat people in Huntington, West Virginia, and they said it was okay to work the wreck because the cars were not placarded "Explosive". I was not worried about the bombs or the shells for the bombs were in racks and not fused and the ammunition was in wood boxes and pretty safe. The powder worried me, so I called Crane Depot back. He told me to open one door very carefully, light my flashlight before going in and check the load. If any loose powder was evident, I was to leave the car, stop all work and call him immediately.

When I opened the door, I found the car was loaded with waxed cardboard boxes, each weighing 50 pounds. The car was loaded completely end to end with no void in the doorway so there was no evidence of shifting. I climbed up on the boxes to inspect the load for loose powder. There was an acid-like smell which was almost sweet. When I walked on the boxes, they crunched like walking on frozen snow. I inspected the entire load; and because of the way the load was packed, no boxes had come open and no loose powder was seen. I closed the door and called the officer at Crane Depot with the report. He said it was okay to work the wreck. I told him there would be sparks from the cables since the car was off the trucks and had to be raised with a crane. He said that was okay since no loose powder was evident.

Jackie Harmling and the X218 250-ton Brownhoist wreck crane from Cincinnati cleaned up the wreck with no complications. The military loads were returned to Crane Depot for further disposition.

I often wondered if the hazmat people at Huntington would have heard the blast if I were blown to the "Happy Hunting Ground" in the sky had there been loose powder in and around that car.

Off Track

Lloyd D. Lewis
October 2011

T'was mid-February of 1988 but it could have been February of 1989. Should have kept a diary. I was on beeper duty for media calls all that weekend and, sure enough, on Sunday evening I got a call from the "round building" (the Dufford Dispatching Center in West Jacksonville) office that handled such things. At that time, I was Director of Media Relations in CSX's Corporate Communications Department.

My orders were to report to Cecil Field about 11 p.m. that night to meet with men from Operating and Engineering to fly to the Akron, Ohio, airport to cover the major derailment of a CSX freight on Conrail tracks in South Akron.

When I arrived at the appointed time and was shown our aircraft, I knew without a doubt that the good days of jetting around the CSX and Chessie Systems were long gone!! Before my colleagues and I was a quite small propeller plane that held all five of us - and with NO room to spare.

As soon as I climbed aboard, I realized that I'd left my heaviest coat at home in Atlantic Beach, forgetting ever so quickly what a winter in Cleveland could be! Not to worry, I did not suffer at all due to a lack of body heat during my ensuing FIVE DAYS IN AKRON!!

Of course, none of us had expected to catch any sleep at all that night - and we were soon looking around quizzically (also read it nervously) at each other in the very dark, cold cabin - colder as we flew north, naturally.

Neither of the two-person crew - a man pilot and a lady co-pilot - had ever flown anywhere near Akron or Canton, which was quite understandable because our destination was at least 850 miles due north of Dear Jax.

But things got a little tense amongst us railroaders as the crew switched on the lights and began to consult their maps! That was something NONE of us had EVER experienced in the "good old days" of flying around to lots of destinations in comfortable Chessie corporate jets out of Cleveland, Baltimore and Huntington.

Although I did not let on to my colleagues, I had the funniest feeling that here in the dead of a dark winter's night flying up through central Ohio — getting colder by the minute! — and not only by dint of the temperature — that we were going to overshoot Akron AND Cleveland airports and be found sometime the next day beside a wrecked plane on an iceberg in the middle of Lake Erie!!

Needless to say, my fiercest fears did not happen and modern aviation technology won the day — and all that very long night. Dawn was breaking in a snowstorm as we descended past the Akron airport control tower and landed safely. WHEW!!

[You really cannot make up this stuff!! Stay tuned!]

We were met by very friendly division personnel, who, as I now recall, even brought us breakfast following our something like six-hour flight. Off to the derailment scene we went.

The "command center" for railroad, police and fire personnel was a small brick building behind a funeral home in South Akron, which could have been (come to think of it now) the local crematorium. But I sure never thought to inquire about this.

Upon arrival, I introduced myself to all the railroaders and first responders as the "PR Guy from Jacksonville" and telling them that I was the fellow who would answer all the "hovering media's" questions. Like the guys from the federal government who say, "Say, we're from Washington — and we're here to help you!!" Right on!

Then looking across the parking lot — which was just across the street from the track upon which the multi-car derailment had occurred the night before — I spied Ohio Senator Howard Metzenbaum, without a doubt espousing "the wicked evils of that nasty railroad business" to any media within earshot. I forget his party affiliation but it did not matter even a whit when I just knew he was "taking on" my very valued employer in Surely Scurrilous Terms!

Quite needless to write, I steered clear of the distinguished looking white-haired Senator on that cold, snowy Monday morning in South Akron and never did have the pleasure of meeting him in any venue.

I soon discovered that the track over which our CSX freight was running was probably one of Conrail's worst examples of roadway maintenance. Thus, I maintained this fact in my many public statements and one-person (ME!) impromptu press conferences during nearly the next week but I was never sure how much the "great unwashed public" cared — or even care today — about such technicalities.

What the television and radio viewers and newspaper readers knew was that a train with a bunch of loaded chemical tank cars had derailed in the Kenmore section of South Akron — and several of those suckers had blown themselves to Kingdom Come!!

(I also discovered — as an aside after all these ensuing years — that this is the very same Kenmore neighborhood which gave its name to the Sears Roebuck & Company brand of washers, dryers and such — a few years before their manufacture was surely shifted to China!)

Never did I think to keep track of the number of interviews I had with the local, state and national media — plus those usually three- or four-times daily (and very live!) impromptu press conferences at a good safe distance from the re-railing operations. Sometimes they were nearly in the middle of a public street closed because it had not been plowed for several days. After one of those 11 p.m. late TV news sessions — which I really relished and which always featured a dozen or more live microphones directly beneath my closely shaved chin — I decided to call my brother and sister-in-law in Greeley, Colorado. Just to let them know where I was.

So, I made my way in the semi-darkness through about three feet of snow and found a public telephone right next to a parking meter that was virtually hidden by the white precipitation.

When my sister-in-law Margie answered, I said, "This is Lloyd. Guess where I am?" "You're in Akron, Ohio," she quickly answered. "Well how in the world did you all know THAT?" Back she came: "Because your name is all over TV, "The Denver Post' and our "Rocky Mountain News!! " All I could think of to say was, "Well, what do you know?"

The days passed quickly and I, of course, stayed in touch at least daily with Our Great Boss in Jax, Diane S. Liebman, VP of Corporate Communications, and my Eminent and Extremely Knowledgeable PR Spokesman Colleague, the Unforgettable R (for Robert) Lindsay Leckie, who taught me nearly as much about "Real Railroading" as My Own Dear Dad.

Author's Note Follows: "By the way, Lindsay, if you read this, PLEASE CALL ME in Kenova, WV, at 304/730-4092!! I can't find you, Brother!! Don't you DARE forget, 'cause I been a-knowin' you a LOOOOOOONG TIME!!!!]]

I must insert here that Our CSX Railroad Guys were always great to provide me with any information I needed to give "the press". For all my 12 great years in PR -- many times as the only spokesman for Chessie and then CSX -- I constantly found that if the Operating and Engineering, Finance, etc., officers think you know the business of railroading -- in all its various forms and sometimes quite complicated machinations -- especially including The Dreaded Derailments -- they trusted me.

THAT, Ladies and Gentlemen, is a Genuinely Very Good Feeling!

My company rental car came in very handy all those days and nights as I drove the streets of Akron from the derailment site to our official railroad place of residence, the unique Quaker Square Hilton Hotel on Quaker Square right downtown. That was a fun place to stay! After Quaker Oats Company left town to move to Chicago (I think) a few years before the late 1980s, the Hilton hotel chain converted the former concrete oats silos to hotel rooms.

Thus, the outer walls were round — which reminded me of my office on the 39th floor of Terminal Tower just a few miles north of us in Cleveland. Ah, Terminal Tower:

What a wonderful building I was privileged to inhabit for nearly seven years, 1979-1986!

No matter how much sleep we got the night before, we officers met at 7 a.m. the next morning after breakfast in an equally round conference room on the Quaker Square Hilton's first floor for an update of the day before and for me to learn what The Real Men Of This Railroad hoped to accomplish that day. It was just a GREAT way to make a living!!

Then when we from Jax had been in Akron about four days — I should've kept a diary — we had yet another derailment!! OOPS!! One morning while transporting at a very slow speed on flat cars about half a dozen bodies of empty and scorched tank cars from South Akron to a storage yard on the city's north side for all sorts of testing and investigation, several of them tipped over on the double-track mainline and blocked the westbound track on a steep curve!

So, that required much consultation — right now! -- with my officer colleagues and with my Jax compatriots. My job was determined to be CSX liaison with the Mayor of Akron so I met with him several times and helped him at news conferences, taking the heat for CSX, as was written right there in my job description!!

Late on the Thursday afternoon of my longest-ever visit to Akron, Ohio; I visited the small yard where the tank car bodies were stored awaiting visits from the National Transportation Safety Board. And I soon found out that these guys really WERE from Washington and they really WERE here to help us!

Right off, I met several NTSB men roaming through the wrecked tank cars. When I introduced myself, one of them allowed as to how he was the official NTSB public spokesman — and he had just arrived from Washington, of course. In a polite but firm way, he promptly allowed as to how he would henceforth from that very moment take over all communications with the public through the media.

Well, sir, that sure shut me down. So I called Diane Liebman in Jax to inform her and, being as the next day was Friday, asked her if I could take the weekend off and spend it in Cleveland visiting old friends.

Her answer was a very pleasant yes, so I drove the rental car north about 50 miles, had a fine time and flew home from Cleveland Hopkins International Airport on Sunday evening, my seventh day of absenteeism from 500 Water Street and my lovely home four blocks from the ocean in Atlantic Beach, Florida!!

That was the longest I ever spent out of town to cover a Chessie/CSX derailment in my 12 years (1979-1991) in PR Departments in both Jacksonville and Cleveland. However, others were just as interesting in their own ways. Once again, A TERRIFIC way to make a living!!

Section B

SALES and MARKETING

Chapter 7   Selling Railroad Freight and Passengers Services

Bush's Best Beans

By Harry Hinds
April 2009

Back in the 1950s, I was a Traveling Freight Agent working out of our Memphis District Freight Office and traveling the state of Arkansas. We did not get a lot of business to or from the northwest corner of the state but, now and then, we would handle an inbound carload originating in B&O territory, moving through the St. Louis gateway. Therefore, I made just one or two trips a year into that area.

At the time, on one of my semi-annual (or annual) trips, our records showed that we handled a carload of can stock to a canning plant near Rogers, Arkansas. That plant was one of the early Bush Brothers baked beans plants. (Incidentally, in 1962, Rogers was the site of the first Wal-Mart store.)

Never having been there before, I stopped in the local SLSF (Frisco) agent's office and asked the agent who at the plant I should see about their rail traffic. He told me I should talk with John Winchester.

When I arrived at the plant, I told the receptionist that I would like to see Mr. Winchester. She told me go down a hall to the third door on the right; just walk in and I would find Mr. Winchester.

When I entered the room, I found three men who were gathered around a table on which there were five or six plates, each containing pork and beans. The three men were in a heated argument over which plate contained the best beans.

I stood at the door for a few minutes when one of the men noticed me there. He looked at me and then said, "Come here, Bud, and tell us which one you think best." There was a plate

Bush Baked Beans were produced and canned in the old Bush Brothers factory in Rodgers, Arkansas. It was here that Harry Hinds voiced his opinion on the best beans. Today, the factory has been converted to a museum and gift shop featuring Bush Baked Beans memorabilia.

containing some little wooden spoons (the flat ones that you used to get with a dish of ice cream). So I started in on the beans.

I finally made my decision and said, "Well, they're all good, but I like this one best." The man who called me over (who apparently was losing the argument) got a little hot under the collar and told me that I didn't know what I was talking about and that I obviously didn't know anything about beans. I told him that I was a child of the "Big Depression" and that I had probably eaten more beans than he had ever seen.

A few more heated words were exchanged (the other two men were really enjoying the show). Then he asked me, "Who the hell are you, any way, and what are you doing here?" I replied, "My name is Harry Hinds. I represent the Baltimore & Ohio Railroad and I'm here to see John Winchester about any rail traffic the company may be shipping to the Northeast and any inbound traffic from that area you may have in the future".

He said, "Well, I'm John Winchester!"

The other two gentlemen were practically rolling on the floor at this time. Very intelligently, I then said, "Uh huh—tell me again, Mr. Winchester, which one of these beans do you think best?" I could only agree.

After we all had a good laugh, we went across the road to a small cafe and I bought the coffee. Whenever I see a can of Bush's Pork and Beans, I can't help but wonder if they were the ones I liked best.

Sales Blitz—Timesaver Service
By Ken Roloson
January 2002

It has been a long time since LCL (less-than-carload freight) was a household word on the Baltimore and Ohio Railroad. Back in 1950, the B&O was very much involved in the LCL business, along with the freight forwarding companies, many of which the railroads promoted to operate over their lines.

Mr. A. S. Baker (Al), no relation to the other B&O Bakers, was Manager Merchandise Traffic in Baltimore and an enthusiastic supporter of our LCL Service. Mr. Baker would occasionally come up to Philadelphia, where I was stationed as a Freight Traffic Representative at the time, and hold breakfast meetings at one of the better hotels with our large LCL shippers. He was extremely well thought of by traffic officials of the large LCL shippers, such as F. W. Woolworth, S. S. Kresge, Sears Roebuck, Montgomery Ward and others. The freight forwarding companies were very active at this time. On the B & O, we had General Carloading Co., Republic Carloading and Distributing Co. and later the ABC Freight Forwarding Company. Some of these companies were created by the B&O in order to compete with forwarders operating on NYC and PRR lines. Universal Carloading and Distributing Co. operated primarily on NYC and Acme Fast Freight and National Carloading on the PRR. These forwarders did a huge business. There were some specialized freight forwarders, i.e. Ohio Fast Freight (New York‑Cleveland),

While some readers may find the inclusion of a photo of a railroad car model in this book as a step away from reality, it is included here as it best depicts the paint scheme employed on B&O's Timesaver equipment. It was distinctive as to style and choice of the bold colors of blue and orange. The box cars were rolling advertisements of the less-than-carload service. They also were easily stopped by the railroad employees who well knew of their priority handling requirements.

Terminal Freight Handling (Sears Roebuck & Co.) and Springmeir Shipping Co. There was plenty of freight for all, including the railroads' own LCL service. Some people, at that time, made statements that the forwarders were "parasites"-- skimming the most profitable traffic off the top and leaving the railroads' LCL service with the lamp shades and other balloon freight. In any event, the revenues derived from this traffic were substantial. The long haul truckers had not yet moved into the picture at this point.

The Philadelphia Traffic (Sales) Department was quite large at the time, consisting of: the General Freight Agent, two District Freight Agents (one for Central States Dispatch "CSD" Routes), two Perishable Representatives, three Traveling Freight Agents, and five Local Freight Sales Representatives, plus the supporting clerical personnel.

At that time, a sales blitz was instigated for the entire railroad to generate new traffic. Steve Taylor was designated as the coordinator for the "Blitz". The entire sales force participated in the "Blitz," which lasted for about a week, as I recall. At this particular time, the Freight Traffic Department was awash with

"Giveaways" provided by management, such as book matches and scratch pads, which assisted in making the "Blitz" a success. People were called on who had never seen a B&O Freight Representative.......ever! The program was concentrated in the northeast section of the city, where most of the LCL shippers were located. At the same time, management inaugurated "Time Saver Service" on the B&O and several of our red-hot merchandise trains were named "Time Savers." This era was not to prevail for the long term as clouds appeared on the horizon. The New Jersey Turnpike was built in the early 1950s which was the forerunner of the coming Federal Interstate Highway System. The long-haul truck era began moving into the picture, gradually eroding the LCL traffic over time. Individual railroads started embargoing LCL and eventually the system collapsed. There were other factors, not the least of which was labor. Now, we have UPS and FedEx, and the USPS and AMTRAK are making inroads on the truck lines. They say history repeats itself but I will not be around to witness this one.

Customer Service

By Bob Frost
October 2003

There were several unique ways railroad sales people could assist customers and, often, we didn't realize the scope of the tools available to us. In the early 1990s, I was working with Michael Day, President, Francis Day Company in Rockville, Maryland. The Day Company was a major supplier of asphalt in the Baltimore/Washington marketplace. Mike Day was concerned about their long-term future and was looking for expansion into the stone market.

Accordingly, he had spent significant funds to purchase a quarry near Martinsburg, West Virginia, and was looking for rail access to enter the Maryland market. Accompanied by Pete Hitchens, Day's Comptroller, Mike and I went to the quarry site to determine whether rail use was feasible.

In viewing the site, we noted a long stretch of land adjacent to CSXT's trackage which would accommodate new turnouts and siding capability. Mike was pleased, as he felt he could go forward with his project.

Mike then asked what would be the shipping location since we were about five miles from Martinsburg and there wasn't a town at this location—all farmland. I thought a second and then said, "Well, why don't we just call it Dayco, West Virginia?" Mike asked, "What do you mean? How can you do that?" I explained the railroad stations and that it was relatively easy to add another. I would handle with Bob Patterson and it would be accomplished within 60 days. We were walking back to the car and I heard Mike carrying on an earnest conversation with Pete Hitchens. Later, I asked Pete if there were any problems. Pete said, "No. Mike just was saying to me that here he spent years of his life and millions of his dollars to make sure his name goes on after he dies and Bob Frost says 'Why don't we just call it Dayco? It can be done within 60 days?'" This, free of charge, accomplished his main aim and I had treated it as no big deal.

If you review the Open and Prepay, you should see Dayco, West Virginia. Many other people were involved behind the scenes to have this happen. Many other people don't realize the impact these minor actions have on the lives of our customers. As Paul Harvey would say, "Now you know the rest of the story."

Local Area Management on the B&O RR
The Story of the Sidney, Ohio, Piggyback Ramp
By Ken Roloson
April 2000

Back in the early 1960s, ALCOA, Inc., headquarters Pittsburgh, Pennsylvania, approached the B&O advising they were contemplating the construction of an aluminum siding plant at Sidney, Ohio. They wanted to move the structural steel and accessories on flatbed trailers in TOFC (Trailer on flat car) Service to Sidney, Ohio, if we would provide a Piggyback Ramp at that location. Several hundred trailers were involved. This occurred before the Chessie era began on the B&O RR.

B&O people were agreeable and a ramp was constructed at minimal expense. A ramping and deramping contract was negotiated with the Sidney Truck & Storage Co., a local trucker, also at minimal expense. Rates were established to move this traffic and the entire matter was handled in an expeditious manner.

Our Sidney agency was a one-man station and no additional help was required. The movement took place without incident and, in retrospect, I believe it involved about 250 trailers.

Now that the movement was completed, what do we do with this new ramp? There were no rates available to and from Sidney, making it impossible to solicit any traffic. Some officials in Baltimore wanted to close down the ramp. Ray Blayney, our Traveling Freight Agent, working out of the Dayton, Ohio, office, was finally successful in prevailing upon our Rate Department to publish "Plan III, Freight All Kinds" rates to and from Sidney. At this particular time, these FAK rates were utilized for most TOFC and COFC (Container on flat car) movements. Another problem was the fact that Sidney was served by local freight train service; Lima to Dayton on Monday, Wednesday and Friday and northbound Dayton to Lima on Tuesday, Thursday and Saturday. Ray was a former Agent-Operator and he had a very close relationship with the Dayton Dispatcher and the Trainmaster at Dayton. From a service standpoint, it was agreed and outbound loads would move on the

The early B&O piggyback ramp shows how a flatcar can easily create a "circus style" loading ramp. "Circus style" takes its name from the way circus trailers were traditionally loaded on railroad cars.

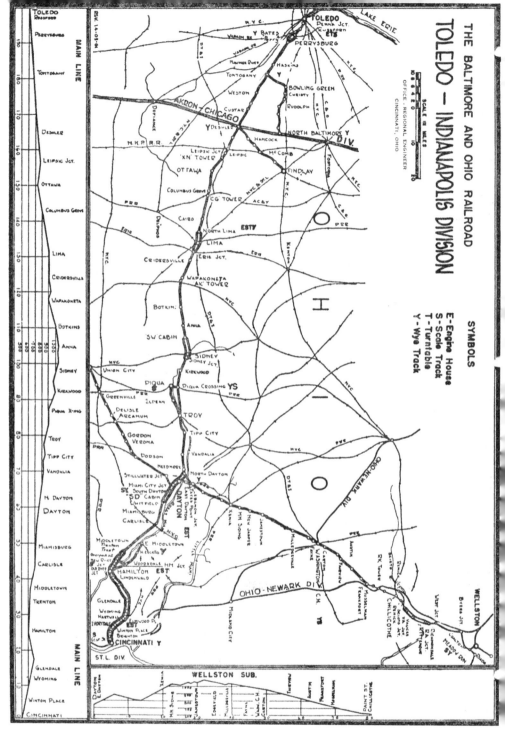

Toledo-Indianapolis Division April 26, 1964, employee timetable map showing the Cincinnati-Toledo main line and branches.

Ray Lichty collection.

local North on Tuesday, Thursday and Saturday for connection with Train 294 to Willard, thence Train 94 beyond. On days the local did not operate, northbound arrangements were made for Train 86 to pick up the trailers and move them into Lima for connection with 294 - 94 as above. This arrangement provided daily service with 2nd day arrivals at Baltimore, Philadelphia and New York. It wasn't long before the steamship companies got wind of this and began positioning containers at Sidney for outbound loading to the ports. A flawless and economical operation developed by local people! I am sure that Bill Johnston at Cincinnati was aware of it

I recall two movements in particular: A lumber company at Minster, Ohio, received a very large contract to supply custom-cut and polished lumber for bowling alleys in Japan. Several hundred containers were involved. Ray also latched onto a regular and substantial movement of cigar boxes to Tampa, Florida. Cigar boxes being a light loading commodity, over-the-road truck rates were very high and we were able to reduce this shipper's transportation costs considerably.

As time went on, the austerity programs engulfed all departments and Ray Blayney's job was abolished. My office in Dayton was reduced from eight to four people. When I retired on September 1, 1976, the Sidney ramp was still operating but I understand it was later closed.

That's the way it was back in those days!

The "Ohio" in Baltimore & Ohio meant the Ohio River and Wheeling, West Virginia, was its first terminal at the river in 1853. It was still a busy spot in the early 1950s when P-7 Pacific 5300 was on the point of a passenger train at the B&O's impressive 1908 Beaux-Arts station. The tracks here are now gone, but happily both the locomotive and station survive -- the 5300 at the B&O Museum in Baltimore and the station as the home of West Virginia Northern Community College.

J. J. Young photo, B&O Railroad Historical Society collection.

Chapter 8

The Baldinger Collection

Steve's Stories

By Steve Baldinger
As told to Mark Craven
July 2007

N&N Editor's Note: I was recently contacted by Mark Craven who volunteered to write a RABO Bio on Steve Baldinger. The two had worked together in the Sales Department and now lived relatively close together in Arizona. Steve had turned 95 earlier this year. I was, of course, delighted to get Steve's bio. It will appear in the next issue of News & Notes.

In the conversations associated with that task, Mark mentioned that Steve was "full of stories!"—as you would expect of any good salesman. Mark offered that he would be the writer and Steve the talker and the two of them would record some of these tales. So, the effort is underway. What follows is the first three installments of "Steve's Stories". More will come in September and even more after that.

I am very pleased that these two have undertaken such a task and would encourage others to join in such collaborations.

Late 1940s – Omaha, Nebraska, Office; Part 1

Traveling out of the Omaha Office, Steve got the company car one week each month. He used this week to make calls in Sioux Falls and Sioux City, Iowa. On these trips, there was a lot of open road; and on his first trip, nature's call caught up with him between Sioux Falls and Sioux City. He started looking; and finally about midway between the two cities, he found the C&NW Station at Hawarden, Iowa. It was a neat little station with an agent-operator, a coal burning stove and a clean warm restroom. Steve gave the Agent his card and asked if he could avail himself of the facilities. Like many small agencies, the Agent took Steve's calling card and tacked it to the wall.

This station became a regular stop for Steve when he was making the swing through this part of his territory and for more than one reason. On some occasions, the Agent would be too busy on the telegraph; and Steve would just wave and leave his card. Over the years, the Agent continued to tack Steve's card to the wall.

After Steve was transferred to Chicago, Murray Campbell, the District Freight Representative-Omaha had an occasion to take two officials to meet with some Morrell people at Sioux Falls. Morrell at that time was the largest B&O traffic producer within the Omaha sales territory. Well, all was going well with Murray; but just about halfway between the two cities, all three men needed to stop and they, too, found that little C&NW station. After introducing themselves and giving the Agent their cards, each visited the restroom.

After leaving the station, one of the officials said to Murray, "Did you see all of those calling cards from Steve Baldinger tacked to the wall? I want you to follow up with Steve and find out why he was stopping there so much." So, upon his return to the Omaha office, Murray picked up the phone and reached Steve in Chicago. Murray explained what had happened and said the officials wanted to know why Steve stopped there so often. Steve said to Murray, "Why did you stop there?" and when Murray said, "Well all three of us had to 'go'". Steve answered, "Well see, you can't even 'go' without your bosses asking why?"

Late 1940s--Omaha Office; Part 2

The C&NW ran a Motor Car out of Sioux Falls with the capability of hauling one passenger car. Steve was going to take this to Mitchell, South Dakota. It was 5 below zero when Steve showed the conductor his pass and the conductor said he would take him on but on one condition and that was Steve would tend the stove. They laughed about that but Steve had already learned being part of the gang always paid dividends, so he took care of the stove on the trip.

Along the line to Mitchell, a line crossed from Worthington, Minnesota, to Sioux City and they were to wait for a train at that point. Well, the train was late and the conductor said they had to wait because of the mail. So they waited in below zero weather with a B&O'er tending a C&NW stove.

They had been waiting for over an hour when one of the passengers suggested singing a few songs would pass the time more quickly. Since it was near the holidays, everyone agreed and the singing started. A little while later, the train arrived from

Worthington; and when pulling close to the waiting Motor Car, the Engineer heard the singing and said to the Fireman, "Call the sheriff, they're all drunk over there!"

Late 1940s--Omaha Office; Part 3

Steve left Omaha on a BN Rail Motor Car to Beatrice, Nebraska, where he called on Beatrice Manufacturing. This company made windmills that were shipped all over the world.

When Steve talked about the BN, he mentioned they had also developed Burlington Trailways Bus Line that was operated separately from the railroad. He said when he used this service, it was always on time, the employees were courteous and the equipment was always clean.

Steve then took a bus to Fairbury, Nebraska, where he called on the headquarters of Heasted Stores. This was a variety chain with stores in Nebraska, South Dakota and California. They received small quantities of goods from all over the east and Steve arranged for these goods to be channeled through Camden Station with a Trap Car (LCL) sent to Fairbury.

He then took a bus to Superior, Nebraska, where several creameries were located. Steve was after the sweet butter they manufactured and shipped to New York City. After making his calls, he stayed the night in Superior.

The next day he caught a MP mixed train from Superior to Hastings, Nebraska. He presented his pass to the conductor who said, "I haven't seen you here before." The caboose was an extended version and could carry four passengers. On the way to Hastings, the crew stopped to switch a large grain elevator. Steve had stepped off the caboose with the conductor; and the owner of the mill, seeing a man in a suit, came running toward them. The conductor said to Steve, "Show him your pass and introduce yourself and make sure he understands you are a traveling freight agent for the B&O." Steve later learned the shipper could only ship cracked corn and he was sure by their actions they were shipping whole kernel corn. He did get two of the carloads they had switched out for Early and Daniel Company, Cincinnati, Ohio, via E St Louis – B&O.

Upon arriving in Hastings, Steve checked in at the local hotel. He had invited the Traffic Manager of the Naval Ammunition

Depot for dinner; and after meeting in the lobby, Steve invited him up to his room for a drink. During this time period, many counties, cities, etc., were dry so every good sales person carried a bottle for these occasions. No sooner did they get to the room and had their drinks than the phone rang. Steve answered and a male voice said, "This is the front desk and you have a woman in the room and that is not tolerated in this establishment." Steve said, "I don't have any woman in my room" and the man said, "Oh yes you do!" This went on for a while and then there was some laughter at the other end of the line. Steve Swift, the MP Traveling Freight Agent, happened to be in the lobby when Steve and the customer went to his room. The MP Traveling Agent had to have a little fun. Steve invited him up to the room and they all had a drink!

While visiting with Steve, the MP man said, "What about these carloads of melons you're supposed to handle over the Burlington." Steve asked, "How did you hear about that?" The MP man said, "We know all about it." So Steve had to tell the story about this produce man in Baltimore who figured a way of prolonging the melon season beyond those grown in Colorado (Rocky Ford). He made a deal with some farmers around Eustis, Florida, to plant melons that would ripen just after the Colorado crop. The fall had been a pleasant one and the crop was nearing harvest and the Burlington Traveling Freight Agent had already arranged for 10 reefer cars iced and ready for loading. It just happened that the night just before they were to start the harvest there was a hard freeze. Goodbye melons and Steve's 10 carloads!

Getting back to the Naval Depot: The railroads were handling plenty of traffic but a change came about when Harry Truman became President. There happened to be a trucker based in Kansas City that happened to be a personal friend of President Truman and it just happened that the trucking company started hauling most of the freight. Steve pointed this out but they said that it must have been just a coincidence. It just happened to be!

126

Steve's Stories

By Steve Baldinger
As told to Mark Craven
October 2007

Late 40s--Omaha Office; Part 4

One of Steve's customers in Sioux City, Iowa, was Currie Holman, a hog buyer who shipped to Baltimore, Maryland, and Allentown, Pennsylvania. Every time Steve called on Currie, he would complain to Steve how much he was costing him in profits. To explain, Currie's customers settled and paid on destination weights and any loss of weight in transit translated to less profit for him. This happened regularly on the shipments to Allentown, Pennsylvania, and it was brought up on just about every visit.

The hogs were watered and fed on the B&O at Connellsville, Pennsylvania, before moving through to the destination. Steve had written this matter up several times but the shipper continued to complain about the loss of weight. All will note; it was "Steve" who was causing the customer to lose dollars and no one else and Steve was expected to fix it.

Finally, Al Sherry, B&O's Perishable and Live Stock Agent, was making a trip through the territory and Steve took him to see Mr. Holman. The problem was explained to Al and he said he would look into it. (Currie said Steve had reported it several times but the problem wasn't corrected.) Those readers who have not had the pleasure of meeting Al Sherry do not know the tenacity of the man. The writer knew Al from his days in Pittsburgh and compares him with a bulldog. When he got hold of a problem, he didn't let go.

Al got into the problem. It developed the hogs destined to Baltimore and Allentown were getting the same rest, feed and water at Connellsville. The hogs destined to Baltimore were getting through just fine but the ones to Allentown were taking longer in transit without receiving any more food and water, therefore losing weight. Case solved. Allentown hogs received more food and water and Steve's customer was satisfied.

Writer's note: Now I know why Al Sherry had the statues of the sow and the piglets on his desk in Pittsburgh.

1950s--Chicago Office; Part 5

Steve tells the story about a B&O salesman by the name of John Buckley in the Chicago Office. Steve says John was a top-notch salesman who attended college and finally received a law degree. He used his knowledge of the law to help some of his customers when they received traffic citations.

John would listen to his customers explain their respective situations and then would usually tell them not to pay for the violation but to ask for a hearing. John would represent them at the hearing and his success rate was phenomenal. As a result, he was very popular with his customers, which related to success in securing carloads.

It just happened Ed Keenan, another salesman in the office, got a traffic ticket and asked John if he could or would help him. John's first advice was to not pay but to contest the violation and he would represent Ed in court.

The day of Ed's court appearance finally arrived and both he and John were before the judge. Well, things didn't go as well as John's other cases and Ed had to pay. The whole office got a chance to hear the volatile Ed Keenan rant and rave about John getting his %&*#% customers off, but couldn't get a fellow worker off.

1960s--Chicago Office; Part 6

Here's another Ed Keenan story. First, Ed had an explosive temperament.

Chicago winters were cold, windy and just plain miserable. Apparently, the winter weather had caused quite a pothole in front of Ed's home and he had called various city departments without success. The hole kept getting deeper; and Ed complained that when large trucks went over the pothole, his whole house vibrated!

The lid finally blew. Steve was sitting in his office with another salesman working on a project for Bill Bamert when Ed burst in saying, "That's it! I'm calling Mayor Richard Daley about that %&*#% hole. I can't stand the noise and the house shaking any longer." Steve looked up and said, "That's a good idea Ed. Why don't you call Mayor Daley."

Well, as the story goes, Ed did call Mayor Daley; and when his secretary answered and asked who was calling, Ed said, "This is

Mr. Keenan." It so happened there was an alderman by the name of John Keenan and the secretary thought it that Keenan, so she put Ed on the line with Mayor Daley. Daley said, "How are things going, John?" and Ed said, "This is not John. My name is Ed." He then goes into a hotly worded description of the pothole, the large trucks, the shaking house and why couldn't the city fix a %&*#% pothole. The Mayor thanked Ed for calling and said he would look into it.

Later, before leaving the office for the day, as was his practice, Ed called his wife, Marge, to see if she needed him to pickup anything before coming home. All that Marge could say was, "Ed, what did you do or say? There are so many trucks and machinery in the street one can hardly get through." Well, Mayor Daley got through. As Ed said later, "He had practically the whole street re-paved." And Ed's house shook no more!

1960s-Chicago Office; Part 7

Steve had become good friends with his counterpart on the CRI&P in Chicago, who also happened to be a close personal friend of Mr. Norris, a major owner of the Rock Island Railroad and owner of the Chicago Black Hawks. Through his friend, Steve was able to obtain hard-to-get tickets to the Black Hawk hockey games.

Steve used this friendship during a period when the PRR and C&NW were on strike, which caused the B&O problems at Willard and Chicago. Steve's Operating Department contact asked Steve if he could help relieve the congestion at Willard and gave him the details. Steve called his friend at the Rock Island and asked, "How would you like 80 plus carloads delivered at Chicago for the UP at Council Bluffs?" Steve told him that operations would make arrangements to deliver the carloads direct; however, it may block traffic on one of the main streets for a while. Steve asked, "So, are you on good terms with the local precinct Captain of Police?" Steve's friend said that he was on good terms and he would handle the situation. Well, the 84 carloads were delivered to the Rock Island and the main street was blocked for 20 minutes. Later, Steve's Rock Island friend said that he had really taken it on the chin from the Captain of Police for the 20-minute delay but he had soothed things over with a visit and some gifts. The next delivery only took 15 minutes. This helped relieve some of the pressure on the yards and everybody was happy. During that time, Steve also arranged for some of the sales people to help at Chicago's Barr Yard.

1960s-Chicago Office; Part 8

Tom Keefe, General Manager-Automotive, Baltimore, was working with Sales and Volkswagen in the handling of import vehicles from Locust Point to Chicago. Tom and Steve had requested funds to build a small fenced facility at Forest Hills to handle and secure the vehicles but were not getting the permission to spend the dollars. Tom found a spare portable ramp in Michigan and had it shipped to Forest Hills but they still needed some work.

Steve approached John Rogers, President of the B&OCT, for some support funds. John asked Steve, "How much are we talking about?" and Steve responded, "Around $30,000.00 for a fence and a small shanty." John gave the go ahead and the project was completed.

The first carload was shipped and Tom Keefe, along with Steve and the Terminal Agent, Bill Finnegan, were waiting for the arrival. Representatives of the two Chicago newspapers were going to be in attendance when the first carload was placed at the ramp for unloading and all were expecting a little publicity.

On Friday, the weather changed for the worst as cold wind and rain developed into a terrible ice storm. Tom was going to stay into the weekend and Steve said, "You might as well go home with this weather. The car will not be placed over the weekend." So Tom left for Baltimore. Guess what? On Sunday, the car was placed at the ramp and Tom missed the first railcar being unloaded.

Steve recalls that Chessie handled the profitable VW traffic for some time, prior to their moving to the port of Wilmington, Delaware. As the writer understands, the Port of Wilmington offered much lower rates and better service. Also, when the West Moreland, Pennsylvania, plant was constructed, VW took advantage of using motor carrier in a turnaround arrangement between Wilmington and the plant and mixing imports with local production.

1960s-Chicago Office; Part 9

Bill Finnegan, Terminal Agent, Chicago, had a habit of checking the agencies at night and one in particular was Robey St. where two clerks worked the night shift.

One night, Bill decided to pay Robey St. a visit. Bill had just approached the door and was about to enter when he spotted two young thugs who had the two clerks backed into a corner. Bill backed away and quickly got two brake clubs and hurried back to the door. Upon entering, he raised one of the clubs and brought it down on one of the desks to make a loud sound and get some attention. He swung so hard the desk collapsed from the impact.

Getting the attention of the young thugs, Bill pointed to the door he had just used and said, "There are two ways out of here; one through me and the door or out those two windows over there." Now, the Robey St. office is located where the entrance is on ground level but the windows border the street that is one story below ground level. The young hoodlums pointed out that they were on the second floor and Bill said, "You have the choice and you had better make it now!"

They decided to take the windows and left that way, one story down to the concrete pavement below.

Steve didn't know the results of the landing, but all turned out well upstairs.

Steve's story reminds me of coming into Chicago on the Illinois Central. I was standing on the tail end talking to the conductor. As we were entering through South Chicago, he told me we should step inside as some think it's nice to take target practice. You never know!

Steve's Stories

By Steve Baldinger
As told to Mark Craven
January 2008

1940s-Omaha Office; Part 10

While all of Steve's trips started at Omaha, we'll pick this one up at Sioux City, Iowa. Steve caught a CMSTP&P (Milwaukee) from Sioux City to Yankton, South Dakota; and when he got off the train, he asked the Ticket Agent where he could find the

Freight Agent. The agent pointed to a man wrestling with milk cans on the platform and said, "That's the Freight Agent." I believe Steve mentioned in his biography about each time he shook hands with a particular Freight Agent, the agent would show his hand and say this is the hand that shook the hand of Daniel Willard. Well, this is that guy!

The story goes: When Daniel Willard was President of the B&O, he was invited by the President of the Milwaukee to tour the railroad. Of course, any time Mr. Willard met a Milwaukee employee he would shake his hand and Willard shook the hand of Freight Agent Ferguson, Yankton, South Dakota. When Steve walked up to Agent Ferguson and introduced himself, he got the treatment: "This is the Hand that shook the Hand of Daniel Willard."

Agent Ferguson was not a young man and Steve marveled at the ease with which he handled those heavy milk cans. After discussing business and since it was near noon, Steve invited the agent to join him for lunch. As they walked down the street, they were passing an alcohol plant and Ferguson asked Steve if he had called there and Steve said, "Not yet." The agent said, "Well, let's go in and I'll introduce you." So, they went in and Steve was introduced and found that there were 12 carloads ready to be shipped—all via the PRR to Philadelphia, Pennsylvania. The agent and Steve persuaded the shipper to route six of the carloads via the B&O. It was so important to meet and know the local freight agents in an off-line territory as their knowledge of the local industry and their influence was great.

After returning from lunch, the agent said to Steve, "Go over there and look in the water cooler." Steve went over and took a look and there, buried in the ice, was a pint of bourbon and alongside it was a tin cup. He said, "Help yourself", as those who visited and were in the agent's good graces did. Of course, every so often a visitor would replace the pint.

Agent Ferguson was not the only one in the family to work on the Milwaukee. He told Steve his son also was with the Milwaukee and worked as a Traveling Freight Agent out of Omaha too. Regardless of how many times Steve would call on Mr. Ferguson, the meeting would always start the same, "This is the Hand......"

Steve stayed the night in Yankton and the next morning

Mark Craven stands behind Steve Baldinger in a photo taken during one of their sessions that created this 2007-2008 series of stories in "Rails' Tales."   *Mark Craven collection.*

boarded a train to Mitchell, South Dakota, where he had arranged to call at a local coal yard. In those days, coal yards providing coal for domestic use were called on by Merchandise Sales rather than by Coal Sales, and this particular yard was ordering 25 carloads of smokeless coal from West Virginia. He got the B&O included in the routing. At this particular time, the great majority of homes were heated by coal and practically every town had a coal yard. These days, it's natural gas and electricity providing the energy for most domestic heat, with coal-fired power plants providing a large percentage of the electricity.

1940s-Omaha Office; Part 11

Steve took a train from Omaha that originated on the C&NW at Minneapolis and merged with a UP train at Omaha with an ultimate destination on the west coast. Steve's destination was Lexington, Nebraska, where he would call on Corn Land Products, one of the largest producers of alfalfa pellets. The alfalfa was brought to the plant and was dried, using natural gas supplied by the Kansas Nebraska Gas Company. After drying and processing, the pellet form provided the greatest amount of nutritional value; and as a result, the firm had great difficulty in producing enough to satisfy the demand.

Steve had looked at the timetable and noted the train did not stop for non-paying passengers and he wanted to talk to the conductor about whether they would be stopping at Lexington. He located the conductor introduced himself and showed him his pass and the timetable stating he was going to Lexington, but noticed the reference about only stopping for paying passengers. Steve asked the conductor if he had any paying passengers on the train destined for Lexington. The conductor looked at Steve and told him he did not. Steve said, "Well I guess I'll have to go to the next station and take the bus back." The conductor then said to Steve, "Oh I don't think we have to do that; we'll make an exception here." So the train stopped at Lexington for Steve.

When Steve got off the train and was talking to the conductor, they were throwing mailbags out of the car on to the street very fast and Steve happened to look up at the Engineer who was glaring at him. The conductor had dropped a message off at a previous station to wire ahead so they could give the Engineer instructions to stop at Lexington. Apparently, the Engineer did not appreciate the unnecessary stop. Steve could understand why as the big 4-8-4 would get up to speed and do 65 or better and the extra stop had taken time. While standing and talking to the conductor, he asked, "How many cars are on this train?" The conductor responded, "Nineteen." Steve repeated, "19!" The conductor challenged him to count them but Steve took him at his word and said, "But I don't feel any slack action." The conductor told Steve that the Engineer doesn't have to worry about that. The conductor explained that the engine had a four-wheel booster under the cab. Steve couldn't believe how easy that train pulled away from the station. He said there were people eating in the dining car and they were not affected one bit as the train started to move. The train started out slow and smooth without any jerking or noise other than the engine and the turning wheels on the rail. Steve said in all his years he had never seen a train start so smooth.

The track in that area ran along the Lincoln Highway (old US 22 and US 30); and if you were driving along that stretch of highway and wanted to keep up with a train, you had to go 65 or better.

Steve had asked the conductor where they changed crews and was told North Platte. Steve explained to the conductor it was his first trip after being discharged from the army and he wasn't flush with money but he went on to say, "The day after tomorrow, I'll be at the Pawnee Hotel; and if you and your engineer friend are in town, I'd be glad to meet you in the bar and buy you two a drink for your kindness." But Steve went on to say, "If you have a run the next morning, the deal's off." The conductor laughed and said, "That's okay; we don't have a run until Saturday."

Well, Steve left the passenger station and walked the block or two to the Corn Land Hotel where he was expected as he had telegraphed for a room reservation. He asked at the desk if it they could store his bag as he didn't need to check in immediately and he asked for directions to Corn Land Products. The desk clerk gave him directions and Steve walked to his first call on Corn Land Products.

He met the son of the founder of the company, Mr. Ray Robinson, and Steve found that Ray's father owned a farm just south of Toledo, Ohio, along the B&O and had leased some property from the railroad. Also, the young man told Steve that this was poker night and he was invited. Steve told him he didn't have a lot of money and the fellow replied, "Don't worry; it's only 5 - 10 - 25 cents." Steve's comment to me was, "Have you ever been in a game where there were maximum raises on each card?" I answered that I had, many times, at traffic club meetings. The point was you could still lose quite a few dollars on a run of bad luck.

Well anyway, Ray gives the company's book of orders to Steve and said look through it and see what you can handle. Steve took a look at the book and every carload to the east had a routing of PRR. The owner said to Steve, "Well, what do you think?" and Steve said, "You just stabbed me; there's not one carload in this book that isn't routed via the PRR." It so happened there was a woman that practically ran the whole office and the PRR traveling freight agent was bringing her a box of candy on each visit. Steve said, "Jiminy Christmas, does she smoke?" Which she did.

It was on to the poker game, which included the city electrician, a businessman who had a parts business next to Corn Land Products, Ray Robinson and Steve. There could have been others and I imagine there were; but after the game, these four went to dinner. Steve was a little worried about the dinner; but Ray said, "Don't you worry. Sparky is going to buy as he was the big winner tonight." They went to a restaurant on the shores of a lake outside the town and Steve said he never saw bigger steaks.

The next morning, Steve found a drug store where he purchased a carton of Chesterfield's, the office manager's brand, and a box of Whitman's chocolates. He then went back to Corn Land's office and laid his gifts on the office manager's desk. He said, "There's an order on your books for three carloads to Early and Daniel, Cincinnati, Ohio, and I sure would like to see them routed via the B&O." She took care of Steve and routed the business via B&O. Before leaving Steve had another conversation with Mr. Robinson; and he asked Steve how he planned to get to North Platte. Steve explained that he would get a local freight or the passenger train that stopped at Lexington. Mr. Robinson asked Steve if he would like to drive to North Platte. Steve said, "What do you mean?" Robinson explained that some of the boys weren't married and they like to visit North

Platte on occasion and have a little fun. Steve said, "Sure I'll drive you there". Robinson told him he wouldn't be able to drink and Steve responded that that was not a problem. Robinson also owned the Cadillac/Oldsmobile dealership and he had this big Oldsmobile and he asked Steve if he could handle such a car and Steve replied, "Blindfolded!"

That first trip Steve drove them to North Platte and waited for them at the Pawnee Hotel, then drove them back. That first night was an experience as it was about 5 below zero on the return trip, and one of the guys in the back seat got sick and kept the window down for most of the trip. Steve said he almost froze to death. After dropping everyone off, Steve told Ray that he had better get the car washed and cleaned because one of his friends got sick all over the backseat. Ray was single at the time but got married shortly thereafter. Steve told him he better not let his wife ride in that car.

From then on, Steve did the driving for the next five years. About twice a year, Steve would drive his new-found friends from Lexington to North Platte, a distance of about 60 miles.

Many years later, when Steve was assigned to the Wheeling office, he met Ray Robinson and his wife at the Greater Pittsburgh Airport and they spent three days visiting with Evelyn and Steve.

The things you do for a carload or two of freight!!!!

Steve caught a local the next day and checked into the Pawnee Hotel. He took a look in the bar and there seated toward the back were the conductor and engineer he had invited for the drink. He said he never enjoyed an evening more in listening to the two Union Pacific men talk about their jobs and the UP. Of course, when you get two or more railroaders together, discussions can be long and lengthy. Steve did not reveal to this writer how much sleep he got that night. Only that it was most enjoyable.

Atlanta Office. The Clock: Part 12

Around the end of World War I, "Windy" Mitchell, who was a classmate at Harvard of Daniel Willard's son, became an employee of the B&O and was authorized to open an office in Atlanta, Georgia. When he opened the office, he placed a large eight-day clock on the wall between two large windows. The clock had an advertisement on it and Steve was not exactly certain as to what company it advertised. We agreed that it being

Atlanta, Coca-Cola may have been involved.

Steve wasn't sure whether the clock had ever worked and neither could any of the rest of the office staff. For years, Charlie Young, Traveling Freight Agent, assumed the duty of winding the clock. The pendulum went back and forth in the normal way and the clock sounded like it should but the hands remained in the form of an inverted "V". The funny part is the clock was placed so that any person walking down the hallway could look through the open office door and see this large clock. Year after year, people would stick their heads through the door, look at the clock and ask if the clock were running and the response would be, "Sure! Isn't the pendulum swinging?"

None of the office staff, which included A. A. Irwin, District Sales Representative; Charlie Young and Gus Chastine, Traveling Freight Agents; Bill Moore, Freight Representative; and Steve, Chief Clerk, did not know why the clock remained that way for so long. It was possibly out of respect for Mr. Mitchell, who had passed away years before, and a way to remember him, But it also caused Steve and others problems.

Many re-consignments were handled by the Atlanta Office staff and the exact times instructions were received and transmitted had to be recorded. As a result, Steve would take his wristwatch off and hang it on a bracket on his desk so he could see it while talking on the phone and typing. The easy way would be to look up at a large functional wall clock keeping the correct time.

Well, the day came. Bill Moore and Steve decided to fix the clock! They discovered the hands were not attached and may never have been. All they did was attach the hands and they had a working clock. The funny part was nobody else really noticed the change!

Steve's Stories

By Steve Baldinger
As told to Mark Craven
April 2008

1943-45--Around the Globe: Part 13

Steve was inducted into the Army early in 1943 and became part of the Transportation Corps. He was not a young 18 or even a 20-year-old but was 32. He and another man about his age went through training with much younger men and the deal was the first person to drop out of training that day would buy the beer that night. Steve and his compatriot never bought the beer during the weeks in training. Young whippersnappers!

Steve was eventually assigned to the 749th Transportation Battalion under Command of Colonel Donley who had been an Operating Superintendent of the New Haven Railroad. Technical training for the 749th was on the main line of the Southern Railway between New Orleans, Louisiana, and Meridian, Mississippi, with the headquarters bivouacking at Camp Shelby, Mississippi.

Before we continue with this story, we should look at the U.S. Railroads commitment in support of our troops and country. During World War II, many of the railroads committed volunteer railroad personnel to fill the need for experienced officers in the Transportation Corps. The 749th Transportation officers came from the New Haven Railroad. As Steve remembers, the B&O supported two battalions; one was involved in transporting goods through Iran to Russia and the other supporting transportation needs in Europe. It would be very interesting to hear from any former B&O, Chessie or CSX employees who were involved in the volunteer program and served as a transportation officer during WWII. There must be some good stories.

Getting back to Steve, his outfit was transferred to Camp Stoneman, California, for overseas assignment. All equipment and 1,100 soldiers were loaded on the S.S. Mormac; and as Steve says, "After 39 days of sailing around the Pacific", they anchored off shore in Manila Harbor, Philippines. At the time of the 749th's arrival, there was still a lot of fighting going on and all the cargo had to be off-loaded into LCMs for delivery to the beaches.

The battalion set up its headquarters about ten miles north of Manila in Caloocan, which was a Japanese stronghold not long before their arrival. This area had also served as a storage yard and repair shops for the narrow gauge Philippines railroad. The Corps of Engineers dozed the ground and the 749th was in operation and ready to go. Part of the cargo brought to Caloocan was 2,000 pre-fabricated gondolas that needed to be put together and made operational. They were fabricated so they could be put together with nuts and bolts. Each gondola had two doors on each side so they could be outfitted with benches and used to haul troops as well as supplies. There was not much time for building benches, so most of the troops sat on their gear or on the floor.

Another ship arrived with ten Mikado locomotives, with oil fired boilers, and five diesels. These had to be unloaded farther north where the army had heavy lift cranes. There was an effort to have the Mikado type locomotives renamed MacArthurs, since we were fighting the Japanese, but it never happened. Sometimes they were referred to as just "Mikes".

The photograph below shows a local narrow gauge locomotive that was never used by the 749th. Also pictured is one of six coaches, with link and pin couplers, that were reworked by the mechanics so they could be used for civilian passengers. The man stepping off the coach is John Wilson, a Yale Graduate and New Haven Railroad employee in civilian life. He worked very closely with Steve. The two of them had the responsibility of moving all replacement personnel upon arrival.

Each ship that arrived with replacements was met by Steve and John Wilson. They were supposed to have medics assigned but medics were in short supply and needed for more critical duties. Steve emphasized that the humidity and heat were unbearable. Steve and John learned very quickly that forced marching of troops just off a ship with full gear caused a lot of men to pass out from the heat. They made sure company commanders let the troops walk rather than quick-march. A few company commanders learned the hard way.

With the lack of medics, Steve and John developed a way to get these guys back on their feet. When one passed out, they would be laid flat on their back with the shirt unbuttoned and tee shirt pulled up. Then, Steve or John would start to pour a small stream of water from a canteen starting at the neck and moving down. Steve said most awoke immediately wanting to know what the hell was going on.

General MacArthur had promised the Philippines Government the Army would provide transportation for the civilians so that is why the six coaches were jerry-rigged with couplers. By the way, since the 749th was attached to the General's Headquarters, that was another excellent reason the coaches were fixed.

The regular afternoon train consisted of two coaches for civilians and two or three gondolas with benches for troop replacements destined to the 22nd Replacement Depot about 35 miles south of Manila. The route ran along Lake Laguna and Steve and John made sure the best riflemen were posted at the ends of each railcar as there was still enemy activity around the lake. If the Engineer saw any enemy activity ahead, he would give short toots on the whistle as a warning.

Another train went north to Clark Field and carried gondolas loaded with 500 lb. bombs and others with 55 gallon drums of 100 octane aviation fuel, ammunition and supplies. The trains carried few replacements to Clark Field as most arrived there by air. There were other daily trains, some consisting of just replacements for the 22nd Depot. Once the replacements were loaded on the trains, Steve's and John's work was done and they returned to the beach to pick up the next group of replacements.

Originally, there were some problems with scheduling equipment needs as a separate unit made up the consists but that was overcome when a new commander, Colonel Denny Moore, took over command of the other unit and he made certain the 749th received correct and timely consists.

Steve was in HS Company; A Company had the gandy dancers; B Company had Mechanical; and C Company had Engineers, Trainmen, etc. Steve became good friends with Lt. David G. "Pete" MacLeod, who was the Trainmaster located in the Manila Station, along with the dispatcher who had telegraphers stationed along the line. Many years later when Steve was Regional Sales Manager, New York, he ran into MacLeod at a traffic function and learned he was Superintendent on the NYNH&H at New Haven, Connecticut. After that, whenever Pete MacLeod came to New York, the two would get together for lunch and talk about old times and argue whose turn it was to buy lunch.

Steve spent about 13 months in the Philippines. The battalion was scheduled for a move to Korea but those having accumulated enough points could go back to the States for discharge. Steve was one of the lucky ones with enough points but had to wait another four months at the 22nd Depot for transportation back to the U.S. He came back through Camp Stoneman and was discharged at Fort George G. Meade, Maryland.

Steve returned to Akron where his wife, Evelyn, had been staying with her mother and close to her two sisters. Steve and Evelyn had enjoyed Atlanta before he had been drafted and naturally thought they would be going back there to renew his career with the B&O. Sometimes things don't work out the way you would expect, especially with a railroad. He ended up just a wee bit off course—OMAHA, here we come!

Steve's Stories

By Steve Baldinger
As told to Mark Craven
July 2008

1914--Holloway, Ohio: Part 14

Steve's reading of the article about the CL&W in the Second Quarter, 2007, issue of The Baltimore and Ohio Historical Society's *The Sentinel* publication brought back memories of his youth and living in Holloway, Ohio.

Steve's dad, Fred, started as a machinist with the Baltimore and Ohio and was working at Mt. Clare after learning his trade with the Pennsylvania Railroad at Crestline, Ohio. The railroad needed an experienced man as General Foreman at Holloway, Ohio, and Fred volunteered for the job. So in 1914, Fred and his family moved to Holloway to assume his new duties, reporting to Tom Stewart, Division Master Mechanic, Wheeling, West Virginia.

The Baldinger home was adjacent to the rail yard and the home's yard on the back was bordered by yard tracks. There were no telephones in the homes and, as Steve recalls, the only phone he knew of available to his dad was in the shop office. Quite often, Fred's boss in Wheeling would call Fred when he was at home and someone from the shop would have to come to the house and get him. Quite often, this happened at night and Steve remembers how fast his dad could get dressed. Fred's boss also did not like the food at the beanery near the yard; and when he was coming or in town, he was always angling to be invited to the Baldingers for a home-cooked meal. On one occasion, he said something to Fred along the line, "Do you think Winnie could fix us a little lunch?" Fred said, "I'll have to send someone over to see if Winnie is home and whether she has something on the stove." That day, it was decided that Fred needed a phone in his house so he could communicate with his boss. A phone line was run from the shop office to the Baldinger household; and to this day, Steve wondered whether it was the need to talk business or the need to give his mother ample notice that Fred and his boss would like a home-cooked meal.

Steve attended first and second grade when the family lived in Holloway. Steve's mother, Winnie, would take him along on shopping trips to Wheeling. This involved taking the morning train from Holloway to Bridgeport, a distance of about 31 miles. You will not see this in any train schedule but the locals named the train the "Hoodlebug". It consisted of two passenger coaches; and since the train passed two coal mines on the way to Bridgeport, there were usually a bunch of rowdy miners on the train. The conductor saved one of the coaches for families, women and children, with the miners in the other coach. The conductor would not put up with any foolishness. When Steve and Winnie got to Bridgeport, they would take the trolley across to Wheeling Island and then on to Wheeling to do their shopping. Compare this to backing the good old car out of the garage and driving to the mall in 5 to 10 minutes to do your shopping versus an all-day trip by train and trolley and carrying the packages from the stores to the trolley, from the trolley to the train station and from the train station home.

The B&O had an arrangement with the State and used prison labor to do yard cleanup which consisted mostly of picking up coal that was dislodged from the many hoppers that were switched daily. An old camp car had been fixed up with cots and a stove so the prison labor had a place to eat and sleep. Apparently, there were several sources of moonshine close to Holloway and one night the prisoners had quite a party. The night foreman called Fred at home and told him he had a big problem and needed help. Fred told him to get two new hickory brake clubs and meet him at the camp car. Upon arriving at the car, Fred found the drinking, partying and fighting were in full swing. Fred took one of the clubs and told the night foreman, "You go around the car to the other side and, when I yell, hit the side of the car as hard as you can and I'll do the same thing here." Well, when those two clubs hit the sides of the car it sounded like a bomb going off. There was an immediate silence from the car and the party came to an abrupt halt. Nothing more needed to be done.

Fred Baldinger made trips to Wheeling for meetings; and after one of these meetings, he spotted a new fangled contraption in a hardware store that was called a flashlight. Fred thought it would be perfect for Winnie when she needed to use the facilities at night. The facilities were located at the rear of the backyard next to the coal bin and close to the yard tracks. Steve explained it was real nice—a three holer—with actual seats and covers. Well, when Fred got back from Wheeling, he showed what he had bought for Winnie, plus the extra set of batteries and made it a point that the flashlight was for Winnie's use only. Steve and the rest of the family would continue to use the lantern.

Now don't be guessing about what happens next but you are probably way ahead on this one. It happened that Fred and Winnie got in to a card game with an Engineer and his wife who lived a few doors away. Steve got the urge to use the facilities; and as he passed through the kitchen, he spied the flashlight. Well, Steve remembered what his dad had just told him but he thought, "Ah, dad won't mind if I just try it out this one time." Steve picked up the flashlight and turned in on and headed for the backyard. When Steve got to the facilities, he took the end seat and set the flashlight down next to him. None of the seats were down and you know what happened! The flashlight rolled into the center hole! Steve took one look and there was that flashing eye looking back up at him from the bottom. Steve wanted the last five minutes not to have happened but he knew he was going to have to tell his dad. He walked back to the house and got his dad's attention and got him into the kitchen where he confessed as to what he had done.

His dad went to the outhouse and there was the flashlight at the bottom of the hole still shining up at them. Fortunately, the honey

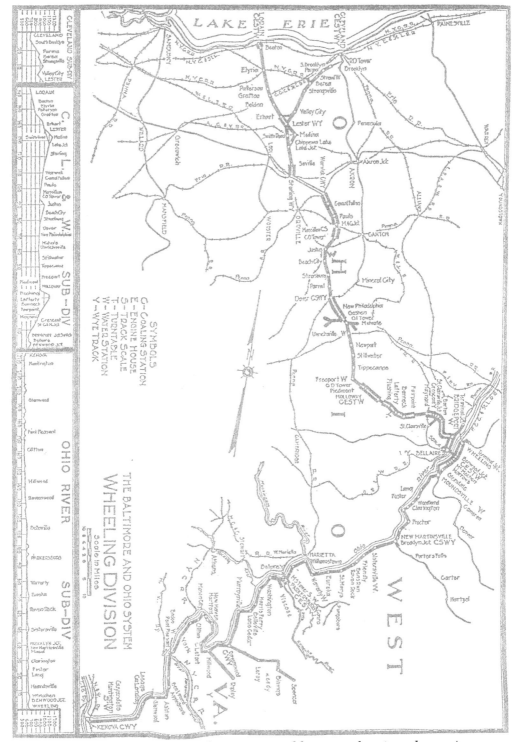

Wheeling Division employee timetable map showing the main line from Kenova, West Virginia, to Lorain and Cleveland, Ohio.. Baltimore & Ohio Railroad Historical Society collection.

145

The Cleveland Lorain and Wheeling, or CL&W, was the backbone of the Wheeling Division north of Wheeling to Lake Erie. Coal, originating in West Virginia and Ohio dominated the traffic flow northbound and steel products accounted for the traffic from the mills of northern Ohio.
Holloway Yard was the main yard serving the coal traffic lining up trains for industrial customers and the piers on Lake Erie.
H. H. Harwood, Jr., photo, 1957.

dipper had paid them a visit not too long before so there was not too much waste down there. Fred told Steve to go get his work gloves and when he came back with them, Fred put them on, then took a garden rake and retrieved the flashlight. Fred took an old pan and put warm water from the stove in it and then proceeded in taking the flashlight completely apart washing each piece. He then put all the pieces in a rack in the stove where they dried for a few days. He then put the flashlight back together and, believe it or not, it worked! When I asked Steve what was his punishment, he said he thought his dad wanted to laugh but looked very sternly at him and said, "Don't ever touch that again."

Steve says he can remember as if it were yesterday when the armistice was signed ending the First World War. He and a friend were chucking stones at a trimmer engine that was running up and down one of the yard tracks near their home. The Engineer was blowing the whistle and ringing the bell celebrating the end of the war. Well, one of the stones accidentally hit the Engineer and it didn't take long for the information from the yard office to reach Winnie, causing Steve's instant punishment.

Steve remembers his dad talking about the Wheeling Division being responsible for Holloway's inbound traffic and the yard operation but the Akron Division called the shots on the outbound tonnage.

1946--Omaha Office: Part 15

Shortly after Steve became Traveling Freight Agent, Omaha, in 1946, the Corps of Engineers, Omaha District, under the Flood Control Act of 1944, commenced construction of the Fort Randall Dam on the Missouri River some 50 miles up river from Sioux City, Iowa. At that point, the Missouri River was bordered by Nebraska on the south and South Dakota on the north.

Steve says there were two large grain elevators in Sioux City that could not use barges to move their product down river. This was because the water levels on the Missouri River were not sufficient for barge traffic above Omaha. Although most of the export grain business was through east coast ports, the Port of New Orleans was becoming more popular with the increase in river traffic. Enough said about the reason the dam was started but it was needed to control the water flow to raise water levels for barge traffic among other things.

The Corps of Engineers selected a firm headquartered in Des Moines, Iowa, for the project. This firm had completed construction of a tunnel for the New York subway system between Manhattan and Brooklyn just before the outbreak of WWII and had stored its heavy machinery on B&O property at Staten Island during the war. After receiving the contract in 1946, it moved this machinery by rail from Staten Island to the construction location via the B&O-Chicago-CMST&P.

Steve was anxious to see the construction site but it was difficult to get there. He was telling this to one of his counterparts, the Traveling Freight Agent of the Milwaukee at Sioux City which served the site, who said he had to make the trip and would be glad to take Steve with him.

When Steve accompanied the Milwaukee man to the construction site and met the Construction Manager, the man said to Steve, "I'm really glad you came as I have been wanting to thank someone from the B&O for its help in loading and moving our construction equipment from Staten Island." He went on to say the equipment arrived with no damage and was in excellent condition. Steve was glad to hear the compliment.

At that time, the Fort Randall Dam was to be one of the largest earthen containment dams. Apparently, there would be a concrete core where the floodgates and spillway were located and the rest of the dam would be earthen. There were not any more business opportunities available for the B&O other than the construction equipment already handled.

Upon completion, the water impounded behind the dam was named Lake Francis Case after a Senator from South Dakota. Upon completion, the water behind the dam would be released to maintain a river stage between Sioux City and Omaha during the grain shipping season allowing barges to be loaded at Sioux City. This action permitted the grain elevators to remain competitive with their rivals down river.

The nearest town to the dam now is Pickstown, South Dakota, and there is a State Recreational Area bordering the lake.

Late 60s--New York Office: Part 16

While Steve served as Assistant Regional Sales Manager and then Regional Sales Manager of the New York Office in the late 60s and early 70s, one of the most significant architectural and construction projects by the New York Port Authority took place. It, of course, was the World Trade Center, which as we all know was destroyed by the terrorist attack on September 11, 2001.

Steve and Mike Perner, Freight Traffic Manager of the CNJ, had many meetings concerning the inbound steel for this project. Steve and Mike had initially met in Atlanta when they were Chief Clerks for their respective companies. They became friends and worked on mutual projects then, as they were doing again in New York, and they met regularly to update each other and to firm up a joint proposal.

The CNJ had recently torn down a pier and Steve and Mike were planning on that property for accumulation and storage with delivery of the steel by tractor-trailer on a strict schedule to the job site. Both Steve's and Mike's problem was the close relationship the Port Authority had with the PRR. They were working on a project involving big numbers. 90,000 tons of steel were to originate in Japan, move through the Port of Seattle for fabrication at Pacific Car and Foundry, thence to New York. Another 30,000 tons would originate at Laclede Steel Company, St Louis, Missouri.

In spite of all of the hard work by the two from the B&O and CNJ, the close ties between the PRR and the Port Authority appeared to be too much to overcome, with the PRR securing the tonnage from Seattle to New York.

There still remained the tonnage from St. Louis and Steve and Mike were successful in securing this tonnage. Coincidentally, at the same time the steel was scheduled to move from St Louis, the C&O was having some gondolas constructed in St. Louis. Steve approached Ned Lemieux, C&O AVP-Customer Service, about loading them and Ned told him he had been advised the first loads would be from a C&O origin. After a lot of discussion, Steve and Ned agreed the loading of the cars would save the transportation and costs of moving the new cars empty. So the new gondolas were loaded with the steel for the new World Trade Center as they came off the production line.

The steel had to be unloaded from the rail cars at the CNJ's New Jersey site, stored, then delivered by tractor trailer as the pieces (each piece was numbered) were needed at the construction site. This required a good deal of coordination to insure the steel was delivered as needed, as there was no room for storage at the construction site. The size of the steel required the shutting down of the Westside Highway to regular traffic while the steel was being moved. This required the intervention of New York's "finest" (Police) who controlled the traffic while the steel was being moved. This delivery service was negotiated for the price of $1.00 per ton.

Steve and Mike Perner worked about a year on this project; and while they were disappointed with the outcome on the Seattle business, they were certainly glad to secure the St Louis tonnage.

Steve's Stories

By Steve Baldinger
As told to Mark Craven
October 2008

In the Beginning; Part 17

At the start of The Great Depression and living in Baltimore with his family, Steve was 19, out of school and looking for a summer job. Tom Stewart, a friend, and co-worker of Steve's dad, Fred, told Fred there was a job opening at Mt. Clare for a janitor and if Steve wanted the job for the summer to report to Mr. Winter, head of the Electrical Department at Mt. Clare, at 7:00 a.m. the next morning.

Fortified with a lunch packed by his mother Winnie, Steve reported to Mr. Winter promptly at 7:00 a.m. the following day. Mr. Winter showed Steve to a cabinet and said, "There is your equipment and you will be working with Mr. Murphy on the lower level." The lower level at Mt. Clare had been "The Blue Line Transfer". This was the area where goods that had arrived by train were transferred to horse and wagon for delivery. Also, the lower level included the stables for the horses; but when Steve reported for work, it was being used as part of the shops. At that time, all B&O Shops generated their own power.

Steve reported to Mr. Murphy with his tools of the trade and Murphy said, "Set that stuff over there. Have you ever cut pipe?" Steve said, "No." "Have you ever threaded pipe?" Steve said, "No." Murphy said, "Well you're going to learn to do it." Steve said after that first morning he did not touch a broom, mop or any janitor's tools. Murphy had him helping cut and thread pipe, among other things. One job was installing automatic train control to engines and tenders, as all engines in the east were so equipped. They had to carry the equipment about a mile to the tender shop for installation. They then had to wait for the machinist to connect the stoker before they could hook up the coupling for the train control that was housed in the tender.

The union agreement covered 20 minutes for lunch and Steve's mother had packed him two sandwiches. Murphy suggested to Steve that he bring three so every day "they" could have one sandwich at 10.00 a.m. At noon, Murphy would always disappear and he would say to Steve, "If Winter wants to know where I am, tell him I went to the rest room." Well, Steve was starting to eat his lunch one day and was sitting looking out the window and here goes Murphy into the back door of a building just across the alley. Within twenty minutes, Murphy is out the door and back on the job. It just so happened, a "Speak Easy" was very well located for Mr. Murphy.

Steve's job was non-union and he continued to work with Murphy . During this time, the Royal Blue was outfitted with air conditioning at Mt Clare. While Steve was working with Murphy, Mr. Winter was visited by the Union Representative who informed him Steve was doing union work. Back to the stables for Steve! Steve still believes Mr. Murphy let it slip to the Union Rep. that he had Steve doing Union work. It didn't take long for Murphy to have Steve doing the same kind of work and the summer job was nearing the end.

A year or so later, Steve was called back to Mt. Clare as an apprentice electrician; but about that time, Fred was transferred to Benwood and Steve moved with the family. Fred would not put Steve on as an apprentice electrician as he said he would have to furlough a married man who needed to take care of a family. So Steve's service was interrupted for a few years.

Early 1970s--A little New York story: Part 18

George Bunyea spent his career in New York and lived on Staten Island. When Steve became Regional Sales Manager, George was Assistant Regional Sales Manager. If you wanted to know what was going on in New York, George was your man. As Steve said, George knew just about everyone when it came to putting business on the railroad.

There was a lot of entertaining which quite often required missing dinner at home and then getting home very late. The New York Traffic Club had monthly meetings and it was mandatory that Steve and George be there. These activities meant traveling home late at night. Usually, Steve and George would part company at the Staten Island Ferry Terminal. George would take the ferry and Steve would take the PATH (Port Authority Trans Hudson) train to Hoboken and then the Erie to Maplewood, New Jersey, and home.

On these evenings, one or the other would make sure to call

Florence, George's wife, to let her know he was on the Ferry and then she would be on hand to pick him up. This worked out pretty well most of the time but sometimes George would end up back in New York. Being a local, George had a special spot on the ferry, a seat against a bulkhead that gave him some protection from getting mugged while he caught 40 winks on the way home. The problem was sometimes those 40 winks became 80 and George would wake up still on the City side.

All this time, Florence would be on the dock knowing George was on board but was prohibited from getting on the ferry to wake her husband.

John Ohordnick to the rescue! John was Superintendent of the SIRT and Steve explained to John they needed a way for Florence to get on the ferry so she could wake George before he made the round trip. John made arrangements to have Florence furnished a badge that would allow her access to the ferry. After that, George got more sleep in bed at home than on the ferry.

1947--To a long time Friend: Part 19

Upon returning from the Military Service in 1946, Steve was assigned as Traveling Freight Agent, Omaha, Nebraska. Early in 1947, Steve met John Howard Moxley, Jr., (who was known as Howard) B&O Passenger Agent, who had been transferred from New York City, and his wife Cleo. They became very good friends and remained so over the years. Howard's daughter, Judy, was two years old and son Jack (John Howard Moxley, III) was twelve when they met. Their son, Jack, became a physician after attending the University of Colorado and interning in Boston. Judy attended Iowa Wesleyan, Mt. Pleasant, Iowa, and then the University of Iowa at Iowa City, Iowa, attaining a Masters in Fine Arts. She taught for many years in Solon, Iowa, and now visits Steve when she heads for sunny and warm Arizona during the winter months.

Jack Moxley eventually became Dean of the University of Maryland Medical School. His reputation spread and the University of California, when opening a new medical school facility in San Diego, hired Jack and some key people away from the University of Maryland to run the school. While there, he met Harold Brown who later became Secretary of Defense during the

Carter Administration. At that time, he recruited Jack to Washington as Assistant Secretary of Defense-Health Affairs, with the duties of overseeing all military health care. Later, Jack joined and became a partner in Korn Ferry International, an executive placement service. With his vast experience, Jack set up a Physician Executive Practice within the firm. Jack is now retired and living in California

After attaining her Masters Degree, Judy Moxley spent 34 years teaching in Solon, Iowa. She spent one year on loan to the University of Illinois teaching freshmen, in order to develop a program for high school seniors that better prepared them for their freshman year in college. Judy spends her summers in Cedar Rapids and now winters in Sun City, Arizona. She has maintained close contact with Steve over the years and visits with him regularly during the winter months. She really is a true friend.

When Howard worked in the New York City Passenger Department, he was the Reservation Bus Coordinator. His job was to insure the buses leaving the four New York stations (Columbus Circle, Times Square, Liberty Street and Brooklyn) arrived inJersey City on schedule to insure B&O passenger trains, such as the Royal Blue, departed on time. Each of the bus stations mentioned above was also a B&O station with a Ticket Agent at each station. Howard said it was a hard job to get those buses through Manhattan to Jersey City on time.

Steve and Howard often worked together. One instance involved Harley Jackson, VP of a grain elevator and one of Steve's customers. He was also an officer in the Shrine. The Shrine was having a large national convention in Washington, D.C., and Howard was having trouble getting to the right person. Steve mentioned this to Harley and he got Howard and the person arranging the transportation together. Howard not only got some passenger traffic but also got to move the Shrine Patrol (horses and all) to Washington.

Howard was tenacious in his quest for passenger business as with other challenges in his life. One of his fears when traveling away from home was the safety and comfort of his family. They had a three-bedroom home in Omaha but it had a coal furnace and his fear was that the fire would die and his family would be subject to the cold without him there to keep the fire banked with new fuel. He had tried to find an oil burner converter for the coal furnace but had come up empty-handed.

Steve and Howard quite often would end up in Sioux City, Iowa; and when Howard was driving, Steve would hitch a ride back to Omaha. One particular day in January, 1948, with the temperature hovering at minus two degrees, Steve was spending time with an independent hog order/buyer cooperating five hog cars which were being shipped to Esskay Company in Baltimore. After completing that job, he spent the rest of the day at the Sioux City Stock Yards with other buyers. At the end of the day, Steve returned to the Warrior Hotel where he and Howard usually stayed when in town. He checked out and retired to Foster's, a watering hole next to the hotel. Steve wasn't sure he would meet Howard as Howard had driven to Yankton, South Dakota, where he planned to book a large women's organization on a tour to Washington, D.C., and New York City. During this period, serving liquor was a local option and Foster's served their drinks in Coke bottles. Howard was there waiting for Steve. They both had successful days and were celebrating with their "Cokes".

Just when they were congratulating each other on having a good day, the door is flung open and in walks this salesman complaining how cold it is and having to drive back to Des Moines. He joined Steve and Howard in having a drink and, of course, Howard asked, "What do you sell?" The salesman said he sold Century oil burners. He had just spent the entire day putting on demos in Mitchell, South Dakota, and had sold his allotment for the entire month. Howard's eyes lit up as he gazed through the window at this large station wagon with a complete oil burner in the back. Steve knew at that moment he would not be riding back with Howard and would need to make the 6:30 pm train. He had $50 on him and some change for the trolley when he got to Omaha. He handed Howard the $50 and said good luck. Howard asked Steve to call his wife, Cleo, when he got home and explain what was going on.

Well, come Saturday morning, Howard arrived with the complete oil burner; and on Sunday, it was installed in the furnace and producing. Tenacious? Yes!

Around 1950, Howard was transferred to Denver, Colorado. Prior to his transfer, the Denver office was headed by a joint Passenger and Freight Agent but it was decided to divide the duties and have both a District Freight, Frank Leskey, and a Passenger Agent, Howard Moxley. Salt Lake City was covered by the Denver office, a hot spot for tours, especially to Washington, D.C., and Howard spent a good bit of time there.

During the Moxleys' stay in Denver, Steve and Evelyn visited with them on two occasions. Steve said on those visits they usually ended up playing penny ante poker as Cleo was addicted to it. They had lots of fun and many enjoyable evenings playing that game. And, by the way, Steve still manages to play poker with some friends every Thursday afternoon; however, the game might now be nickel–dime.

Howard's last position was Assistant General Passenger Agent in Chicago, Illinois, with responsibility for calling on the high schools and helping them plan tours, primarily to Washington, D.C. Steve remembers him talking about one tour that involved, for the primary tour, a little boat trip down Chesapeake Bay to Norfolk and return to Washington, D.C., then back to Chicago by the B&O.

These tours were priced to include transportation, room and other items, which meant making contacts and dealing with many people putting together these packaged tours. This eventually led to a large problem within the Passenger Department and the release of many from their positions. It was believed that a lot of people were let go because they happened to be in the wrong place at the wrong time, if that makes any sense to those of you who were working on the railroad at that particular time.

Howard Moxley was one of those, as Steve says, "Good People", who got hurt. After leaving the B&O, Howard and four other former B&O Passenger Agents opened a Travel Bureau in Chicago, which became very successful.

Howard was so proud of his son and daughter and their accomplishments. I think they were also proud of their father and mother. Howard was a Jr., his son has the same name and is called "Jack". Jack's son has the same name and is called "Jay" and Jay's son is the fifth and is called "Jet". Judy remains single and is called "Judy".

Steve is still very close to Judy, with the friendship lasting more than a half century.

1919--Living on the B&O: Part 20

Around 1919, Tom Stewart, Steve's father's (Fred Baldinger) boss, transferred Fred to Gassaway, West Virginia, as Master Mechanic on the old Coal and Coke Railroad. He was the second Master Mechanic appointed, with the first not staying long before being transferred to Cincinnati, Ohio. There was no restaurant and no place to stay. Maybe that's why the first one didn't stay long.

Fred began to look for a place. He started at Mrs. Longwell's boardinghouse where he found the family could have its meals. He learned from Mrs. Longwell that her daughter had a home and the second floor was available for rent. The Baldingers rented the second floor and had meals at the boardinghouse.

While in Gassaway, Steve attended the third grade, after attending first and second grades in Holloway. Ohio. This was a one-room schoolhouse; and if you were smart and fast, you could find out what was going on in the next grade.

Being a good cook, Winnie offered to help Mrs. Longwell in the kitchen, but she would not hear of that. She had learned that Winnie Baldinger played the piano and suggested she play the old upright piano for her guests, which Winnie did prior to dinner. Steve said every day Mrs. Longwell made four great big apple pies and then cut four pieces out of each. A serving was a quarter of a pie!

Since the writer considers himself a fisherman, Steve just had to mention he caught his first fish out of the Elk River in Gassaway.

Steve's Stories
A weekend in New York City

By Steve Baldinger
As told to Mark Craven
January 2009

First, Steve wanted to tell this story before he passed away but it sort of got away from us because the writer was trying to locate some photographs that would have added to the story. We didn't find the photos and Steve has left us for a better place but this is what we talked about.

On August 1, 1971, Steve was transferred to Baltimore as Assistant Vice President-Sales; and, just prior to that, I was transferred from Pittsburgh to Baltimore as Manager-Special Equipment, Customer Service. Steve initially worked for VP Tom Keefe and I was working for AVP Ned Lemieux. Over a period of time, the four couples (Tom and Pat Keefe; Ned and Dee Dee Lemieux; Steve and Evelyn Baldinger; and Doris and I) had talked about spending a weekend in New York and seeing a Broadway show. Steve was anxious to be our tour guide as he had just moved down from the "Big Apple" and George Bunyea, his Assistant in New York and a native New Yorker, had shown Steve some of the finer parts of the city.

There always seemed to be a problem about getting a weekend where all of us could get away. Tom Keefe was having a birthday and everyone thought New York was a good place to help Tom celebrate. Plans and reservations were made. There was no question about how we were going to get there; we took the Metroliner from Baltimore.

On the train, Ned commented that the first thing he wanted to do was to get a hot dog "with everything on it" from one of the street vendors. We had no sooner checked into the hotel than Ned wanted to check out the surrounding territory. He bought his first New York hot dog while walking back to the hotel, right through the lobby and into the elevator munching on his "foot long" with everything. New Yorkers have seen just about everything so Ned got just a few stares, mostly from us.

Steve was a wonderful guide and we saw a lot of New York. We attended a Broadway show Saturday afternoon, "A Little Night Music", and enjoyed it very much. Since there were eight of us, we were taking two cabs everywhere.

After the show, Steve surprised us by taking us to the "21 Club" for dinner. That famous spot gets its name from its address, 21 West 52nd Street. Steve had a shirt pocket full of ten-dollar bills and explained this was how you got around in New York. Upon arrival at the "21 Club", the doorman got a "10"; inside, the Maitre d' got a "10" and I can't recall how many others.

We had a lovely dinner and were treated royally. If you took a sip of water, a waiter would immediately be on hand to refill the glass. I believe we had three people plus a sommelier attending our table of eight. We lingered over our dinner for some time, enjoying the evening, and then finished with a birthday cake for dessert.

After dinner, we were asked if we wanted to tour the wine cellar. Of course, we said "yes" and were led through the kitchen and down a pair of narrow wooden steps into the basement. Our tour guide stood before a stone wall where there were some small holes in the mortar between the stones throughout the wall. Our guide picked up a steel rod about a quarter inch in diameter and very dramatically counted so many up and so many over to select one of the holes, then inserted the rod. The stone wall swung open and there before us was a large wine cellar with row upon row of wine bins. During Prohibition, the wine cellar was a speakeasy and that was the reason for the hidden room and the swinging wall. Some of "The 21 Club's" famous members had their own private stock stored there and we walked up and down the rows looking at the names on the bins and the wine they favored. Ironically, "21 Club" today is owned by "Orient-Express Hotels, Trains & Cruises"—the same folks who were running the American Orient Express.

Before we departed, each couple was given a medallion about the size of a half dollar with the Club's insignia on it. It had a small raised spot in the center so it could be spun on a flat surface. We were told it could be spun to see who paid the bill. Doris and I have kept our coin and it reminds us of a good time with fine friends.

When we exited the club, there were drivers with their limousines double-parked on the street waiting for their customers. The doorman said to one of the drivers, "Your people won't be finished for some time. Why don't you take these good people back to their hotel?" The driver said that it would be his pleasure and we all climbed in to the limo and went back to the hotel in style. Ned took over for Steve and placed a few bills in the driver's pocket.

We did a little more sightseeing Sunday morning and then boarded the train for Baltimore and reality.

The week before Steve passed away, he told me the story about joining the "21 Club". Not long after he was transferred to New York, he realized a membership to "21" would be very beneficial and asked George Bunyea if he had any information about the application or recommendation process, not realizing it was not a private club. George accompanied Steve to the club where they were met by the Manager. Steve thought at first he might have been the bouncer. Steve introduced himself as the new

Steve Baldinger, on the left, is talking with Bill Ollerhead, Senior Vice President Sales and Jim Suthann, Regional Sales Manager, at a Chessie System Sales Department staff meeting at the Greenbrier. The Greenbrier resort, owned by the C&O, was a favorite location for such meetings.

Regional Sales Manager of the Baltimore and Ohio Railroad in New York and said he would like to join the "21 Club". They had a brief conversation about mutual business acquaintances. The Manager then put an application on the desk, told Steve to sign on the bottom line and welcomed him as a new member. Steve mentioned that the application was blank and the manager answered, "That's okay. We'll take care of that later."

N&N Editor's note: Steve Baldinger passed away October 23, 2008.

Section C
HEADQUARTERS

Chapter 9   The GOB
(General Office Building)

Burglary in Progress

By Bob Chilcote
July 2009

This story is an example of how strange things can happen to railroaders even when they are minding their own business and going about doing their normal pursuits.

One day in Bill Stockdale's office on the 19th floor of Baltimore's One Charles Center, Bill and I were discussing some routine industrial development projects as we did more or less daily. Now get the picture: Bill was sitting in his office desk chair talking to me. I am sitting in one of the office chairs with my back toward the window. Now, it so happened that his sight line past me was to the top of the Lord Baltimore Hotel, next door to the old B&O Building. All of a sudden, some movement beyond me caught his eye. He stopped talking about our project and muttered, "What are those guys doing?" We both looked to the top of the hotel and we saw a weird sight, indeed. Two men on top of the building were throwing down to the alley below big plastic bags. The bags must have been at least three feet in diameter and, one after another, bags were being hurled to the street below.

For a while, we were bewildered but we decided the bags must be full of bedding, pillows, linen and other cloth materials that could survive such a drop. We realized it must be a burglary in progress. Charlie Geyer's office was nearby and we knew he could contact the railroad police. Accordingly, Bill immediately talked to Charlie and he notified the railroad police; they in turn called the local Baltimore City police.

While Bill was doing that, I had ample time to observe this extraordinary scene; and I decided I better get descriptions of the two men. Accordingly, I made careful note of the type and color of clothing and their height, weight and hair style. When the police came, we could give them a fairly good description. The police did, in fact, apprehend the two men; and we found out later that they were hotel employees. I don't believe I ever knew what happened to the case but the police did tell Bill, "Your buddy sure had those guys down cold."

A curious thing happened shortly after that. The police called me over to the hotel and they asked me to look at another man that they had in custody. I never quite understood this because I had already told them we had seen only two men. At any rate, they took me to an upper floor and asked me to observe this other man. I advised them that he was not one of the men I saw. The manager later told me that he was pleased that this man was not one of the culprits because he thought him to be a reliable good worker. I could only assure him that he was not one of the men I saw.

There is an interesting sequel to this incident or at least I think the two incidents were related. It must have been about two months later. We were going to lunch in the Federal Building. Suddenly, a man was immediately in front of me, saying, "You are a detective, aren't you?" Actually, it was quite frightening. I didn't know if I was about to be stabbed or shot. Since he was less than two feet from me, there was no way to avoid whatever confrontation that might be coming. I replied, "No, I work for the railroad." The man walked away and nothing happened. I have always wondered what that was all about. I could only conclude that my appearance in the hotel must have been noted by someone there at the time when I showed up and advised the other police that the third man was not one of the burglars I saw and that there was no apparent reason to further hold him in custody. I recall only that I was conscious of several other people being present at that moment in the Federal Building.

Lucky 7s

By C. Norman Murphy
July 2007

This memorable date (7-7-07) sixty-four years ago (one which will NOT go down in history) was the first day of CNM's B&O employment. He was still in high school but worked as a messenger in "GO" (General Office call letters) telegraph office on the mezzanine floor of the Central Building on weekends (Fridays: 4PM to midnight; Saturdays: 10AM to 6PM; and Sundays: 8AM to 4PM). Fortunately, that was enough time to "count" in his seniority.

The Sunday shift was particularly "enjoyable" as that was when he (via a 10-cent Baltimore Transit Company bus ride) delivered accumulated telegrams to the Agent's office at Claremont stockyards where the aroma was somewhat "outstanding" and not easily forgotten.

A messenger's "leisure time" in "GO" was occasionally devoted to setting up an empty metal message carrier in each of the twelve pneumatic tubes (one for each floor above the mezzanine floor) and then timing their release so that all "arrived" about the same time on each of the twelve floors--this being done, of course, when no officer was in residence (we hoped). The loud and simultaneous arrival "bangs" of the metal carriers--echoing throughout each of the twelve vacant, marbled hallways and lobbies--startled (awakened?) many of the clerks who were on duty. That was the objective, of course .... and those were the good old days!!

The Afternoon Show

By Charlie Geyer
April 2009

From my years with the railroad, I came across many interesting tales involving the B&O Central Building. That headquarters location at Baltimore and Charles Streets in Baltimore was the railroad home for many of us for a long time.

Along about 1977 when I was Superintendent of Buildings, including the jurisdiction over the headquarters building, I had a call from the ladies using the 12th floor restroom that an indecent act was being performed by two males over in the Lord Baltimore Hotel. At that time, the 12th floor housed the Real Estate Department and the Cafeteria.

Since the east wall of the hotel and the west wall of the B&O Bldg were so close (only an alley apart) it was easy to see into the windows of the hotel. Also, the window in the restroom led to the fire escape and could not be locked. Plus, there was no air conditioning in the B&O Building so the window was open most of the time.

Chessie System's new headquarters building, the Ludwig Miles van der Rohe designed One Charles Center, is shown on the left and the former GOB headquarters B&O Building in on the right. At the very right-hand edge of the B&O building is the adjacent Lord Baltimore Hotel. Fayette Street runs between the B&O Building and the One Charles Center building in 1962, the year before the Hamburgers men's store was built over Fayette Street. Hamburgers building was removed in 1998. In the background to the left of the B&O Building can be seen the Mathieson Building, later Maryland National Bank Building, and the Blaustein Building where some Chessie offices were located, specifically the Planning Department.

B&O Railroad Historical Society collection.

As seen from Baltimore Street, the Lord Baltimore Hotel is on the left and adjacent to the east is the edge of the B&O Central Building. These two buildings took up the entire block at the northwest corner of Baltimore and Charles Streets.

There were a lot of "shows" going on daily over at the hotel that were visible from our building.

When I went to investigate the 12th floor complaint, the restroom was so crowded with women that I could not get into the room to verify the reported action. So, I took the ladies' word for what was happening and asked the matron, Mary Turner, to close the window. Mary was the one that attended to the ladies restrooms, providing supplies and keeping things tidy.

I called the manager at the hotel and told him what was going on but he said there was nothing he could do except go to the room, knock on the door and ask the subjects to close the shades.

One of the 12th floor ladies was so "upset" she had to take the rest of the day off sick!

Oh, if only those walls could talk!

Chapter 10   Administration

Nearing One Hundred
Old Pete Reflects

By L. S. "Pete" Hartley
July 2003

As I drift toward my 100th birthday (September 26, 2003), I reflect upon an eventful 100th anniversary party in which I had an active part the summer of 1927, i. e., the B&O Centennial and The Fair of the Iron Horse. What a different world then from my world today.

Although plans for this B&O birthday celebration had had the attention of several B&O officials and associates for several months, (Mr. Hungerford had begun assembling material for his two-volume The Story of the Baltimore and Ohio Railroad, Margaret Stevens was composing the song "Hail The Baltimore & Ohio" for the well-known B&O Men's and Women's Glee Clubs) the "kick-off" event was a big banquet the evening of February 28, 1929, held in the Lyric Theater, which had been "taken over" by the B&O for this event. I was a relatively new employee, just completing my first year as B&O Agricultural Agent, and was very appreciative of being on the invitation list for this historic event.

The Centenary Exhibition and Pageant staged at specially-constructed facilities on B&O property at Halethorpe on the B&O main line near Baltimore, ran from September 24th to October 15th and was visited by more that 1,225,000 people.

The Pageant featured the development of transportation over the 100-year period and this required oxen to pull those early vehicles. Landscaping required shrubbery for beautification. The B&O Agricultural Department was called upon and I was assigned to the task. In 1927, suitable oxen for use in a pageant were few and far between. It was known that in the Winchester, Virginia, area there was a large landowner who had several oxen so I went to Winchester, borrowed a car from a B&O employee there and drove down the Valley to this "plantation" to try and rent two yoke of oxen. I had a very pleasant visit with the gentleman owner and succeeded in leasing the oxen, plus necessary equipment and two men to handle and care for them. B&O motor truck subsidiary, Blue Line Transfer, provided the transportation to Baltimore.

Now for the shrubbery. It was already too late for regular planting so I headed for my native land, the West Virginia hills, arranged with my friend J. A. Wolfram, County Agricultural Agent for Webster County, to have six of his 4-H boys help me dig some native Hemlock, Spruce, and Rhododendron plants in the Cowen vicinity. We loaded those plants into a 36-foot boxcar and "deadheaded" the car to Baltimore.

On the "exhibition" tracks at the Fair of the Iron Horse, there was assembled an "Agricultural Demonstration" train to show the visitors the type of education work in which the B&O was engaged. I was "on duty" most of the six weeks of the "Fair".

I expect I am one of very few former B&O employees still living who participated in that memorable event—The Fair of the Iron Horse.

A Different Kind of Cash Crop
By Norman Murphy
January 2000

In the early 1950s when I was beginning to climb the real estate managerial ladder, I was assigned to the leasing group under George Woessner, a member of RABO who passed away in 1982 (and whose son is now a RABO member). Over the years, the B&O had found itself many times purchasing much more property than actually needed for rights-of-way, yards, etc., primarily because the owners would insist the B&O purchase all of their property - not just what we needed. Therefore, the company had thousands of acres of so-called "surplus property" which was available for lease or sale.

Like many others in those days, our department was understaffed. As a result, the lease group devoted the vast majority of its time responding to mail and phone inquiries and negotiating leases from the office, with little or no time being available for the checking of changing field conditions.

When it came to leasing large acreages for agricultural purposes, the department's policy was to get enough rent to at least recoup the land taxes. While these farming leases were on a month-to-month basis, they usually continued unchanged for years.

Not long after the end of World War II, the department leased quite a few acres near the Columbus, Ohio, airport to a farmer named Clarence Tucker. It so happened the property abutted the large North American Aviation plant which still had many Defense Department contracts to fulfill. The plant was working two shifts with hundreds of employees. Parking on company property was at a premium, and "exiting" at the end of a shift had become a nightmare.

Everything with farmer Tucker was going along smoothly until one morning the boss received a letter from the Newark, Ohio, Division Superintendent with which was enclosed an article from the Columbus newspaper regarding the entrepreneurship of farmer Tucker. It seems that farmer Tucker - noticing the North American Aviation employee parking problems - had stopped planting corn, soybeans, etc., and had "cultivated" the B&O property into a North American Aviation satellite employee parking lot. Farmer Tucker was grossing thousands of dollars each month, while paying the B&O a yearly rental of far less than $1,000. Adding "insult to injury" was a front page picture of a smiling farmer/entrepreneur Tucker in his coveralls with his foot on one of the hundreds of cars in the photograph.

Needless to say, the boss had one of the department's senior agents on a plane that evening to Columbus. A new lease was signed in a few days by farmer Tucker under which he was required to pay the B&O sixty percent of his gross parking receipts and also carry public liability insurance.

Incidentally, that "senior agent" was Irv Bromwell, another RABO alumnus who died in 1982 and whose family's contribution to RABO started our Memorial Fund.

Out of the ashes of that incident came a comprehensive lease review program that involved a review of all leases on a five-year cycle and field reviews of those in metropolitan areas, resulting in thousands of dollars of increased and recurring annul income to the B&O. That program was also a helpful factor in the sale of millions of dollars of surplus railroad property in later years.

"Fair" Visitor

By Ken Roloson
July 2003

Regarding "The Fair of the Iron Horse", I was there for a day. My dad was Foreign Freight Agent at New York at the time and he took a few days vacation and brought the family down to Baltimore to visit relatives. We took a special train from Camden station directly to Halethorpe. The "Fair" was Daniel Willard's party. There was no admission charge and no commercialization, as I recall. I was 10 years old at the time.

The 100th anniversary of the B&O was celebrated by the Fair of the Iron Horse held at Halethorpe, Maryland in 1927. (See page xix for more details). A parade of people, equipment and trains passed the grandstands to the delight of the thousands that attended.

Chapter 11   POTUS
(President of the United States)

Not a Chance!
By Harry Eck
July 2011

Back in 1948, I was firing the Baltimore Beef train (Baltimore 94). One day passing Halethorpe in the wee hours of the morning, the Train Dispatcher advised that he was going to hold us on No. 1 track at Mt. Winans for a POTUS (President of the United States) special. He also instructed us to inspect the right side of our train to make sure that nothing was fouling the westbound main, along which the POTUS would operate. After a long wait on the No. 1 track, we saw the headlight of the Special approaching. I dropped down to the ground, walked forward past our locomotive and observed the Special as it passed us. It was carrying Harry Truman, who was returning from a difficult time at the Democratic Convention in Philadelphia where he secured the party's nomination for President.

When I got back in the cab, the other three members of the crew (the Engineer, Head Brakeman, and the Conductor, who was riding the head end to assist in the Ma & Pa set off on the Belt Line) gave me the "raspberries". They said that guy would never be elected President. So, I'll end the story here because everybody knows how that turned out!

King of the Mountain
By L. Byrne Waterman
July 2001

When the President of the United States traveled by train, a code name of POTUS SPECIAL was assigned. (POTUS—short for "President of the United States"). To insure smooth operation of such a move, all Division personnel involved in the move were contacted and each was assigned specific duties, both prior to and during the actual movement. The Division Superintendent would issue a "phone-book size" document, outlining the duties of each line officer and delegate to each certain responsibilities for

169

inspections, operations, coordination, etc., for the move.

I was involved in a POTUS SPECIAL on 1 November, 1956, when then President Eisenhower would be enroute to Cleveland, Ohio, and his train would be traveling over the East End of the Pittsburgh Division on a Monday evening. In the "Work Book" given to me, as the Assistant Division Engineer at Connellsville, Pennsylvania. I was to make an open motor car inspection trip on Sunday, the day prior to the special, over the main track between Cumberland (Viaduct Junction) and Connellsville with the respective Track Supervisors. The purpose of such a trip was to insure that nothing unusual was out of line along the right-of-way, giving attention to possible gapping switch points on all facing point switches; briefly inspecting culverts and bridges to see that no unusual erosion or washes had occurred; and also, at each interlocking tower, taking time to stress the importance of the special movement with the tower operator and the signalmen on duty. At the end of the approximately 90-mile trip, I had to notify the Superintendent that I had made the trip and took no exception to the general overall condition of the track, bridges, tunnels, towers, etc. and could see no reason why the special move could not be made.

On the day of the movement, each Track Supervisor would speak to each of his track foremen about the impending movement and have each again check any potential trouble spot. The Signal Supervisor would check with his signal maintainers at the various towers along the route to insure that all signal and switch mechanisms were functioning properly. The entire Division was again made aware of the forthcoming special and its importance.

The train enroute from Washington, DC, would be passed to the Pittsburgh Division at Cumberland, Maryland. According to the printed 'work book', the long, heavy train would be headed by two Diesel units needed to lift that equipment up the mountain grades and curves leading to Sand Patch, one of the B&O Railroad's biggest physical barriers and a route that normally took extra helper engines on the front end of passenger trains and helpers, either on the front end or the rear end, or both, on freight trains heading towards Pittsburgh and the west.

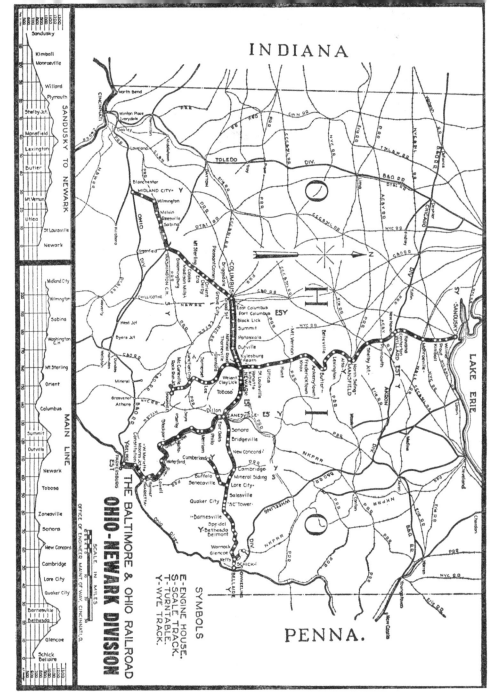

Ohio-Newark Division October 25, 1964, employee timetable map showing the main line from Bellaire, on the Ohio River, to Midland City, where it joins the Chillicothe Sub Division, and the Lake Erie Sub Division from Newark to Sandusky.

Ray Lichty collection.

By the special instructions, all Division personnel were to be in their assigned places by an hour prior to the scheduled departure time in Cumberland. A roll call was taken via phone assuring that each and every staff member was in his place. My assigned duty was to be with the Connellsville wreck train, on the phone in the office of the engine roundhouse, Connellsville Yard. I had to verify that the wreck train was all assembled with its engine attached and its crew aboard, ready to move east at a moment's notice. For safety reasons, the boom on the big hook had to be facing towards the rear of the wreck train. Once the special train passed the Connellsville Yard, the whole wreck train had to be turned to the west (towards Pittsburgh) should it be needed.

About the appointed hour of the train arrival in Cumberland, the phone line became quite quiet, except for some questions and answers by the Superintendent, Art Colnot, in Pittsburgh. Everyone was on the line: tower operators, track supervisors, signal men, Trainmaster, mechanical forces, other staff members, etc.

Then came the announcement that the special was in Cumberland station being serviced and inspected and was expected to leave on time, as per the pre-arranged schedule. Then the comment: "It is starting to pull." Within 0.6 of a mile, the train would go by Viaduct Junction, the beginning of the Pittsburgh Division and the beginning of the Central Region--the Region that extended to the outskirts of Chicago, Illinois. The responsibility was now ours; it would be up to the Pittsburgh East End people to push that train over Sand Patch summit for its downhill run towards the City of Pittsburgh and on to Cleveland. All silence; then the operator at "ND" tower, Viaduct Junction, reported the train clearing (passing) by his location, two minutes late of the posted schedule. Immediately, the Superintendent's voice asked "What happened?" The operator said he did not know. A comment was heard that "Maybe he can make it up across the flats", the twelve and one-half miles between that point and the Hyndman Tower, Pennsylvania, over almost flat terrain.

Everything was quiet again. Hyndman Tower, "Q", would be the next reporting point. Hyndman sits at the base of the Sand

A "POTUS" (President of the United States) train is any carrying the U. S. President. Andrew Jackson rode the B&O from Baltimore to Ellicot Mills but Lincoln is considered the first to travel on a POTUS train. Since then, particularly in the heyday of the railroads, many Presidents have ridden the railroads. Some have used the rails for ordinary transportation, especially before the advent of modern air travel. Others have used the trains for campaign trips with the frequent stops coining the phrase "whistle stops." A campaign train is not a POTUS train unless the candidate is a sitting President.

This photograph shows President Reagan's Re-election Campaign train on Chessie making a stop in Deshler, Ohio, on October 12, 1984. Even the grain elevator's silos are announcing "Reagan".

Patch grade--that challenging twenty miles of sharp curves and heavy grades, an engineering marvel even in today's railroad physical plant. The small town is used to seeing trains literally roll through town running for the hill and, long after the caboose has disappeared, hearing the struggling train fighting to keep up its momentum in its westbound thrust. Hyndman is the east side helper station and very few westbound freights get out of town without one or more helpers on their rear for that push over the summit of the Alleghany Mountains.

The operator at "Q" tower reports the special is on his bell, an indication that he has a train coming. When he gives the "OS", (the telegraph code reporting that the train has passed) another four minutes have slipped behind the special's pre-arranged schedule. Things are beginning to get touchy and there is the feeling along the phone line that tensions are starting to build.

The next reporting tower is a place called Foley Tower, "FO", about eight miles west. It is right in the middle of a mountain wilderness reached only by a dirt mountain road. No other buildings are anywhere in that area; yet the tower is manned around the clock. It is a very important point on this uphill, westbound track because another westbound track begins here so slow freight trains can be diverted onto this track to permit passenger and fast freight trains to run around the slow movers, permitting the latter to continue as they fight for the summit about ten miles away. The Operator at Foley, under the direction of the Dispatcher in Pittsburgh, has the ability to line the switch at this location for either the main track or the sidetrack.

The POTUS train was now somewhere between Hyndman, "Q" Tower, and "FO", Foley Tower. The clocks across the entire Pittsburgh East End Division continued to tick, seemingly more loudly than usual; everyone listening on the phone, beginning to wonder, just where was that train. The phone carried no idle chatter--only evidence of heavy breathing and everyone waiting for something to happen. Finally, the Superintendent in Pittsburgh spoke quite loudly "Foley" he called for the Operator. The Operator at "FO" answered, "FOL.....ey", with a touch of a mountain drawl, giving the tower name in two syllables, with about an octave difference between the first and second syllable. The Superintendent immediately shot back "Foley. Where is that train?" The answer, "I do not know, sir," again in that relaxed, slow-speaking manner. Then, more wait; tensions started to build to even a higher level. Faint mumbles are heard in the background but are not intelligible. More wait. Then a real blast as the

Superintendent shouts into the phone "FOLEY!" The answer, "FOL.....ey", in that slow relaxed mountain drawl. "Where is that train?" the Superintendent shouts back. That is answered by "I have no idea, sir." More wait....more silence. Across the entire east end of the Division, everyone listening begins to wonder-- where is our special train, the one we were expected to push over the mountain on its way to Pittsburgh and beyond? Tension has just about become unbearable. A comment is heard that is best not printed. Heavy breathing, more silence, more mumbles in the background. Then, the reverse takes place. Foley calls Pittsburgh with the familiar "FOL.....ey". Pittsburgh immediately replies, "Go ahead Foley." The operator says very slowly in his relaxed manner, "The train is on the bell (an advanced indication that something was coming his way). Then the question, "Do you want him to go up the main or put him through the siding?" The phone almost exploded by the comments from Pittsburgh. "Of course the train was to go main." (Then there were other comments, best not printed). Some remarks did include references to the importance of the movement and everyone should have remembered that this train would be main-tracked. In a pause by the speaker in Pittsburgh, the Foley Operator was heard to say, loud and clear in his slow, relaxed, mountain manner, "I was only doing my job, sir."

True. Despite the tensions, the apparent harassment and the importance of the President of the United States being on the special train, the mountain man put his job and his responsibility first, performing his duty as the man who had to throw the switches and set the signals whether our special went the main, or up the siding. He was literally the "King of the Hill".

I often think about this incident. When at times I have thought that some tensions were a bit too demanding, or when accomplishments seem to fall short of expectations, I think I hear in the background of my memory a "FOL.....ey", in a slow, relaxed drawl. Immediately, I know a smile pops across my face and I hear a voice saying, "I am only doing my job, sir."

The next tower, "SA", Sand Patch, gave the "OS" for the train by its point, over ten minutes late. From Sand Patch, the railroad virtually is downhill all the way across the Central Region, to

Chicago in fact. By the time the train passed the tower near Connellsville about sixty miles farther west, that "behind time" was back to about six minutes, and when the special stopped in Pittsburgh for servicing and crew changes, it was posted "on time".

Immediately following the dialogue at Foley tower, the whole attitude on the phone changed. Seemingly, everyone calmed down; the extreme tension was gone. Now all efforts became to one of "Let's get this train over the system as quickly as possible."

Later, it was told of how the electric generators in the Diesel units keep shutting down as the train was enroute, much to the frustrations of the special mechanic and others on board, resulting in the loss of time. Once those interruptions ceased, the train performance went well.

A POTUS SPECIAL is an experience; hopefully only one is enough. But it does bring out some unusual things not easily forgotten. While I never got the chance to meet the 'King of the Hill' in person, I will never forget him.

Editor's note: I was a Telegraph Operator on the Akron Division when this POTUS special operated. I was off duty when it came through Akron. However, I went to Akron Junction where the train would leave the Main Line and head up to Cleveland on the CT&V branch. I joined the crew on the wreck train. As Byrne said, we were lined up with an engine, air tested, ready to go towards the train as it approached from the east. After it passed Akron Junction, the train was turned and lined up to follow it towards Cleveland. It arrived in Cleveland without incident.

My Two Conversations with
President Harry S. Truman
By Herbert Ray Samples
October 2008

In late January of 1960, I was working the Yard Brakeman's extra board in Grafton, West Virginia. On this particular night, I had been called to work the yard turn that switched the passenger trains which we called the "Midnight Passenger Drill". I was working the head end and the Conductor told me to get the engine out of the spur and take it down to D Tower and the Operator would put us in the pocket to wait for the passenger train to be switched. When the train came in, I noticed that it had the Anheuser Busch Brewing Company private car on the rear.

The Operator gave us the dwarf signal and I took the engine up and coupled it onto the car. While I was down between the engine and the car coupling the air hose, a very prominent-sounding voice said, "Young man, what city or town is this?" I looked up and, lo and behold, President Harry S. Truman was standing on the platform of that car! I said, "Mr. President, this is Grafton, West Virginia", and he said, "Thank you and how are you this morning?" I replied, "Fine, sir". I then said, "I presume you are going over to D.C. to the inauguration." The President replied, "Yes, I am headed over to see the Boy (meaning JFK) get inaugurated." He then added, "I am just not sure that young man fully realizes what he is really getting into." Spontaneously I said, "Well, Mr. President, you surely ought to know." Obviously, that struck him as funny because he put his head back and laughed rather heartily.

That was the second time I had the pleasure of talking to President Truman. The first had been a couple or three years earlier when my wife, Doris, our two oldest daughters, Lori and Susan, and I were attending the Mountain State Forest Festival in Elkins, West Virginia. After watching the parade, for which President Truman was the Honorary Parade Marshal, my wife, daughters and I went to the city park to watch the wood chopping and wood sawing competitions.

A short time later, President Truman and his small entourage came into the park and they came over into the area in which we were sitting and sat down beside us. That was a most wonderful experience! He was an awesome conversationalist, a very affable person and he seemed to enjoy talking to us. He asked us where we lived and also asked me what I did for a living. I told him I was a railroad Brakeman and he confided with us that when he was young he had wanted to be one also but could not pass the vision test. He held our young daughters, who were toddlers, on his lap. He also told us how much he enjoyed his daughter Margaret when she was a toddler. My wife and I were totally enthralled to have the opportunity to meet and talk with him.

A few years ago, I went to the Truman Library in Independence, Missouri, and as I visited there, I was constantly reminded of and kept getting flashbacks of those two very memorable and highly enjoyable face-to-face conversations with the President of the United States. It was very fortuitous to have had two conversations with a very great human being, President Harry S. Truman.

Chapter 12   Presidential Material

I Met the Man

By Ray Lichty
April 2010

Dave DeBoer's great article in the January issue of this newsletter related wonderful vignettes about John W. Barriger III. His stories brought to mind my meetings with Mr. Barriger.

In the summer of 1956, I was working as a Telegraph Operator on the Akron Division of the B&O. At some point, I worked all of the jobs included in my seniority district of the Order of Railroad Telegraphers (ORT). On this particular day, I was working at Ravenna, Ohio, on the east-west main line. A hi-rail vehicle was reported to me by the tower to the east of Ravenna, Newton Falls. I was told the car was occupied by New York Central officials.

The NYC and PRR had trackage rights on the B&O's line between Ravenna and Niles Junction, Ohio, a distance of approximately 23 miles. Therefore, the NYC hi-rail car was operating on the authority of its trackage rights, not as a visitor.

NYC's forerunner in Cleveland was the Lake Shore and Michigan Southern Railway. In 1910, the LS&MS Railway's Cleveland Short Line Railway. was completed from Rockport, on Cleveland's west side, to Marcy, Ohio. Two years later, the Cleveland Short line was completed to Collinwood, Ohio, forming a freight bypass route around the city of Cleveland. A year later, the LS&MS and the bypass route were merged into NYC. (Today, this is all part of CSX.) The Lake Erie and Pittsburgh Railway (owned 50/50 by NYC and PRR) built a line in 1911 from Marcy to Brady Lake, Ohio, where it connected with the Pennsylvania Railroad's main line from Cleveland to Alliance, Ohio. The LE&P acquired trackage rights over the PRR from Brady Lake, Ohio, to Ravenna, Ohio, and then both the LE&P and PRR acquired trackage rights over the B&O to Niles Junction where the PRR line headed off to Youngstown with the LE&P enjoying trackage rights. This gave the LE&P a connection in Youngstown to the already NYC-controlled Pittsburgh and Lake Erie Railroad. Eventually, the NYC acquired the LE&P and was still operating over the B&O when I worked that location.

When the hi-rail arrived at Ravenna tower, the vehicle's driver came up the stairs to the office to get a lineup to go onto the PRR line and up to Brady Lake. Right on the fellow's tail was a nattily dressed gentleman. The fellow stuck out his hand to me and said, "I am John W. Barriger, President of the Pittsburgh and Lake Erie Railroad." I introduced myself and we had a brief but pleasant conversation. As quickly as he had arrived, he and the driver were back down the stairs and on their way.

That was the first railroad president I had met.

In the late 70s, Chessie System was sending some of its managers to Columbia University's Arden House seminars for transportation managers. Arden House had been the Harriman estate along the Hudson River north of New York City. It was located in the town of Harriman, New York. You will recall that Harriman was the station on the Erie Railroad where the superintendent is credited with issuing the first train order by telegraph.

I was fortunate enough to attend the transportation seminar in the winter of 1979. It was a one-week session starting on a Sunday evening and wrapping up the following Saturday. "Van" Vander Veer drove the two of us up to Harriman. John Collinson and Ken Blyth came from Cleveland. I was fortunate to get a bedroom in the original estate—a magnificent room with a very high ceiling, a fancy private bath and elaborate decorations. Some of the attendees stayed in a new wing addition built onto the estate house. That wing was much like hotel accommodations. The public areas of the estate house had very large fireplaces that were always ablaze with cheery, roaring fires.

Another addition had been made to the other side of the estate house to accommodate a large, tiered, lecture hall. In that hall, the 100 or so attendees were treated to presentations on a wide range of topics by distinguished leaders of industry.

We stayed at Arden house the entire week. You were discouraged, if even permitted, to leave the grounds. After dinner, the four Chessie fellows would withdraw to the intimate little bar in the basement. There, along with other attendees, we would engage in the usual lively railroad story-telling. The bartender would attend to our every request for libation.

Our group always sat at the bar. It was laid out in such a way

John W. Barriger III (1899-1976) was one of railroading's legends – a serial railroad president (of the Monon, Pittsburgh & Lake Erie, M-K-T, and Boston & Maine), executive of several others, author, amateur historian, and all-round salesman and enthusiast. During the Depression he helped rescue financially ailing railroads as head of the Reconstruction Finance Corporation's railroad division. Among numerous other things, Barriger had a bottomless knowledge of railroad history and, as this story proves, an unmatched memory for details. His legacy is the John W. Barriger III National Railroad Library in St. Louis, probably the country's largest railroad history collection.

John W. Barriger Library collection.

that it wrapped around at one end and the bartender could only enter the bar from the other end. We discovered that, when the bartender's back was turned away from us, we could reach the shelves behind the bar and snatch a bottle of booze. We entertained ourselves snatching bottles and putting them on the floor below the bar. Now, I would expect that many of you wouldn't be surprised to hear such a tale from the likes of Blyth, Vander Veer or Lichty but I assure you that John Collinson, Chessie System President, was right in the middle of our escapade and clearly enjoying himself.

After this had gone on for quite a while, the bartender came over and said the caper was over. He then came out from behind the bar to see how many bottles we had snatched. We had 18 or 20 bottles on the floor. He declared that we were "pikers" and that others before us had done much better. And we thought we had invented the "game"!

It turned out that about mid-week, one of the speakers was John W. Barriger. He gave a delightful and spirited presentation that was very well received. At a coffee break, I went up to him and introduced myself. I said, "We have met before. I was the Telegraph Operator at Ravenna, Ohio, when you stopped on a hi-rail trip." "Oh", he replied, "I remember that trip well. It was in July of 1956 and Al Perlman (President of the NYC) and I were going from Pittsburgh to Cleveland for a meeting with.............." He went on to relate the details which I, unfortunately, don't recall. Amazing!

When the seminar was over, I ask Van on Saturday morning if we could put our bags in the back seat as I had something I wanted to pick up before we left. Van agreed but was very curious as to what I was planning. As we left, I had him drive by the firewood pile and quickly loaded three very large pieces of split firewood into the trunk. Van was sure we were going to be arrested, if not fired. He said later that he was actually relieved as he thought maybe I was planning to abscond with some large artifact from the house.

Some years later, I made four checker boards, cutting veneer off of contrasting colored logs from my back yard. I trimmed those checker boards with veneer cut from the Arden House firewood.

Power Lunch

By Fred Yocum
July 2011

During the time that we were working on the project of what parts of the Penn Central Chessie should try to buy, there was a seminar on the future of the Penn Central held in Chicago. Dick Rayburn sent me to it.

While there, I ran into an old friend, Bill Collins, who had worked in the Planning Department but had moved on to take a regulatory position with the Canadian Government in Ottawa. He told me that he had dinner lined up with two friends and invited me to come along. It turned out that the two friends were legends of the industry, Jervis Langdon, former President of the B&O and then Chairman of the Rock Island, and John Barriger, who had turned around several railroad properties, including the Pittsburgh & Lake Erie and the Monon.

I was quite brash at this point but even I had enough sense to just sit back and listen. Jervis and John got talking about the difficulties they encountered upon being named the president of a railroad for the first time. This was a subject on which Jervis waxed eloquent because he had ascended straight from corporate attorney to President. Jervis said that one of the big problems for him was that he had to suppress much of his intellectual curiosity because subordinates assumed that you wanted to change anything that you asked a question about. "I've always wanted to know how high the B&O Building is, but I wouldn't dare ask because I was convinced that someone would jump off the roof with a tape measure in his hand."

No Problem

By Walter Vander Veer
October 1999

Shortly after being transferred from Assistant Superintendent Chicago to Superintendent of the Monongah Division at Grafton, West Virginia, in 1962, the enlargement of the 21 tunnels on the Parkersburg Branch was nearing completion. As this was a major construction project to provide additional clearance for high cars and piggybacks, it was decided to have a special train open the line from Grafton to Parkersburg.

As was typical, little time was given to the division personnel to prepare for this historical event. There were numerous cars on the sidings that had been used in the construction of the tunnels and upgrading of the track. It certainly would not be appropriate to have President Langdon and other dignitaries see this equipment. Thus, two days prior to when the branch was officially placed back in service, Trainmaster Eddy Kincaid, Road Foreman of Engines Walter McCahill and I, with locomotive, spent one entire night collecting cars and moving them to Parkersburg yard. There was no problem with the brotherhoods as the track was officially out of service. I had to buy breakfast as payment to Eddy and Walter. They stated that was a night they would never forget.

On the special train trip, we stopped several times to review the tunnel work; and at one location, Mr. Langdon asked if it was ok for him to walk up the nearby hillside for a view of the railroad. I replied very quickly, "No Problem."

Upon arrival at Parkersburg, while everybody was enjoying lunch in the dining cars, I was inspecting the train when a small gentleman approached and asked if Mr. Langdon was on the train. Fortunately for me, I had seen a picture of Walter J. Tuohy, President of the C&O, and I quickly introduced myself and escorted him to Mr. Langdon. I never did get my lunch.

Thus, as I titled this article, "No Problem". Just another day's work.

Testimony to Jervis Langdon, Jr.

By Ron Dunn
January 2005

Some of you who may barely remember me may also barely remember (Bill Johnston and Mil Hodges excepted) my dad. He was a locomotive engineer for the B&O and was obviously the genesis of my life long professional career in railway civil engineering, starting with my first summer job after graduating from Baltimore Polytechnic Institute in 1955. After the B&O and Johns Hopkins, I went on to become Chief Engineer-Track for Jim Caywood on the Washington Metro project and so on and so forth.

I don't recall that I personally ever met Mr. Jervis Langdon; Jr., and if I had, I'm certain that I would have remembered, so that is my loss. My dad, Delmas Dunn, certainly met him and had an unusual direct line of communication with him that I will always remember, as he vividly did until he passed away in 1984.

In the mid-late 1960s, dad had a regular passenger run between Baltimore and Washington. Mr. Langdon made a habit of riding the head end on his travels. On one of those trips with my dad, he learned that dad was a Scoutmaster for the Boy Scout troop sponsored by his church in Govans, where I grew up and had also been a member.

Mr. Langdon, on repeated trips, asked dad to start a Boy Scout troop at the Mt. Clare Shops in an effort to get the juveniles off the streets into some meaningful activities and hopefully to reduce the vandalism and broken windows. Graffiti wasn't the problem then. Dad agreed and became the Scoutmaster of two troops, at opposite ends of the socio-economic scale!

Shortly, the obvious became obvious! Dad told Mr. Langdon, as best I can remember dad telling me, "These boys can't afford to buy their own canteens much less cook kits, sleeping bags, knapsacks (before they were called backpacks) and pup tents." Mr. Langdon told dad to let him know how much money he needed and the B&O would provide it. Dad did and the B&O did! The troop was successful and vandalism decreased!

Mr. Langdon then told dad that whatever and whenever he needed something for the Boy Scout troop to not hesitate to come to his office at any time; and if he wasn't in, his secretary had standing instructions to address those needs. I'm sure that his secretary didn't have a "blank check" but dad was always impressed and personally touched with Mr. Langdon's "open door policy", for him especially.

After a year or so, Mr. Langdon asked dad, "If there is anything you would like to have from the railroad as a memento for your outstanding work with the boys, please let me know what it is." Dad didn't ask me for my suggestions so a steam locomotive or even a brass bell from one of them wasn't mentioned. Dad modestly and reluctantly mentioned "a caboose stove". The next day, a Royal Blue B&O truck showed up at my

185

Jervis Langdon, Jr. (1905-2004) served as B&O's president from 1961 to 1964 , and was the railroad's last "true" president. (His immediate successors came from the C&O and managed both railroads in the same capacity.) When he took on the job, he quickly moved to challenge traditional ways of doing business and to bring in new and creative thinking. Although his time on the B&O was short (he moved on to become chairman of the Rock Island, then trustee of Penn Central), he has been ranked as one of the B&O's most notable leaders, in company with Daniel Willard, Leonor Loree, and John W. Garrett. He had been the RABO Honorary President.

Ray Lichty collection.

parents' home and the crew unloaded a caboose stove in dad's garage, where he used it to heat his workshop until he passed away. I'm still consulting and that caboose stove is now in the conference room of my office where it draws many questions and admiring comments.

For many years later, some of those boys looked up my dad and thanked him for what he had done for them and for how his selfless act had changed their lives. Some of them even invited him to their weddings! Needless to say, dad cherished those contacts as I cherish the memories of his enthusiasm in telling them to me. Thanks dad and thanks Mr. Langdon!

Jervis Langdon--Our Hero
By Keith Rader
July 2011

Jervis Langdon was a godsend; he came to the presidency of the B&O when we had hit bottom. As I recall, it was 1961 and we had ended the year $3 million in the red. Mr. Howard Simpson was President before Jervis. He came from the Central Railroad of New Jersey where he had been head of the Passenger Department, I believe. A good passenger man but that's one place where we were losing money and he did not know the details of the freight operations of our railroad, with which we had all grown up.

His belief was that we should set our sights on earning X number of dollars per month. For example, he said we are going to earn $2 million in January; and if we only earned $1 million, then he said we had lost $1 million and had to make it up in February. To accomplish that, we had to defer maintenance and the purchasing of M of W materials and other supplies. Our maintenance-of-way folks buried their inventory of needed rail and other material so that it would not be charged against them. The result was derailment after derailment. It was a sad situation!

A. W. Colnot was General Manager at Pittsburgh about the time Mr. Langdon became President. At a morning regional conference, Mr. Colnot asked, "Gentlemen, what are we going to do about these derailments?" A familiar voice said, "Quit running trains!" And would you know, it was our newly-appointed

Assistant Superintendent at Chicago, Bill Booth. When asked who had made the comment, Bill confessed.

We had a meeting at Baltimore and any officer from the Trainmaster level on up was present. Mr. Langdon mentioned we had lost $3 million dollars the previous year. He said, "If we lose $3 million this year, most likely you and I will not have a job!" We had just been given an across-the-board 10% pay cut and Mr. Langdon said he was giving it back to us. He said, "As long as I am president, there will never be another officers' pay cut!"

He came out on the property; his was a familiar face. He was one of us. He didn't travel on the railroad with an entourage like his predecessors had done. He was a commoner who understood how difficult it was to run our operation on a dime.

He had the mannerisms needed to motivate his people. He wanted suggestions and said if it looks like any part of your proposals have merit, we will work on it. Some made suggestions at the Baltimore meeting and were laughed at by some but not by our President. Someone, as I recall, said we should do away with our passenger station attendants to save a dollar. Mr. Langdon said if that is what you think is needed, you submit your recommendation and we will look at it. "However", he said, "it is my personal belief that if we are going to run a passenger business we should run a good one. If not, we should get out of the passenger business." We loved him and I was told the following year we were $3 million in the black.

Every railroad in the country was trying to duplicate the rapid turnaround in our financial position. It may have been roundhouse gossip—however, we were told at the time that we were paying debts that were incurred during WWI when the government controlled our railroad. It was said that nothing was ever paid on the principal; only the interest that accrued was being paid. One thing that did take place about that time was a real estate boom. We were able to reduce the size of our railroad going from four main tracks to two or two tracks to one utilizing new signal systems instead of train orders in some places. As a result of improvements, real estate made surplus and available for sale brought premium prices at some locations. I was Terminal Trainmaster at Pittsburgh in 1961-1963 when we sold our Allegheny Yard to the city for $3 million and the Three Rivers Stadium was born.

I think someone once told me to tell them what I wanted to say and explain it later when more time was available. All I really wanted to say is Jervis Langdon was our hero of that day.

A Birthday Party for Jervis
By Dick Nickels
July 2011

I cannot be absolutely positive about this but here goes.....

I think it was in 1961 that a new B&O Railroad president named Jervis Langdon, Jr., arrived in Baltimore to help the "Best and Only" get out of its financial troubles and return to being an outstanding rail carrier.

Some of us wondered about this gentleman named "Jervis" but most soon learned what kind of a gentleman he was. We found out quickly that he was friendly, courteous and very attentive to what was going on...and he looked and asked for suggestions from many to help lower our operating costs and liabilities.

And he did get some help...but one of the most visible cost reductions occurred when he said, "Let's get rid of these limousines and reassign the drivers to 'real jobs'".

He had looked at where our Baltimore Central Building was (three blocks from City Hall and the courthouse, three and a half blocks from the Inner Harbor, two and a half blocks from our retail center...i.e. May Company, Hecht's, Hutzler's, Hoschild Kohn, Stewarts, etc., and only three blocks from the Lexington Market). All of this, including Camden Station (four blocks away) was within walking distance. So, we really didn't need limousines, chauffeurs, etc.—we can walk!

At first, his action shocked a few...but not many. Ultimately, we all felt a great, sensible decision occurred benefiting all of us. Our only regret was that we had too short of an experience with him because, looking back, it would have dramatically minimized B&O's problems.

After he retired in 1986, we were fortunate in finding him interested in our RABO organization. He joined us and attended many of our meetings....especially our annual reunions.

Not many people realized the "super pilot" flew his own plane from Elmira, New York, to our BWI airport in order to join our RABO meetings. His son, Halsey (a pilot for USAir) and his wife Jacqueline and his son, Charles, also live in our area...so he was able to accomplish two goals at the same time...meet with us and visit with his family members in the Baltimore area!

Jervis' becoming a private pilot was a rather natural thing as he was in the Army Air Force during WW II; a Colonel who flew the "hump" to get supplies over the Himalayas.

Because of his age and other reasons, he gave up his license to fly and sold his plane, thereby residing more permanently in Elmira. But his impact on us was so real that we decided to make an impact on him.

So, we decided that because his 95th birthday would be on January 28, 1999, a group of us wanted to go to Elmira and celebrate that event with him before winter weather would rule out such a trip. With help from Jack Campbell, an "executive coach" was secured to take 11 members, together with our wives and "significant others", to go north and celebrate with Jervis and his family on Friday, September 28, 1998. Jack made sure we had good stops north and south. We visited the new U.S. National Park Service's Steamtown National Historic Site at Scranton, Pennsylvania, and the Corning Glass Works and Museum in Corning, New York.

However, upon our arrival at our motel in Elmira, we were advised that instead of us honoring our Honorary President with a party, the Langdons had arranged for us to join them at their private club for dinner. We did and even now we cannot forget how wonderful an evening they had arranged for us. The food and service were better than even any "Royal Blue" experience, without the train. Halsey joined his parents and our gang for the festive affair and he made a video recording of the "speeches", the most notable being the one by Jervis wherein he suggested that he join with the members of RABO and buy back the B&O from CSX. Might not have been a bad idea! The video of that speech is in the RABO archives if anyone would like to view it.

But, the high point of this event was that Jervis and his wife, Irene, talked with every one of us. We were amazed at his cool but contributory responses dealing with railroad problems here,

The high regard for Jervis Langdon was shown when a bus load of RABO members and spouses travelled from Baltimore to Elmira, New York, to celebrate his 95th birthday. The Langdons graciously hosted a dinner for the travelers at their private club. That trip, arranged by RABO member Jack Campbell, taught the Club the advantages of travelling in an Executive Motor Coach which became the "standard" for all future trips.

RABO members shown with Halsey, Jervis and Irene Langdon at Jervis' 95th birthday party are, l to r; Jack Campbell, Ray Lichty, Allan Baer, Dick Nickels, George Bull, Bob White, Dick Lang, Norm Murphy, Al Best, Bob Keyser and Bob Breiner.

Dick Nickels photo.

there and everywhere.

We couldn't help but smile when his wife said, "Jervis, enough, you are talking too much!"

Also, after we got back home, we received a lovely note from Mrs. Langdon thanking us for visiting them in Elmira. She was so gracious to us all.

So, in spite of our desire to honor Jervis and Irene with a party, the Langdons threw one heck of a party for us, instead!

The Days of Hays

By Robert J. Frost
July 2004

Reading in RABO *News & Notes* that Hays T. Watkins had joined our rolls brought back some wonderful memories of the golden years when Hays headed up the Chessie System. For those of us working in the Pittsburgh Sales Office, you might call the week of the Pittsburgh Traffic Club Annual Dinner something we looked forward to every year. In the 1970s, Pittsburgh, along with Chicago and New York, had "The Annual Dinners". Pittsburgh would have a table for railroad presidents and Mr. Watkins was present for most, if not all, of the dinners during his tenure. There are fond memories of the down-to-earth Hays Watkins during those times recognizing the Sales personnel who were responsible for getting Hays and company to/from the Hilton Hotel and the county airport. Either Ron Bernick or I would normally get the enjoyable duty of taking Hays to the airport. We would always get a room for Hays and John Collinson to change into and out of their tuxedos before and after the dinner. One year, they were late coming out and I was asked to check and make sure everything was all right. I knocked on their door and entered to find both Hays and John crawling on the floor. Mr. Collinson had lost one of his cuff links and Hays wouldn't leave until it was found.

One other year, we were heading for the airport and Mr. Watkins mentioned that this was a rare occasion when both he and John Collinson would be on the same plane. It was humorous when he said to John Collinson, "Boy, John, I'd like to be a mouse in headquarters if this plane goes down. Everyone will be running around trying out our seats." I'm not certain but don't think Mr. Collinson was a lover of flying but a great leader.

When Chessie was in the process of merging with Seaboard System, Hays shared the story of his AAR meeting in Chicago when every other railroad was asking for some part of Chessie or Seaboard. I believe one railroad asked for the former B&O main line from Chicago to Baltimore. Hays stated to the effect that he told the other Presidents, "We'll keep what you're asking for and you can have the rest."

Hays T. Watkins, Jr. came out of the C&O's Finance Department and, beginning in 1971, led C&O, B&O, and their successors for 20 years. Watkins was a major force in the 1980 creation of CSX when he became its president and co-CEO, later moving to chairman and finally retiring in 1991. Also a long-time railroad enthusiast, he was a strong supporter and savior of the B&O Railroad Museum.
Hays is the Honorary President of RABO.

The best sign of Hays Watkins was after the CSX merger was approved and the NS merger was going forward. Remembering Hays's comments about what other railroads asked for during the CSX hearings, I asked Hays whether CSX would gain something from the NS merger. Hays responded to the effect that it wouldn't benefit CSX nor the rail industry to hinder mergers. It is my belief it was his stance that CSX would not seek to benefit from any other merger.

There isn't any doubt in my mind that he was the finest I worked for in over 34 years.

WORKING on the RAILROAD

Chapter 13   **First Work on the Railroad**

Old Pete Recalls and Reflects

By Pete Hartley
January 2003

Today is November 11, 2002--day number 36,214 that I have been alive on this earth. Of this number of days, 100 of them have been on November 11th. Of this 100, there are two that I vividly remember--1918, when the armistice was signed ending World War I and 1932, when my son and only child, Ken, was born. All others have been "just another day".

Although these two days were only 14 years apart, there was a great difference in my two worlds. On November 11, 1918, I was a sophomore in high school at Buckhannon, West Virginia. It was the time of the nation's first influenza epidemic. Schools were closed and no large gatherings of people were permitted. The radio had not yet come upon the scene so we got our news via the newspaper. It was rumored that the war was coming to an end and everyone was anxiously awaiting the news. The local Western Union telegraph office posted on its office window reports of developments and people gathered on the street eagerly reading every message. When the good news came, the church bells rang and whistles blew. That evening, we had a big bonfire in a vacant lot near the junction of Florida and Main streets. There was great jubilation.

On November 11, 1932, the scene was much different. At the beginning of that year, 1932, my wife Elma and I were happily living in a fourth floor walk-up apartment on High Street in Morgantown, West Virginia. I enjoyed the position of Agricultural Agent for the Baltimore and Ohio Railroad. We were in the early stages of the "Great Depression". During the first three months of that year, it became necessary that my secretary be furloughed and I took a ten percent cut in salary and Elma

The RABO Club threw a party to celebrate Pete Hartley's 100th birthday. Members, spouses and friends gathered at a restaurant in his home town of Morgantown, West Virginia, for the festivities. Pete arrived by stretch limo provided by his family. George Bull, who was 78 at the time, said if someone was told there was a 100-year-old man present they probably would pick out me!

Pete died in October, 2003, having been the first RABO member to reach the age of 103.

became pregnant.

To eliminate the four-flight walk-up, we decided to move to a second floor duplex on South High Street with an increase in rent from $40 per month to $50. I also purchased additional life insurance, assuming that life would continue uninterrupted. Then the bomb dropped. On May 15, I was informed that due to the depression, our department was being placed on furlough. I was suddenly unemployed.

I was successful in getting another job but at half the salary, so we had to reduce expenses. We moved to a $25 per month apartment and managed to keep going.

November arrived and the baby was due. Elma entered the

hospital Sunday, the 10th, and, after considerable difficulty, delivered a nine pound, healthy, boy on Armistice Day, Nov. 11, 1932. I remember it well.

Yes, I will always remember those two November 11th days out of the 100 I have witnessed.

A Century Has Passed

By Keith Rader
April 2010

This photo of my children's great, great-grandfather, Henry Ginniman, who was a yard foreman on the Baltimore and Ohio Railroad at Cumberland, Maryland, was taken over 109 years ago. Henry was run over by a switch engine and killed at the Virginia Avenue switchbox in July of 1900.

During the 1943 World War II era, I was attending high school and working part time at that same switch box in Cumberland as a Car Checker.

I remember my first tour working second shift at that location. My assignment required me to identify every car on the inbound trains by writing down the car numbers as the trains went by me and matching those numbers with their waybills. We had twelve inbound trains that evening. I missed most of the numbers on the first train and walked the rest of the night, after the trains were yarded. I was furnished all the necessary tools including a kerosene lantern, which I can still identify, if one is near me in the dark, by it aromatic aroma.

As the trains came around the curve and up Hog Pen Grade that runs parallel with the old Chesapeake and Ohio Canal, there was a constant chug-a-lug. It was a mortal sin to stall coming up this grade, especially when your train consisted of 100 cars or more. Any train in excess of 100 cars in length would not clear the Baltimore Street grade crossing, which was the main artery in downtown Cumberland. The switch box that served as an office and shelter was equipped with a potbelly stove that was fueled by coal or wood, whichever was readily available. It was very small but comfortable. The stove also had a distinctive aroma.

The photo also shows Yard Foreman Ginniman posing in a sitting position on the front of his switch engine Number 1110.

A classic posed turn-of the century photo of a B&O yard crew and their engine, in this case taken at Cumberland. The existence of such photos shows the pride of the crew in their assignments and the equipment with which they worked. The author's, Keith Rader, great-grandfather, Henry Ginniman, is the crew's foreman and he stands in the center of the photo dressed appropriately for the job.   *Keith Rader collection.*

The engine's catcher had been modified, by replacing it with a footboard for yard service. With his crew standing nearby, Henry can be seen outfitted in his suit-style jacket and bow tie which signifies his rank as Yard Foreman.

Henry was run over by a switch engine and killed at the Virginia Avenue switchbox in July of 1900.

Number 1110 was a rugged-looking locomotive and was equipped with a link and pin coupling device. The automatic coupler had not been invented at that time. The link and pin coupler was a dangerous feature even for an experienced crew member. The loss of an arm or finger was not uncommon; even the loss of life!

These engines were often referred to as "tea kettles" or "yard pots" because they were steam-powered. Standard equipment included a carbide headlamp and a whistle which was invented by B&O's George Washington Whistler.

The long-spouted oil can was replaced by an engine-mounted device that lubricated the bearings which could be activated from the locomotive cab. It was invented and patented by a railroad laborer from Bristol, Tennessee. His name was McCoy. This device was referred to by all as the "Real McCoy". When the Storekeeper would order one, he would specify that he wanted the Real McCoy, no substitute.

Number 1110 was built for the Baltimore and Ohio at the Baldwin Locomotive Works in Philadelphia, Pennsylvania, in 1892 and was retired in 1925.

The last of the 1100 series were built in 1892 and all were retired by 1946. They were the work horses of their time. Even to this day, steam power is considered to be one of the most widely-used sources of power known to man.

Other specifications of this class D-3, 0-6-0 locomotive included her 19x24 inch cylinders and 50 inch drivers. She weighed 97,700 pounds; t. p. (tractive power) was 22,000 pounds; and the s. p. (steam pressure) was 150 pounds.

My First Day at the
Baltimore & Ohio Railroad Company
By Dick Kraft
January 2001

In 1945, Just prior to my 16th birthday, I applied for a job as a Yard Clerk at the Grafton, West Virginia, yards.

I had been born and raised just across from the Yard Office and the Chief Clerk to the General Yardmaster just lived down the street from our house. I had been employed at the local cemetery cutting grass.

My grandfather (on my mother's side of family) had been employed as a Carman. He had died while on duty when I was but three years old. I also had two uncles (mother's brothers) employed as Carmen at the Grafton Yards.

It had long been my dream to work on the railroad. I had just

The B&O's Grafton, West Virginia yard office.
Baltimore & Ohio Railroad Historical Society collection.

finished my junior year of high school. I asked for and got the application at the Superintendent's Office, which was located on the second floor of the Passenger Station. I completed it and turned it in to the Chief Clerk. I was told that they would call me when and if I was accepted.

I knew that they were short of clerks, as the War was going on. I received a call and was told to report to the Medical Examiner. That was a great experience as this was my first employment physical. When I got the "finger", I wondered what this was all about.

I passed the examination and was told to report to the Chief Clerk at the Yard Office for further instructions. On reporting there, I was told that I would be on my own and had to qualify and work one day before my seniority would start. So it was up to me to get busy and learn one of the clerical jobs. I asked if I could come out that night and he told me he would arrange to have someone take me under his wing and show me the ropes. He gave me a slip to go to the Storekeeper's office and get a lantern.

I reported at the Yard Office at 11 PM. The Yard Office at that time was two old railroad coaches placed together in the middle of the leads at the east and west yards. One of the coaches was for the lunch and locker room for the switch crews and Carmen. The other was for the Yard Office. One end had the General Yardmaster's, and Chief Clerk's office; In the middle was the Yard Office and on the other end were the Police and the Switchtender's small offices.

In the main Yard Office, there was a desk for the Eastbound Yardmaster and one for the Westbound Yardmaster. There was a center desk for the Night General Yardmaster and the Booker Clerk. (He was the one that took the lined up waybills and recorded them on a Wheel-Report for the outbound train.) There was then only one desk left and that had to be shared by the Eastbound Checker Clerk and the Westbound Checker. There was also a caboose stove right in the middle. Needless to say, there was not much room left.

That night was a life-changing experience for me. As I walked into this office, the first thing that I noticed was a cloud of smoke that hung from the ceiling. I think that everyone in the office was smoking. The next thing was that you could hardly hear, as it seemed that everyone was talking at the same time. Some of the language would make your ears burn.

All at once I saw this person (later learned he was the Night General Yardmaster) jump up from his chair and throw the phone across the desk. The phone was one of those that was on a hanger and would extend out from the wall. Well, the phone hit the wall and came balancing back and out the door he went. I thought to myself what in the world have I gotten myself into.

All that night I was lost. This was a new world to me and I wondered to myself how in the world did this all fit together. After about a week, I became a part of the action as I started to understand some of the madness that was involved in getting the job done.

I guess my instructor told the Chief Clerk that I was qualified to work the outside checking job in the East Yard. I began my seniority, July 10, 1945, on the second trick at Grafton Yard Office. I ended my railroad employment on August 30, 1986. But, that is another story.

Memories

By Bill Lakel
July 2003

My first contact with the B&O Railroad was in 1940. My family moved into an old farm house near Reels Mill, east of Frederick Junction, Maryland. The home was located on a dirt road with no electricity or running water. There was a pump located just outside the back door where we would get our water. I was 12 years old and attended a three-room school in Urbana with two grades in each room.

Looking down the big hill, I could see the sweeping curve with the double tracks just east of the old service area at Reels Mill. The westbound trains would mostly have to stop for water at Frederick Junction in case Brunswick could not handle them. The rear end crews would take three torpedoes and twist the lead together and throw them off the MW caboose while moving. Hoping one of the three would land on top of the rail. This eliminated the long walk back for the Flagman to put down his caps.

Needless to say, the curve was a bonanza for torpedo lead used for fishing sinkers. You could pick up as much lead as you wanted to carry. In the summer I would take my fishing rod and walk down the track from Reels Mill to the Monocacy River in Frederick Junction to fish. The river was full of fish and I caught enough to keep the family supplied.

There was one particular locomotive that had a very different sounding whistle. The sound was so distinctive that you could hear it miles away almost from Monrovia blowing for the road crossings. The sound was almost a low growl instead of the usual shrill sound of a steam whistle. I was at Frederick Junction one day when this locomotive pulled up to the penstock for water and blew signals for the Flagman to go back to protect. I asked the

Engineer, John Earle, about the whistle and he said that this engine had a very different sound and that it must be the whistle itself. He also invited me to "climb aboard". This was my first experience on a locomotive and I was immediately hooked on railroading.

I turned 16 on March 13, 1944. My best friend and classmate's father, I. D. "Ira" Ausherman, worked as Track Foreman of Section 17, B&O Railroad Company, running from Lime Kiln Station to just east of Reels Mill, a distance of eight miles. His son, Marion, and I were both seniors in high school and he asked if I wanted a job on the railroad. Due to the war, the B&O was hiring 16 year olds for Trackmen.

I was hired in Ira's kitchen; the only formality was my mother had to sign a waiver to pay wages to a minor. Ira hired four of us that day, all living in the area of Frederick Junction. Three of us had family with the B&O already. We all went to work at the Tool House at Frederick Junction on June 6, 1944; "D Day".

During that period, the Trackmen worked six days per week, Sunday off. I took Friday off from school working two days a week or four days a half. The pay was 67 cents an hour. I would make about $20.00 a half, which was good money in 1944. 1 believe my father made about $25.00 a week working full time.

I survived the track work (although, at times it was doubtful I would) boring bolt holes with a hand bicycle chain drill and sawing rail with a hand hack saw. We sawed into the base and then broke it with a hammer blow. Handling 36 ft. 130 lb. rail with four men was not an easy task. We would pick one end up and put it on a push truck, then push the truck under the rail. When the end was up in the air far enough to balance, we'd run like hell hoping it would stay on the truck. There were days when we would just swing a mowing scythe all day. We cut the entire eight miles every summer, both sides, from the berm to the fences, fighting snakes and bees regularly.

I turned 18 and got a Draft Notice to appear for an Induction Physical. I joined the Navy. I got married on March 2, 1946, turned 18 on March 13th and left for Boot Camp in April, after requesting a leave of absence from the railroad.

When I came home on leave after Basic, I looked down on the

curve at a huge derailment. I went down and found the Park Junction Stock Train had wrecked. There were horses, cattle and pigs everywhere. People were butchering animals from the trees. Calves and cattle were walking the road and the stock cars were full of dead animals. Several local farmers had opened fences and herded the live animals into their fields. The Claims Department later paid these farmers and recovered the stock. Before I went back to base, the roadway had been cleared and opened for traffic. The stock cars had been pushed off the roadway with the dead animals still inside. What a mess to clean up but it was all gone when I came home in November. The Navy had demobilized the USNR and I was discharged.

While at Frederick Junction one day, Operator C. O. Warfel told me that the Division Operator was hiring Telegraph Operators for this area. He got R. S. Schenck on the phone and I was headed to Baltimore to be hired as a Student Operator at 50 cents an hour for 90 days. I was sent to "MA" Tower under F. J. "Frank" Esworthy to be trained as a Telegraph Operator. After about 45 days, Dispatcher "PSA" (Percy Asher), told Ross Schenck I was ready for work and, needing people, I went to work posting at the different towers. Posting pay was the lowest-rated job on the district but a lot better than 50 cents an hour. My first daughter had arrived and the increase in pay was a godsend to my family.

I got a call one day to go to a huge derailment just east of Reels Mill. A coal train had derailed just west of Hartman Tunnel. It seems that the train had struck a track maintenance machine, derailing almost the entire train into the Bush Creek bottom on the south side. The three-unit consist were diesel locomotives of the F7 Type, one of the first diesel engines we had on the Division. A helper steam engine was shoving the train from Brunswick. This probably contributed greatly to the many cars being shoved off the tracks. On arrival, I found the lead engine (I believe engine number 245) derailed, but upright, just as it entered Hartman Tunnel. The Engineer stayed on board. The Fireman had jumped off the left side landing on the westbound track hitting his head on the rail and was killed.

Further investigation revealed the train had struck a BDK

Ballast Regulator operated by Jack Farley, a friend from my old Track Gang of Section 17, and the Flagman was Durward Sines, a fellow trackman and a neighbor.

Dispatcher W. L. "Larry" Cosgrove had given the regulator, through the Operator at "FE," Frederick Junction, good figures on the coal train at both "KU" Tower, Point of Rocks and Frederick Junction. For some unknown reason, Jack backed up to pick up his Flagman and, instead of running to get in the clear, continued toward Ijamsville or Monrovia, Maryland, with the Flagman aboard the BDK with the right regulator arm extended.

The train had no warning the Regulator was on the rail and struck the machine, critically injuring the Flagman who was thrown in the clear to the south side. The BDK was shoved east with its arm extended until it struck a small trussed bridge just west of the tunnel. Upon striking the bridge with the arm extended, the machine turned sideways and was crushed by the train. Jack was killed instantly. Most of the machine ended up in Bush Creek under the bridge. Most of the coal still remains in the creek bottom long covered by brush and trees.

On a recent visit to my old home, I drove to Reels Mill. I went by the cable blocking access to the road and drove up the right of way to the first bridge, then walked east to Hartman Tunnel. There is still evidence of both accidents--steel scrap from car parts and pockets of coal along the creek banks. Most evident are the dents in the trusses and braces of the bridge where the Ballast Regulator was crushed by the Extra 245 East as the train derailed.

Remembering many days working with Jack, and we also married girl friends in 1946, while coaxing my 75-year-old legs back to my car, I noticed a tear on my cheek, maybe from some sentiment of days gone by. I can almost hear John blowing the whistle on the 4844 from Ijamsville as it echoes west through the hills of the Bush Creek bottoms.

NOTE: Engineer John Earle worked many years on the Old Main Line Way Train. He was very seriously injured in a freak derailment at Gaither, Maryland, in 1945, while Engineer of an eastbound freight. The engine derailed to the center ditch, picking up the south rail of the westbound track. The rail went between the drivers of the engine, piercing the firebox, boiler and crown sheet coming into the locomotive cab just missing John's head to the left. The escaping steam blew John out the engine window saving his life. The Fireman also escaped but was severely scalded. Brakeman Willowby was trapped in the brakeman's seat and killed on the locomotive. The accident happened in front of Brakeman Willowby's home at Gaither.

A Stroll Down Memory Lane

By Ed Willis
October 2005

In the July issue of *News & Notes*, a story written by Allen Brougham about the Old Bay Line and its steamers City of Norfolk and City of Richmond, triggered memories of my early youth and my involvement with the Old Bay Line Steamship Co. Due to constant harassment and pressure brought upon me by Ray Lichty, 1 agreed to share those memories with the readers of *News & Notes.*

I grew up in the Locust Point section of Baltimore on Haubert Street. At the foot of Haubert Street, only two blocks from my home, was the Procter & Gamble soap factory; and on the Hull Street side were the B&O Railroad piers. Sandwiched in between those giants was a little tugboat company named the Harbor Towing Corporation. It was owned by George E. Rogers. Many of you older members of Boumi Temple in Baltimore may remember him.

It was 1943, during the war years, and I was fourteen years old. All of my spare time was spent hanging around this towing company, I would constantly be chased away by the dock foreman until one day Mr. Rogers had him bring me into his office for a little chat. He said since I would not stay away from his dock he may as well put me to work, which was great for me. My work schedule was after school (Francis Scott Key #76) on weekdays, and Saturdays and Sundays doing odd jobs such as carrying buckets of coal to the tugs for their heating plants, gasoline for their generators and other needed jobs that could be done by me.

During my summer school vacation, I turned fifteen; and since manpower was scarce due to the war, I was assigned as a Deckhand on the B.F. Huntley, the diesel tug assigned to service the Old Bay Line Steamship Co. located on Light Street across

The Old Bay Line operated the two steamships. City Of Norfolk and City of Richmond, in and out of Baltimore seven days a week. Our day would start with the arrival of either ship which we would follow up the harbor to its berth at 6:00 A.M. We then spent the rest of the day shifting loaded barges to various locations to be unloaded onto the steamer and going around the harbor to various can companies and packing houses located in Fells Point and on Boston Street where we placed empty barges to be loaded. We also pulled the loaded barges to be delivered to the steamers for loading their contents onto the steamers. After loading the freight and passengers, the steamer would back out of its berth at 6:00 P.M. Our tugboat would go against its bow to shove and assist it in turning around to head it on its trip down the harbor. After the steamer's departure, we would wait for the Bay Belle moonlight ship to depart at 8:00 P.M. which we would also assist in turning for its trip down the harbor. We would then tie up at our dock at approx. 9:00 P.M. Believe it or not, this was our regular schedule, 6:00 A.M. until 9:00 P.M., seven days a week.

H. H Harwood, Jr., photo.

from the McCormick Spice Company. Due to my age, I was also told, if asked, I was not to say I was employed but just say my uncle was Captain and he was letting me ride around with him.

Our paydays were every two weeks but Mr. Rogers, being the kind soul that he was, would pay us our regular pay one week and the overtime pay the next week. My first regular paycheck for two weeks was $40.00 and the overtime check for two weeks was $20.00, making a total of $60.00 for working from 6 A.M. until 9 P.M. seven days a week for two weeks! I thought l was the richest kid in the neighborhood and I probably was at that time.

When summer was over and I had to return to school, I continued to work my after-school schedule and many times I would be used on a tug to deliver loaded oil barges to ships waiting to come into their piers. After unloading, we would deliver the barge back to Standard Oil to be reloaded and 1 would get home about 1 or 2 A.M. but I would still go to school the following day.

Later in my deckhand career during summer vacations, I was assigned to one of the bay boats that would tow oil and fertilizer barges to various places in Delaware, Norfolk and Richmond. On these trips, I would be on duty six hours and off for six hours. When I calculated my pay. I figured I was only being paid fifty cents an hour. I knew I was worth more than that and I told Mr. Rogers so. He said "Hells, Bells, young man, you are only on duty six hours and off six hours." I pointed out to him that when I was off, I couldn't go anywhere either. He relented and gave me a five-cent increase which satisfied me.

I continued with the Harbor Towing Co. until after the war when an old friend, who was Chief Engineer on a seagoing tug owned by the Boston Iron & Metals Co., offered me a job as an oiler with him. I accepted his offer.

This job took me to various places where surplus ships were anchored, such as the upper Hudson River, New York, the James River below Richmond, Brunswick, Georgia, and other places where ships were anchored for storage. We would tow these ships hack to Baltimore to be cut up for scrap, This was a great job but all good things come to an end. After a time, we had towed enough ships into Baltimore to create a surplus. The company

Ed Willis was in the second engine of a train headed by doubleheaded Q-class Mikados much like this pair, when he got his memorable introduction to Mt. Airy Tunnel. One can understand Ed's problem with smoke in this circa 1946 view of a westbound freight nearing Lansdowne, Maryland, -- also on its way to the Old Main Line and Mt. Airy.

H. H. Harwood, Jr., collection.

decided it would be cheaper to contract future towing to an outside company than it was to keep and maintain their own tugboat and the nine-man crew. That ended my five-year career on tugboats and started my search for a new career.

After a time working various jobs in which I had no real interest, I was employed by the B&O Railroad as a Brakeman on July 24, 1951, my 21st birthday. At the start, I wasn't sure how long it was going to last. My first assignment, which got me off to a very rocky start, was Bay View 97, which incidentally, at a later time in my career, got me in hot water with our Division

Superintendent, A. W. Johnston. But that is another story.

On this my first trip, Bay View 97 was scheduled to depart Bay View Yard at 11:59 P.M. After our departure, I was on the Brakeman's seat behind the Fireman and was looking at those steam gauges and wondering what would happen to me if the boiler exploded. I didn't know our location at the time but we stopped at North Avenue for a red signal. While stopped, the Engineer and Fireman were talking, not to me but loud enough for me to hear. The Fireman said, "The company sure is hiring a lot of new Brakemen." To which the Engineer replied, "No wonder, the way they are killing them!" That certainly didn't go over very well with me and almost ended my short career right there! I was trying to determine if I got off the train how would I get back to my car when, fortunately, we got the signal and departed. We made a pick up at Mt. Clare and departed to the Old Main Line for our trip to Brunswick.

There were quite a few encounters on this first trip up and back that made me wonder if I had chosen the right career. The first was arriving at Mt. Airy Tunnel where we attached another steam engine to our head end to assist us through the tunnel and up the grade. For those of you who have never experienced going through a tunnel on the second engine of double-header steam engines, you don't know what you have missed and I don't recommend that you try it.

It was the old timers' policy to "initiate" new employees on their first trip though the tunnel. In this case, I was initiated! I did notice the Fireman and Engineer soaking wads of cotton waste in water and packing it with ice but I had no idea why. When we started through the tunnel with those two steam engines chugging for all they were worth, I soon found out why! The cab filled with smoke, which made it hard to breathe; and the heat got so intense it felt like the skin was burning off my face. I started to panic and would have jumped off the engine but we came out of the tunnel just in time and I could breathe again! The Engineer and Fireman thought that was very funny but I didn't. The waste, packed with ice and soaked in water, allowed them to breathe through it and keep the heat from their faces.

My next encounter was when we arrived in Brunswick. My

eyes and head were full of cinders and I was as black as the Ace of Spades. After getting settled in, having had a shower in the old YMCA building and breakfast of creamed chipped beef and toast, which in all my trips to Brunswick was the only thing I could ever eat, I retired to my assigned room, which cost fifty cents. The rooms were not air-conditioned and the windows had to be opened in the summer. July was the hottest part of that summer. At that time, Brunswick was full of steam engines. While I slept, the soot was pouring in the windows; and after sweating, tossing and turning during the day, when I awoke I was just as dirty as before I showered. After my second shower and dinner that evening, which was creamed chipped beef and toast, we departed Brunswick for our return trip to Baltimore on Baltimore 94.

We arrived at Frederick Junction to set off and pick up. The Engineer, in his gruff voice, instructed me to cut off five cars, which we would set off on one track, and pick up five cars off of the adjacent track. He would then go down to take water on the engine and I was to reline the switches and couple up to the train when he returned. His last comment was, "Do you think you can do that?" I assured him I could. After relining the switches, I sat down on a crosstie with my light out to await his return. It was a pitch black night. After a while, I heard him chugging back and, not being experienced in judging distance to couple, I waited until he was about one car length away before I turned on my light. When the engineer saw the light go on, he made a desperate attempt to stop but he couldn't before ramming into our train. When he hit, it looked like the engine was going to turn over. Lucky for me, the coupling was made without any damage to the draw-head. I could hear the engineer hollering and cussing and I decided to couple the air hose, wave him ahead and stay where I was.

After about a ten or fifteen-minute wait, the Engineer climbed down off the engine, walked back to me and told me to get my ass on the engine, which I did very quickly. The Fireman told me later that the Engineer had a cigar in his mouth; and when we made that coupling, he went forward and smashed it in his face. Much later, the Engineer always accused me of doing that on purpose, although I didn't. I let him know it served him right for his treatment of a new employee.

Brunswick's huge, barnlike Railroad YMCA provided meals and beds for B&O crews out of Cumberland, Baltimore, and other Eastern terminals round the clock. Maybe not surprisingly, it was also a major social center for the town of Brunswick itself. Originally built in 1907, it was later expanded to this appearance with new top floor and roof -- but along the way lost its large porch overlooking the tracks. Sadly, it was lost to a fire in 1980 and replaced by a modern facility off-site.

H. H. Harwood, Jr., photo, 1966.

After arriving back in Baltimore, again eyes and hair full of cinders and again black as the Ace of Spades, I really wondered if I had made a wrong decision about my future. However, I decided to give it one more try.

My next assignment was to report to Riverside to "deadhead" to Brunswick. Our crew was taxied to Camden Station for the morning Local to Brunswick. On arrival at Brunswick, I was informed I was relieved and would be paid a day's pay which sounded good to me. After breakfast, (of course, it was creamed chipped beef and toast) I settled down to await our return trip to Baltimore. That evening, after dinner of creamed chipped beef and toast, we were called for the Time Saver. When our train arrived, I climbed up on that big diesel engine, departed Brunswick on the "Met Sub" to the Washington Branch and on into Baltimore and was relieved one hour forty-five minutes later. Another day's pay! After that, I knew I had found a new home.

After working a wide variety of positions in Baltimore, being transferred to Philadelphia, Cumberland and back to Baltimore, surviving six Superintendents, five Division Managers and four General Managers, I retired as Assistant Superintendent of Operations on the Maryland Division after thirty-seven years of service.

Looking back over my working career with all of its trials, tribulations, disappointments and successes, I know I lived and worked in the best of times and the best of places. As a result, my favorite quotation is, "With All Of Its Shams, Drudgery, And Broken Dreams, It's Still a Beautiful World."

It's in the Details

By Byrne Waterman
July 2002

I don't know why he asked but Ray's question was, "How long was the Training Program when you were a Trainee?" Well..... as I recall the program—52 Years later—it was on 5 July, 1950, that the eight of us met for the first time in C. H. Holtzworth's office for the beginning of the Management Training Program. It was to be a 104-week program—52 weeks of the Preliminary Phase and 52 weeks of the Intensive Phase, the first being a similar program for all Trainees, spending the same amount of time in each of the four principal departments. Then, on the completion of that preliminary program, each Trainee could choose, subject to the approval of the department head, the department in which he would like to take his intensive training. I believe that the second year of the program was flexible because I do not believe all eight of us got assigned at the same time— assignments depended on the department and the "need" or an opening in those departments.

Since I asked for the Maintenance-of-Way Department, I was assigned to the Central Region and transferred to Pittsburgh. I spent several weeks at a time on various M of W projects all over the region, from the Track Supervisor at Hyndman to the Track

Maintenance of Way machinery was pretty much unheard of on the railroads until the 1950s. Some of the first equipment to replace manual labor were the pneumatic ballast tampers, the huge ballast cleaning machines and spreaders for maintaining the ballast configuration. Later advancements brought on devices capable of doing almost every track task that existed including laying quarter mile long stretches of welded rail. Such large equipment brought on operating problems since they had to be treated like trains occupying a section of track. The ballast cleaner was notorious for causing problems on a double track railroad where the "wings" of the machine fouled the adjacent track.

Supervisors at Willard, Ohio, and Walkerton, Indiana, and the Master Carpenters at various locations; Bridge Inspectors and Tunnel Inspectors; the ore and coal piers at Rochester, Lorain, Fairport; etc. I cannot say if the early semi-permanent assignment was originally a part of the overall program or was it an answer for the various departments to rid themselves of continuing programs for we "non-productive" assignees but to those of us that did get assigned, it was a great relief as now, hopefully, we could really get down to work and not be carted around and shown this and that. I was most happy.

But before the second year was finished, it was decided that "Some return should be derived from the original investment" and we were shipped out to our initial assignments. I was sent to the Akron Division as the Assistant to the Division Engineer, a position which the Division Engineer, Guy Long, told me that he did not ask for and did not care whether I was there or not and that I should come prepared to work. He farmed me out to Track Supervisor at Ravenna; Bill Childress, the Track Supervisor at New Castle; and to the Track Supervisor at Akron, Roland Hedrick. I was sent to work with an extra gang, for several weeks, in Clark Avenue Yard at Cleveland, hopefully to learn to drive spikes, tighten bolts, tamp ties—as I was told, "You do not have any knowledge about that type of work." Then, it was to Youngstown to work with two extra gangs relocating tracks in the area. The Extra Gang Foremen were Patty Russo and Veto DiPiolla, the two of them and myself being referred to as 'the blind leading the blind'. Division Engineer Guy Long gave me the Baltimore-prepared plan for the track work, relocating several switches, etc., and informed me that the job would only be completed after he made an inspection; and I had better "be sure that every detail had been covered." It did not exactly pass his inspection because I failed to insert a cotter key in a bolt that anchored the switch bar running from the switch stand to the switch point. It was an oversight because the bolt goes in from the bottom and the washer and nut are on top and the bolt itself has a hole for the cotter key. Of course, I was told that I should be more alert to details. You would be surprised over the next twenty-plus years how many switches I looked at and how many I found with that cotter key missing. Just could not carry that many kegs of keys around replacing the missing! For every one that I saw, I made the statement, "I wonder who will get chewed out for that missing key?" But of course, Division Engineer Long has gone on to the "Great Engineering Office in the sky" and I was not responsible for that omission.

I really enjoyed my stay in Akron, meeting Terminal Trainmaster Tom Ready at Akron Junction who became a very good friend, Track Supervisor Teeple on the Lake Branch, and loads more.

I then moved to the Newark Division as Assistant Division

Engineer—ironically was transferred on the same day I moved my furniture from Pittsburgh into an apartment in Cuyahoga Falls, Ohio. I replaced 'Little John' (Collinson) who had been stepped up to Division Engineer. I enjoyed that relationship for several years. We became very good friends and John, Patty, my wife and I spent many a Saturday evening together, watching their children and my son grow up.

Then entered Assistant Road Foreman of Engines, Sam Myers and his wife May, and Assistant Trainmaster, Andy Huber and his wife Betty. Golly, the four of us fellows were ready to take over the Western Region. First, we had Clarence Jackman in Cincinnati and T. Earl Johnson coming to Newark as Superintendent. We had one h--- of a good time.! (I found a lot of cotter keys missing on the Newark and C&N Divisions.)

I then went on the Pittsburgh Division East End and who was my new 'mentor?' No one but "Big John" Collinson, father of Division Engineer John at Newark. Now that was and is another story, believe me! It was surprising when "Big John" told me that I did not know how to install a switch!—saying that anyone who grew up on the railroad should know what to look for and he had heard that I was lacking in certain details. I never told him I found a lot of switches on the East End that lacked cotter keys!

I moved six times in ten years. My wife, carrying our first son, had three different doctors in Pennsylvania, Akron and Newark areas and my son was born in Newark in May, 1953—34 months after I started the Training Program.

There are only three of us from the first group still around— Art Alberg, Bob Downey and myself. Bob was one of the Civil Engineers and Art was one of two Electrical Engineers.

Sorry for this discourse but Ray's question brought back a few of the many memories of the 31 years I enjoyed working on the B&O. You know what?—I must dig out some cotter keys—I might find a switch rod bolt nut that has the key missing. Gotta stick to details! That's what I was told!—Switch Builder—long ago.

Professor Morse's Foreign Language
By Gifford Moore
July 2008

The announcement read "Baltimore & Ohio Railroad Seeks Young People to Learn Morse Telegraphy for Positions with the Railroad as telegraphers and Tower Operators". It sure did sound attractive and interesting; in fact, downright fascinating. I had been somewhat interested in radio of late. No, not The Lone Ranger or Jack Armstrong kind but the use of radio in two-way conversations in business or just for the enjoyment of contact through the ether. So I signed up. I was confident I could learn.

There were several young people who showed up at the first meeting. It was in the home of Mr. Richard Gliddon, a regularly-assigned operator locally, who would be our instructor in learning Morse code telegraphy. I knew none of the rest of the group; and to this day, I can only remember one person, a young woman, Miss Black, who bowed out early on. Mr. "Dick" Gliddon was a small, slender man, who appeared to me to be "real old" although he was nowhere near retirement age. He smoked big black cigars; and as a consequence, he smelled of tobacco smoke when one was near him. He was rather gruff but kindly helpful and did not

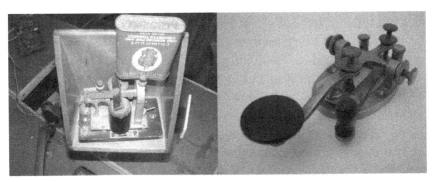

The telegraph added a level of mystique to railroad offices when that was the preferred communication device. The interlocking tower operator and the train dispatcher used Morse Code to move trains safely across the railroad. Often, a Prince Albert can was placed next to the sounder to amplify the clicks. The telegraph key was a simple device whose operation was only perfected through hours upon hours of use.

use many words in explanations. I was both awed by him and a little afraid of him.

He informed us that we would receive 25 cents an hour from the railroad for producing and learning the code as well as some basics of railroad operating rules and regulations. We would keep track of our own time and every so often turn in the information on the appropriate form through our teacher, Dick. He also said we needed to secure a Morse practice set known as a KOB set. KOB stood for "Key on board" and was a Morse code sounder, a telegraph key powered by a 6 or 9-volt battery screwed on a square wooden board. He had two or three and so I borrowed one of his. Thus, I was off to the races.

I would practice sending at the kitchen table. I would go to Dick's house, about two miles away, and he would send Morse code to me. Also, I spent time in the main telegraph office of the division (K office) in Akron, Ohio, where the sounds of telegraph, teletype and telephone abounded like three people singing together but each with a different song.

About that time, I had a chance to work part time (weekend, holidays, vacations) at the railroad LCL (Less Car Load) freight transfer platform. It was hard manual work, but I persisted with my Morse training. So I was working for the railroad, although not full time, at two jobs. But I was not satisfied with my learning Morse code. No one person sends perfect Morse code by hand. A machine can do it but, generally, a person cannot. I found that out very quickly in the K office. I would struggle to understand by listening carefully and sometimes trying to write down the transmission if it wasn't a message. Sometimes I thought they were "speaking in tongues," a different language, but the same Morse characters. I was counseled to keep trying as I was doing and that someday - perhaps soon - the curtain would lift, and it would be simple: I would listen, hear and understand effortlessly, or almost!

Then one day, an operator at Nova, Ohio, Mr. Asa O. Fair, asked me if I would work his job second shift at VN Tower Nova for his Christmas vacation. My first telegraph challenge! My first assignment! Nova was a hot job with lots of trains, some message work, train orders from the dispatcher by Morse, all alone in the tower in the dark with a cantankerous coal stove. I asked Dick and some others if they thought I could handle it. With various words (e.g., "You've got to start sometime, kid.") they affirmed me to do it. My first telegraph assignment!

Well, I got along fine. A new and fascinating experience for a sixteen-year-old. For getting "comfortable" with the foreign language of Morse code, it was a "baptism of fire". I even copied my first military death message on the Western Union wire that came into the tower. Thereafter, I had a new confidence about my telegraph skill and felt that I could "hold my own" with most of the old timers.

I Inherited My Railroad Career
By Spence Sullivan
April 2009

My father, Al Sullivan, Jr., appears in the vintage photo shown on the next page, taken in the mid 1920s, during his short career as a B&O employee, working at Mt. Clare Shops. He's in the middle of the front row--the good looking guy with all that hair, both attributes which were passed on to me. Perhaps someone can identify the type of locomotive shown in the background but I certainly cannot.

Alfred Sullivan, Jr., was born in 1899 in Baltimore. He married Gertrude Spies in 1918. I was born in 1923--one of four children; one brother and two sisters. Only my sister, Marty, survives and still lives in Maryland but literally a foot this side from the Pennsylvania line in Parkton. Somehow, my father, being a "Junior", acquired the nickname "2D" (or 2nd) which stuck with him all of his life. Dad served in WW I.

His B&O experience was followed by his lifetime position as a Court Reporter in the Baltimore City Superior Courts. He was an expert both in shorthand (the Pitman method) and typing. At one point early in his life, he was selected to represent Baltimore in a national typing contest to be held in Chicago but an illness prevented him from participating. Unfortunately, he passed away at a very young age in 1941.

In a way, I followed my father's career when I started my B&O career in mid-1942 as a Clerk-Stenographer in the Maintenance-of-Way Department headed by Mr. P. G. Petri. In March of 1943, Uncle

Sam needed me more than the B&O, so I joined millions of other young men in the U. S. Army. I spent a considerable amount of that time overseas in the European Theatre of Operations. I returned home in November of 1945 and, by early 1946, returned to the MofW Department. Shortly thereafter, I obtained a position in the Insurance Department, then under Clarence Dawson. From there, I moved to the Industrial Development Department where Gayle Arnold was at the helm. I next moved to the President's Office, in the very fine quarters on the 3rd floor of the Central Building. As I recall, this coincided with the retirement of Colonel Roy B. White and the appointment of Howard E. Simpson as the new President of the B&O. I remained in the department when the Presidency was awarded to Jervis Langdon, Jr.

As the C&O presence became increasingly evident, many changes occurred in the Executive Department. I became a part of the C&O Secretary's office and reported to Howard Keelor. During his tenure, I was made Administrative Services Officer and was responsible for the Records Management Program and Central Mailing Division in Baltimore. My final assignment was as Manager of Special Services under Jack Harbert. After 40 years of railroad service from B&O to CSX, I decided to discard the suit and tie, retired and became a member of RABO and CHEERS.

Hiring Out – 1953

By Walt Weber
January 2011

Back in the "good ol' days" of the early fifties, when engineers fresh out of college were a much wanted commodity, there were recruiters from all around the country making the rounds of the universities and colleges looking to round up soon-to-be graduates to fill positions that were still depleted from the wartime years. While college graduates in general were wanted, graduating engineers were the most in demand. We were wanted to fill positions all the way from selling soap to performing actual engineering-type functions. It was apparently a kind of a fad among the corporate personnel departments to particularly go after the engineers.

Such goodies as all-expense-paid trips for further interviews at their headquarters in cities located all around the country were offered to entice candidates into their folds. Many signed up for interviews with companies that they weren't really interested in, just to take advantage of the paid-for visits to far off "exotic" cities that were offered. The only two that I took advantage of from my home base at College Park, Maryland, were Wilmerding, Pennsylvania, (how exotic can one get?) and Niagara Falls, New York. I actually had some interest in Westinghouse Air Brake and the company that I visited in Niagara Falls but now being well into my codgerhood I don't any more recall the company's name. The two that I was really interested in were located in Philadelphia and in nearby Baltimore, neither one of which offered much in the way of reimbursement for away-from-home expenses.

After a train ride to Pennsylvania Station at 30th Street in Philadelphia, I met with a gentleman by the name of H. H. Haupt whose office was located in that building. He held some kind of an advanced position in PRR's Mechanical Department. (I was a soon-to-be Mechanical Engineering graduate.) He was immaculately dressed in a tailored suit, shirt and tie and what I remember most about him were the frilly cuffs of his shirt which slightly poked out from under the ends of his coat sleeves (very stylish). My interview with him was quite friendly, during which we chatted about many things. I thought that we were getting along rather famously and I could see myself stationed somewhere along the PRR in the near future doing many exciting things. That is, until this question came up at about a half hour or so into the interview: "And where does your daddy work on the Pennsy?" Oops! I didn't have the required response to that one. My father, nor any of my family, had no professional association with any part of the PRR and I had to own

The first is of the Lee Street entrance to Camden Station. In the left center of the image is the B&O Central Building and to its left the Lord Baltimore Hotel, both standing out all by themselves with none of the intervening buildings with which we are familiar today. The tower is the leaning tower of Lee Street. Its right wall rested on the stone wall above the lower level main line tracks into Howard Street Tunnel. The foundation of the left wall was imbedded into plain old Mother Earth, which, after settlement of the foundation into the ground, caused the tower to lean over to one side. It was said at the time that the only thing that kept the tower from falling over completely was the mechanism of the mechanical interlocking emanating from the bowels of the tower. Walt Weber photo.

up to this bitter fact. (Going in, I had no idea that this would be a requirement for employment with the Pennsylvania.)

Then, abruptly, the interview came to an end with the following (and Llew Davis has heard this one from me many times): Mr. Haupt swiveled slowly in his chair slightly away from facing me and with an arm extended in the direction of the Schuylkill River and with his frilly shirt cuffs poking out from under his coat sleeve and, hanging palm down, he flicked his hand up and down a few times, frilly shirt cuffs flapping around a bit and said: "Have you tried that outfit across the River?"

And boom! That was all she wrote! Goodbye, Irene! There's the

There at the front of the line shaking hands with the Colonel is, of course, Charlie Heck. He is followed by a person whose name escapes me, then Leon Daciek, Johnny Grant, Marshall Street, Dick Priddy (my assigned "buddy" during the program), me and Vernon Garrett. Of this group, Heck, Street, Priddy and I stayed with the company and the others departed sometime after completing the training program for opportunities elsewhere.

Baltimore & Ohio Railroad photo, Walt Weber collection.

door and don't let it hit you in the rear on your way out! Your train south leaves from the lower level and hurry up or you'll miss it! (He didn't really say all of these things but from his statement above, the implication was quite clear.)

So then, for that "outfit across the river", my next train ride was much shorter--from Riverdale to Baltimore on a Budd Car. There, I was interviewed by a number of B&O notables--George Elste and Clarence Holtzworth among them. While there, I was shuttled around for interviews with representatives of the different groups within the Operating Department and the upshot of it all was the arrival of a letter a month or so later inviting me to join seven others to form the third group of the B&O's Technical Graduate Training Program, the class of 1953, starting in July of that year. Above is a photo of us being welcomed by "the Colonel", President Roy B. White.

Thirty-two and a half years later, December 1st 1985, twenty-five years ago, I retired in Baltimore from the Chessie System; and in the spring of 1986, Marcia and I ran away from home and moved to Brevard, North Carolina, and have been here ever since.

A latter-year wish of mine, when Conrail was dissolved and its different parts were to be shed off to the surviving railroads who had made it on their own during the intervening years, was that CSX would have taken over the Pennsylvania Railroad as part of that deal. What poetic justice that would have been for the "outfit across the River!" that survived as one of the key segments of CSX Transportation.

What's in a Name

By E. Ray Lichty
April 1996

Growing up in Ohio, I was known as just plain "Elvin". My parents wanted their children to have first names that were not easily converted to nicknames. Elvin met that requirement.

When I started to work for the B&O in 1955 as a Bridgetender and then a Telegrapher, it was common to be identified by your telegraphic "sign". In my case, that was "ER" and that is how I was known on the Akron Division. There were a lot of people there that didn't know my first name.

It was and is the railroad practice to identify men, in correspondence, by their initials. (This was not the case for women. They were identified by their first names. Can anyone tell me Virginia Tanner's middle initial?) When I started in the training program in 1960, I traveled with C. S. (Stu) Burgess (who retired in October as GM Operations Planning and Industrial Engineering in Jacksonville) and Pete Pacheco. The three of us would show up at a training site and introduce ourselves--Stu, Pete and Elvin. The usual question to me that followed was, "What do people call you?" Obviously, they didn't think it should be Elvin.

When Judy and I went to Ohio for the holidays, I told her that when we returned to Baltimore I was going to begin using Ray, my middle name, as my name.

The first assignment of the New Year was with Baine Edwards, Track Supervisor, at Rowlesburg, West Virginia. Baine received the usual correspondence advising of the pending visit of

E. R. Lichty, so when I introduced myself as "Ray", that sounded fine to him.

About an hour later, when we were up on Cheat River grade watching an M of W gang, Baine called out to me in the cold and blustery air, "Ray." I just kept walking along. He again hollered out, "Ray," clearly directing his call towards me. My response, or lack of response, was the same; he is not calling me, and I kept on my way. Then I realized, that's me!

I suspect Baine sent word back to Baltimore that this guy, Lichty, is the dumbest trainee yet. He doesn't even know his own name!

A postscript: I mentioned how my parents didn't like nicknames. Therefore, my middle name is Ray, not Raymond. Now I have the problem that when people want to get formal with me, in writing or verbal, they address me as Raymond!

My Early Railroad Days
By Fred Yocum, Jr.
October 2001

By far, the most important person in giving me the opportunities that I have had was Dick Rayburn. Probably the only noteworthy thing about me besides what I've been able to do in the railroad industry is the fact that I am well-traveled in the United States. At this point, there are 94 counties in which I haven't been. As I like to say, "You may know someone who has seen more of the United States than I have, but I don't." However, I do know that there are some.

None of my close relatives are (or were) railroaders. I have been interested in railroads since I was quite young, partly, probably, because I traveled on them some during World War II when my father served in the US Navy. My first sentence (at 13 months) was "Thank you choo-choo book." I'd like to claim that it is the last one in which I have omitted the verb.

While I was in graduate school at Case Institute of Technology (now part of Case Western Reserve University), I changed my major from Chemistry to Science, Technology, and Public Policy. I wrote my Master's thesis on high speed passenger rail transportation. I thought that I needed to learn more about the

Being a member of the first class of the B&O Technical Training Program was a perfect start for Dick Rayburn, a man who was to become the epitome of the new style of railroad manager. A Civil Engineering graduate of Purdue University, he finished the Program in 1952 and was assigned Assistant to Division Engineer at Cumberland. Successive promotions took him to Grafton, Baltimore, Wheeling and Connellsville. He became Superintendent of the Toledo-Indianapolis Division in 1963; then Regional Manager at Pittsburgh. After several years in Cleveland staff positions, he was named General Manager Transportation in Baltimore and then Assistant Vice President Transportation. He returned to Cleveland as Vice President Transportation, when this picture was taken, and retired in 1986 as Executive Vice President.

Dick was a mentor to many bringing them along with him as he advanced through the Operating Department. He took a compassionate but no-nonsense approach to his work and expected the same from his staff. He died in January 1996.

Tom Rayburn collection.

currently used dispatch systems in preparation for my writing. I knew Carl Stephanus from having served on a regional YMCA committee with him He had just completed the Management Training Program, so I contacted him for help. Ray Walker, the husband of a cousin of mine, had been in the Program some time before with Ray Lichty and Stu Burgess. Carl put me in contact with Matt Bradway who agreed to make arrangements for me to have access to the dispatching office in Akron, through Assistant Superintendent Tom Jenkins, for whom I later worked with much respect and admiration. Matt added one condition. I had to agree to consider a job with Chessie upon the completion of my graduate program.

Les Roig interviewed me in Cleveland and suggested to Matt that I was worth a trip to Baltimore. My interviews there were a harbinger of things to come. Bill Bammert, Dick Rayburn and Hy Laden all thought that I should be hired….to work in someone else's department. I was most interested in Transportation and Dick consented to allow me to be there for the intensive phase of the program. Thus began a close association.

The single professional accomplishment of which I am most proud is my role as part of the team with Bob Stender, Bill Hart and Dan Sabin that led the Campaign Train for President Reagan on October 12, 1984. Getting to meet the President and the head of the Secret Service were nice rewards for the successful trip.

One of the unusual experiences that made me a better person occurred at the beginning of my Senior year in high school. I am not much of an athlete but I worked at a sports camp with many people who were. The other fellows decided to teach meX something that would allow me to get a letter for doing something other than being the equipment manager. I played a little tennis but they decided for something grander—they were going to make me into a place kicker. With their considerable attention and help, I eventually got good enough that my extra point percentage was better than our team's performance in getting the point from scrimmage (before the days of the two-point conversion). As the equipment manager, I picked out the best equipment. Everything was going along well until the coach came to me the week before our first scrimmage and said that someone had transferred to our school and wanted to be the place kicker. I asked him where he was transferring from but he wouldn't tell me. He forced a logical proposal from me on how we would decide who was the better kicker. Well, Bob McDougal beat me out fair and square and went on to be proficient at both the high school and college level (Gettysburg). The coach wouldn't tell me where he was transferring from because the answer was Overbrook School for the Blind and blind he was.

Chapter 14   It's a Hard Knock Life

Wired

By W. G. "Gifford" Moore
January 2002

The Superintendent Car Service sent his crack Car Service Agent on a special mission, checking cars, to the St. Louis Division. It was about December 20, 1938 and he was in the area of Beecher City (BC), Illinois, doing his work.

On this (say) Thursday morning while out in the country checking spurs, a heavy snow started and before long it was a blizzard. He could hardly walk in the heavy snow but he was able to beat his way to a nearby farmhouse where the farmer and his wife took him in.

Fortunately, the farmer had a telephone; and after much cranking and hollering, the Agent was able to send a telegram to Baltimore and the operator obliged him. It read, "Superintendent Car Service B&O in Baltimore, Md; Am marooned in Beecher City, Ill. account blizzard. Unable to travel now. Wire instructions." (Signed) Agent Jones.

The Agent spent the night with the farmer and the next afternoon the Cowden operator called the farmhouse for the Special Agent, with an answer message. "Yes, yes," the Agent said, in a frantic voice, "What does it say?"

"Well," the operator said, "here it is:" "Special Agent Jones B&O RR at Beecher City, Ill. Start vacation at once." (signed) Superintendent Car Service.

The Worst 6 Years of the 40

By Jim Sell
October 2011

I worked for the B&O Railroad and its affiliates and successors for a bit over forty years. During that time, I had various positions at many different locations. All-in-all, I enjoyed my railroad career except for the six years when I was Night General Yardmaster at Parkersburg, West Virginia. I have now been retired thirty-three years and I still resent those six years.

It was a twelve-hour-at-night job. I went to work at 7:00 pm and quit at 7:00 am. Six days a week, I worked that job for six years. During that time, my wife called me a walking dead man.

I worked twelve hours. It took me thirty minutes to get to work and thirty minutes to get home. When I got home, I showered and ate breakfast with my wife and daughter. That's fourteen hours. I slept eight hours – now that is twenty-two hours. When I got up, I shaved and ate dinner with the family – now we are up to twenty-three hours. That left me one hour to talk to my wife and daughter.

My day off was Saturday. When I came home Saturday morning, I went to bed about 9:00 am and slept about four hours. If I had slept longer, I probably would not have been able to sleep that night. I got up still sleepy and groggy. I forced myself to stay awake and to be as sociable as I could be. On Sunday morning, we went to church, went out to breakfast and "whatever". I had to take a nap about 3:00 pm because I had to work that night.

I was on the station platform one night to see that the National Limited make station-time. Mr. Bertrand's car was attached to the train. He got off to stretch his legs; I shook hands with him. He said, "Jim, you look very tired." I told him I had been working this twelve-hour night job for six years and that I was tired all the time. He said, "Jim, you will hear from me very shortly." In about two weeks, I was promoted to Assistant Trainmaster at Cowen, West Virginia. I never forgot Mr. Bertrand for that. The promotion meant Hello, to family; Hello, to daylight; Hello, to sunshine; actually, Hello, to life.

Shortly after that, I was promoted to Terminal Trainmaster at Fairmont, West Virginia. Bob Clark was the Night General Yardmaster. I stayed until Bob came to work and I told him, "Bob, as long as I am Terminal Trainmaster here, you don't have to come to work until 9:00 pm." He said: "How come?" I said, "If the yardmaster on duty can't operate this yard from 4:00 pm until 9:00 pm, he has no business being yardmaster." Bob said: "Gee, Jim, I appreciate that, it gives me two more hours with my wife." I had often thought if I ever attained a position of sufficient authority, the first thing I would do would be to abolish all twelve -hour night jobs. (I never did.)

The Night General Yardmaster job was a stepping stone for

Parkersburg is an unusual location as the B&O lines there are at two different levels. This eastbound train on the east-west mainline has just crossed the Ohio River Bridge, the subject of this story, arriving at the station west of the High Yard. The Ohio River Sub Division, which ran from Wheeling to Huntington, West Virginia, paralleled the Ohio River for its entire length and went under the Ohio River Bridge, being served by the Low Yard.

future promotions but I paid a price. My wife was raising our daughter practically alone. She was also making major decisions regarding the house and car alone - also many other things. I didn't know the neighbors, rarely saw a newspaper or television and only saw a movie during vacation time. When I was going to work, people were going to the park for a picnic or to swim, or going to a movie or otherwise enjoying the evening. When the evening was finished, they went to bed for eight hours sleep and then got up, ate breakfast and got ready to go to work; and I was still working. It paid off, in the long run, but I had six years of working, eating and sleeping. It was the worst six years of my life.

First Jobs

By Stu Burgess
July 2001

I'd just completed the Technical Graduate Training Program and my first assignment was as Assistant on the Corps in the Engineering Department at Akron, Ohio. After a brief vacation, I reported to the Division Engineer, Bob Enderle, at Akron. Over the next several months, I got oriented to life on the engineering corps, found a place to rent in Cuyahoga Falls and moved my wife and our few worldly possessions from Baltimore to Akron. Shortly afterward, Bob Enderle called me in one evening and advised me not to make any financial commitments that I couldn't cover quickly as the Engineering Department was reorganizing and I may be caught up and transferred. My wife had already obtained her Ohio license as an RN and had started working at a hospital in Akron. Several weeks later, Bob called me in again and said, "I've found out where you're going." I asked where and he said, "Right here; we have a vacancy for a Field Engineer and you're it." I thanked him and that evening, told my wife to go ahead with plans to redecorate our rented duplex and get our car licensed in Ohio.

I should have known better!

About a week later, on a Monday evening, I returned from a day in the field and walked into the office. Dave Glaser, the Assistant Division Engineer, and the Chief Clerk, whose name I can't recall, said to each other several times "You tell him.—— No. You tell him." I finally asked what was happening and one of them said, "Mr. Hoelzer's office in Pittsburgh called this morning and asked why you didn't report for work at Grafton, West Virginia, today. We told them probably because you didn't know about it and neither did we." Obviously, I was slightly dumbfounded and a little bit irritated.

I promptly called the office in Grafton and was told to report to Resident Engineer John Packman at Holloway, Ohio, the next morning and be prepared to work in the field surveying for construction of the track to serve a new coal mine (Crescent Valley #7). The next several weeks involved a hectic commuting schedule from Akron to Holloway, work for a full day and then drive back to Akron each night.

We eventually got everything packed up and moved to our new location at Grafton. Needless to say, my wife was wondering what kind of company I'd gone to work for. Anyway, the next year with the engineering corps at Grafton provided a great work experience. In addition to the job at Holloway and numerous others, I got to see most of the Monongah Division (including the former Wheeling Division) and also spent a lot of time working on the preliminary alignment survey for the Parkersburg Branch tunnel elimination project. We thoroughly enjoyed our stay in Grafton and still have many great memories from that period of our career.

Cowen Memories

By Ray Pomeroy
July 2007

Cowen is a sleepy little town deep in the heart of the coalfields of West Virginia. It has a hardware store, a clothing store, a butcher shop and a drug store. The nearest motel is 15 miles away in Craigsville, West Virginia. The B&O Railroad and the coal mines are the largest employers in the area. There are no night clubs in the area, so on Saturday night you are on your own.

It was May of 1957 when I learned that I was being promoted to Trainmaster at Cowen West Virginia. Jim Sell was there as Assistant Trainmaster and Charles Jaco was Engine Foreman. Jim, Charles and I had a mutual friend by the name of Freddie Burkhammer. Freddie was manager and store operator for the local power company, the Monongahela Power Co. Freddie also owned the house which we would eventually rent from him. The rental agreement was brought about by Jim Sell who literally talked Freddie into it, because there was nothing else available. The deal was done over a cracker barrel in Harry Howard's general store. We lived in Freddie's house for the three and a half years we stayed in Cowen.

One of the first things I remember was a trip to the Greenbrier Hotel at White Sulphur Springs, West Virginia. The contrast between poor Appalachia and rich Greenbrier was startling. The attraction at the Greenbrier that weekend was called "The Sammy

There may not have been a smaller 'city' to which B&O managers were assigned than Cowen, West Virginia. The population was 632 in 1954 and most of the workers in that count were employed by the B&O. In this view, WN Tower is on the left with its train order semaphores. The water tank and penstock are on the right and the yard and shop are in the distance looking west (railroad direction). Nearly all of the traffic handled was coal loads and related hopper car empties.

Baltimore & Ohio Railroad Historical Society collection.

Snead Festival". This was a golf tournament hosted by Sammy. It was a three-day tournament with a par of 70. Jim gave me Sunday off so Freddie and I decided to drive to White Sulphur to watch the pros play golf. The previous day, Saturday, Sammy shot a 59, which was 11 under par and probably was the first-ever score in the fifties. When we arrived at the Greenbrier, we caught up with Sammy and his foursome and followed them until they finished. That day, Sammy shot a 63 and, needless to say, Sammy won his own tournament.

It was about 2:00 o'clock in the afternoon when the tournament was finished and Sammy had buried his winnings. Freddie looked at me and said, "You don't suppose we could play this course, do you?" We then checked with one of the tournament officials and he said, "All you need is a caddy." So we went to the clubhouse, paid our green fees, picked up a caddy and teed off on Number 1 of the Old White Course. What a thrill it was to be playing the same golf course the pros had just finished playing. I actually parred one of the eighteen holes and thought, "Sam would be proud of me."

Back in Cowen, there wasn't a whole lot of excitement so Jim and I decided we would create some. We created a softball league, made up primarily of railroad employees—brakemen, conductors, engineers, trackmen, carmen, clerks and officials. The turnout to participate was amazing! We had one 75-year-old conductor by the name of Guy Bush show up wanting to play shortstop. He may have been a real good athlete in his day but somehow every ground ball hit his way went right through his legs. We had permission to use the high school playing field for our games, which started at 6:00 P. M. One game in particular I remember. It had rained early in the day but had cleared up and was still damp when the game started. During the game, Harry Williams came to bat with two outs and the bases loaded. Harry was a big guy and strong as an ox. He hit a ball that went way over the leftfielder's head, all three runners scored but none of them counted. Harry was thrown out at first base. How could this happen? His first step from home plate he slipped and fell, three more times he fell, and half way to first he started crawling on his hands and knees. He didn't make it.

We had a conductor by the name of 'Bigfoot' McElway. One day 'Bigfoot' came into the yard office, threw the bills, all mixed up, on the clerk's desk, with the statement that it was the clerk's job to straighten them out. All the other conductors that brought in coal loads from the mines had the bills in station order. Two nights later, 'Bigfoot' was called to distribute empties on the night Gauley River Turn. George Metro was Assistant Trainmaster at the time and I called George to tell him we were going to make some efficiency tests. We knew the Turn was to pick up a string of empties at Camden-on-Gauley, West Virginia, and we knew about where the caboose would locate. We parked the car, turned out the headlights and waited. We were only a few steps from the caboose; we waited a few more minutes and then quietly got out of the car and climbed up onto the caboose. Lo and behold, there was 'Bigfoot' snoring away! The next morning, 'Bigfoot' picked up his "Notice of Investigation" for sleeping on the job. Two days before the hearing was scheduled, 'Bigfoot' showed up at the yard office with his wife and four of his eight kids. They were begging not to go ahead with the hearing. I made sure that he would never again bring coal into the yard without the bills in proper order. From that day on, 'Bigfoot' was one of the best conductors in the Cowen area

It was during our first year in Cowen when we acquired our son David through an adoption agency located in Baltimore, Maryland. It was the first time the agency completed an adoption outside the state of Maryland. We received a call from the agency stating the person who was to make the final decision was coming to our home for a visit. She was to fly to Charleston, where my wife, Betty, would pick her up. Betty drove the 100 miles to Charleston; and on the way back to Cowen, the car broke down on top of one of the many mountains in that area. Luckily, there was a small convenience store nearby where Betty could call for help. Since neither gal had eaten for some time, they bought some trail baloney, a loaf of bread and some mustard and had a little picnic while they repaired the car. It all worked out because soon after that, we received our little boy, born November 24, 1957. Now we have our son; a neighbor gave us a little kitten; and we acquired an Irish Setter puppy, all legs and floppy ears. We called the dog "Shawn". He liked to hang out at the local high school during lunch period, maybe picking up a scrap or two. One day, he came home with a brown paper bag in his mouth, some student's lunch. Another day, I got a call at the yard office with Betty saying, "Shawn just came home and he has a chicken in his mouth. What should I do?" My first inclination was to say, "Pluck it and we will have him for dinner," but on second thought I said, "Hurry up and bury it before the neighbors see it."

The cat and dog were compatible. One day going to work, I accidentally stepped on the cat sleeping on the middle step of three. From the commotion, I didn't think she would survive. She did and from then on she was called "Tuffy".

Fast forward to 1960. That was the year I was promoted to

Trainmaster on the Baltimore Division, East End. How could any B&O Railroad official not remember that year? We all took a 10% reduction in pay and our rent went from $60 per month to $120! What a promotion! As we were packing up for the move to Baltimore, we decided to keep the dog and give the cat to some friends in Richwood, West Virginia, some 18 miles away. The friend was Joe McQuad, president of Maust Coal and Coke Corp. He and his wife, Marion, had 16 kids and many of them were still at home. About two months after we left Cowen, we got a call from our friend, Freddie. After a storm, he had climbed a pole to repair a pole line. He happened to look down and saw this cat barely able to put one paw after another. It was Tuffy! This cat was trying to find her way home and had covered 16 of the 18 miles. Freddie felt so sorry for her that he took her in and the cat lived out the rest of her nine lives in her original home.

We had some good times during our stay in Cowen, just one of many assignments during a railroad career that required 14 moves in 34 years. The good times were shared by Jim and Vigdis Sell; Charlie and Mary Jaco and Freddie and Virgie Burkhammer.

Once Upon a Transfer

By Jeanne Bailey
January 2008

It was August of 1954. My husband, Glyn Bailey, a B&O RR Traveling Auditor, and I, along with our children Tom and Mary Jo, were happily living in our hometown of Catonsville, Maryland. Glyn received the news that he was being transferred to Columbus, Ohio, as of October, 1954.

With two small school-age children, this presented a problem as school would soon start in September. It was decided Glyn would go on to Columbus on the appointed date and commute back and forth on weekends. The children and I would make the move over the school's winter break in late January. I, however, thought it would be a good idea to obtain the required three estimates for moving and to also check out the Catholic school situation in Columbus. With help from our pastor, I soon had the school information on locations and desirable neighborhoods— and the moving estimates. Life was so much simpler then—no hassles on information flow.

Glyn took off for Columbus, the children were in school and life went on in Catonsville. I soon discovered that Glyn was stressed over the situation—not much time to check on housing possibilities and not looking forward to waiting until January for all of us to be settled in Columbus. What to do?

I contacted our good friend, Pat Hickey, another B&Oer; and on a Thursday evening, he drove me to Camden Station where I hopped on an overnight train to Chillicothe, Ohio. From there by bus to Columbus was no problem. Hey, new country-side to see! Upon arrival in Columbus, I called Glyn from the bus station and asked if he would like to have coffee with me. You can imagine his surprise to find me practically on his office doorstep.

I bought the local newspaper for the real estate ads—rental homes and apartments were no problem back in those years. You had a big selection. We spent the rest of the day with the assistance of fellow Traveling Auditor George Johnson hunting for a suitable home in a neighborhood that suited us with a top-notch parochial school nearby. Exhausting and scary but fun in a city where we knew no one and hoped we would be soon living.

By late afternoon, we had found a lovely brand new semi-detached home two blocks from the school and church and a bus line on the corner. Can you imagine being so lucky in today's world?

After signing the lease, I called the chosen moving company and they assured me they would be at our house in Catonsville the following Monday morning to pack and load our belongings. Today, I think we would be lucky to get a moving van in three or four weeks going to our chosen destination!

With much rushing, we made the stop to pick up Glyn's belongings at the hotel and made the bus to take us to Chillicothe that night. There we caught the train back to Baltimore, arriving home Saturday morning.

We managed to pack our clothes for a week, notify family we would be leaving for Columbus and Glyn made arrangements to have a bedroom on the train for our trip to Columbus instead of the section Pullman car. I was able to get the school records for the children's transfer to their soon-to-be new school in

Columbus. Back then, it was easy to contact the school nuns on a weekend and find cooperation. I, also, was able to get a box; (usually used to transfer fish for your fish bowl) punched some small holes in it and our canary was able to ride the train in comfort.

Allowing time for the moving van to get to Columbus, Ohio, we left Catonsville Tuesday evening with children, a bird and adequate clothing for the balance of the week, arriving again back in Columbus via Chillicothe Wednesday morning. Checking into the hotel, Glyn took off for work. I fed and watered the canary and left with the children to arrange for their admission to school and checked on our new home, etc., etc. Keep in mind, with no car, this all involved street cars and transfers. We were not yet affluent enough on a Traveling Auditor's salary to afford a car. Back then, city transportation systems were great and all areas easily accessible. "The Good Old Days"?

Early Thursday morning, Tom, Mary Jo and I again hopped on the city transportation system and I delivered them to the waiting arms of the nuns at their new school. Tom was in the fifth grade—Mary Jo in the second grade. I walked the two blocks to our new home and met the movers. By day's end, beds were made, some dishes were unpacked, clothes were in the closets, the bird was in her cage, the children had missed only one day of school, Glyn was home from work and we were HOME in Columbus, Ohio!

We had an enjoyable life in Columbus, made good friends, Glyn worked and traveled his territory, I subbed for three months for one of the teachers at school, had my first time on TV promoting a fund raiser for our church and enjoyed visits from our families. Glyn spent about 80% of his time on the road always by bus or train and sometimes getting a ride from someone going his way, traveling to the various stations for auditing.

In late July of 1956, Glyn and I were vacationing in Maryland with our family when he got the call to move back to Baltimore (even then the boss had to know where to reach you at all times). We were off to see the wizard, so to speak, to find a new house. Rentals were not quite so plentiful then but enough of them to

238

have a choice. We found a town house (known as a "row house" then) in Catonsville, an end unit and close to the #8 streetcar line (still no automobile). A grocery store was nearby, church and school about 1-½ miles away and we were set. Weather permitting, instead of getting on the #8 streetcar at Shady Nook Avenue, Glyn would walk two blocks to the Paradise Avenue streetcar loop to save the extra fare that was applicable beyond the city line.

Back to Columbus—again the required moving estimates, school transfer, etc. The children would be going back to the same Catholic school in Catonsville. Arrangements were made for telephone, gas and electric and all the small details necessary with a move.

The children and I enjoyed several farewell parties with neighbors prior to leaving Columbus and Glyn and I had dinners with some friends. While Glyn continued closing up his work in Columbus, the children and I trekked onto the bus for Chillicothe (again) to catch a ten something evening train to Baltimore.

Reaching Chillicothe, we discovered the train would be late—maybe midnight. Plus, there were oat bugs (whatever they are) everywhere swirling about in your face, in your hair and generally awful. Two tired children and a cat in a box this time as our traveling pet and companion waited out this new adventure. Since I wasn't sure whether they would let us on the Pullman with a cat, I had him in a black container hoping the porter would think it was a medical bag.

We traveled in a Pullman section car this time—two children in the bottom berth—the cat and I in the upper. I had to sleep with my foot uncovered and next to the cat box to keep him from meowing all night. The porter was so nice getting us settled in the Pullman after we finally got onboard about 12:30 AM. Tom and Mary Jo slept like logs but bright-eyed and bushy-tailed the next morning. Now—what to do with the cat while we ate breakfast? That wise old porter smiled at me and with a twinkle in his eye said, "Ma'am, I'll just take care of that old pussy cat you have in that box while you see that these children get their breakfast. No one will even know he's here." Kindness can be found in the most unexpected ways.

We arrived back in Baltimore on August 28th, stayed with relatives until our furniture arrived several days later and we were all at HOME again when Glyn returned from Ohio about the same time as the furniture. I remember well when C. S. Everett, Chief Traveling Auditor, said to Glyn—"I have never seen any woman able to move to a new city in such a short time as your wife." Hey—we all do what we have to do—it's called 'Being Family'.

This is the Baileys' home on Medina Avenue in Columbus, Ohio. Mary Jo, our daughter, age 7, is standing at our door of the semi-detached house. In the background on the left you can see the spire of our Catholic Church, St. James the Less, which was close by. The school was next door to the church which is very important when you don't own a car. In those years, children walked to and from school. Several years later, school buses began picking up children who lived a mile or more from school.
Glyn Bailey photograph.

It's a Wonder a Railroader is Married!
By Van Vander Veer
July 2002

I wonder why all railroaders, especially those in operations, are still able to have a married life simply because of the time they did not spend at home. How many times over our careers have we had the telephone ring and the dispatcher say we have a small accident of ten or more cars and the main line is blocked. Naturally, one quickly went to the accident location regardless of the day or time. In my opinion, night calls were by far the worst time to receive this information. We all said to our sweethearts we have a derailment and will see you after we clean up the mess. Thus, we left our sweethearts to handle all the home details for hours, if not days.

I remember one Thanksgiving Day, while Assistant Division Engineer on the Monongah Division, we had invited friends to spend the day with us and enjoy the dinner. Yes, I was not at home but cleaning up a derailment on Short Line Subdivision at Pine Grove. Got home the following day. Wonder how many Holidays that the Operating officers on our railroad, active and now retired, were not at home?

Now, let's discuss the many transfers of our families. It seemed that back in the older days one had to transfer to be considered for promotion. I remember when I was in Baltimore and was promoted to Division Engineer at Wheeling, West Virginia, for the Wheeling Division. The rumors were strong that the Division was being abolished and that the position of Division Engineer would be abolished. I was told by an official to go ahead and move my family. I moved them to St. Clairsville, Ohio, across the Ohio River from Wheeling. The first Sunday in our new home the telephone rang and John Collinson informed me that my position was abolished and I was transferred to Connellsville. My wife was not very happy about that transfer. Oh yes, before I could find a home in Connellsville, I was transferred to Pittsburgh. Thus, my family lived in St. Clairsville about six months with a visit from me on weekends (if no derailments).

My hat is off to the women who marry a railroader. They are the people that made our railroad operate when the men were riding the rails.

Chapter 15   Getting There and Back

It Doesn't Add Up

By Bob Breiner
April 1996

Charlie Geyer recalled his first encounter with filling out an expense account. He was sent to the Big Apple (New York City) on an Engineering Department job. He wanted to get the job done ASAP so he worked continuously, grabbing a burger or something quick for his meals.

Later, when he returned to Baltimore and submitted his first expense account, he charged exactly what he paid for his meals. His boss returned the expense account and told him to increase the amount. Charlie sharpened a pencil and revised the figures upward! But, not accepted again. Charlie tried again! Still returned!

Finally, his boss told him he would make the rest of the department look bad if he submitted expense accounts with such low charges. So, after five upward revisions, Charlie's first expense account was accepted!

My reaction to this story was: (1) Not everybody eats only burgers for lunch and dinner and (2) Charlie was a slow learner!

A True Story and Belated Confession

By: Norman Murphy
October 1998

In the early fifties, after fulfilling the customary apprenticeships in the Real Estate Department, the boss finally felt I had absorbed enough "smarts" from my tutors and would not sink the Real Estate ship if he released me to do some lease negotiations on my own. In those days, that was the first step .on the promotion ladder involving travel, expense counts, etc.

One of my first assignments involved renegotiation of some B&O property leases in Ohio that had been in effect for many years without any change in the rents paid to the railroad. I took the National Limited out of Camden Station one evening, had a great dinner in the diner and reviewed, for the 'umpteenth' time, the leases I would renegotiate the next day. Finally, I retired to the lower berth I had been fortunate enough to have been able to reserve.

Sometime after midnight, the National hit a stretch of roadbed that the Engineering Department must have overlooked, (my apologies to my Engineering friends) because I found myself lying in the aisle, only half awake. Since the lower and upper berth curtains were buttoned from the inside, I hastily tried to get back into what I thought was my berth by lifting, and going under, the curtain. However, in my stupor, I was actually trying to get into Lower 9 rather than Lower 8. A lady's scream brought me to my senses and quickly, believe me, very quickly, I was able to get back into Lower 8. That scream, of course, brought the porter rapidly down the aisle where he listened to the lady's anguished report that "Someone was trying to get into my berth!" All that I could think of was that my railroad career was over because no one—absolutely no one—would ever believe my story.

I kept very quiet and nervously listened while the porter told the lady she must have been dreaming because he saw no one and suggested she try to go back to sleep. She evidently agreed because she didn't press the issue much further. However, there was no more sleep for me that night!!

This true story has been kept to myself until today. My job is no longer at risk.

Wasn't My Brand

By Harry Hinds
July 2001

Back in the early 1950s, I was a Traveling Freight Agent, working out of our Memphis office, and living in Little Rock, Arkansas. About once a month, I would ride the Rock Island Railroad from Little Rock to Memphis and spend a couple of days in the office. There were times when I would get on the Rock Island coach and be the only passenger in the car.

On one occasion, I was sitting at a window seat when a man came down the aisle and asked me if the aisle seat was taken. When I said, "No," he sat down. In "Arkanese," he was "skunky drunk," and I was not looking forward to a 120-mile train ride with him as a companion.

I am sure many of you will agree, there is nothing more obnoxious than a drunk when you are cold sober.

Anyway, after he was well settled in, he pulled a half-pint bottle of whiskey out of his coat pocket, took a little nip and then offered me the bottle. I declined his generous offer (it wasn't my brand.)

This gentleman then asked me where I was going, and when I told him "Memphis," he started describing his girlfriend who he said would meet him at the Memphis station. He and this young lady had what today many call a "meaningful relationship", which he outlined in fine detail.

What with me being a Sunday School teacher and all, I was beginning to wonder, how am I going to get rid of this pest?

Then he told me his lady friend had a sister who was every bit as congenial as she was and, if I was interested, he could arrange for us to make it a foursome. (I feel sure he was not talking about golf). Again, I declined his generous offer.

Soon thereafter, he asked me what line of work I was in and it hit me like a bomb. "I am a Baptist Minister," I replied.

For about 10 seconds, he sat there stunned. Then he said, "Oh! Yes, well - I enjoyed talking with you Reverend," stood up and found a seat at the other end of the car.

What a Coincidence

By John Arledge
July 1997

In early 1973, a significant labor agreement was made with the B&O Clerks and Telegraphers, combining the work of these former separate crafts. The new agreement was to become effective in June of 1973 and I was assigned to conduct a series of meetings at several locations to explain the details of this agreement to company officers who supervised the affected employees. I was accompanied to these meetings, held in May of 1973, by two of my Labor Relations Department superiors: George Seaton and Henry Taylor, and Dick Priddy who represented the Operating Department.

We held our first Meeting at Cumberland, Maryland, and

proceeded on to Pittsburgh that evening for our second meeting the next morning. At that time, Charlie Heck was in charge of the Pittsburgh Division and he arranged for our meeting to be held at a local motel. Some 200 officials were in attendance at the meeting.

Our meeting at Pittsburgh ended around 3 PM and we were scheduled to fly on to Cincinnati, later that night, for our next meeting the following morning. Since we had a few hours to kill before plane time, Charlie Heck invited the four of us to have a drink in the motel lounge, before he took us to the airport.

The motel lounge was not very big; a bar and a few stools on the left side and several booths along the other. At that time, there were only one or two other patrons in the lounge.

We sat down and ordered a drink and almost immediately we heard the telephone ringing behind the bar. The bartender answered the telephone and then called out "Is there a Mr. Heck here?" Charlie got up and proceeded to the bar and I noticed that one other patron, also, got up. I watched Charlie and the other man converse with the bartender.

After a few minutes, Charlie returned to the booth, grinning. He proceeded to explain that when he told the bartender that he was Mr. Heck, the other man said that he was, also, Mr. Heck. The bartender informed the caller that there were two Mr. Hecks in the room and asked for a first name. The caller said he wanted Charles Heck. Charlie said that he was Charles Heck but the other man said the he, also, was Charles Heck. The befuddled bartender then asked the caller for a middle initial. He said "E" and, believe it or not, both men were named Charles E. Heck.

Although they had the same middle initial, it turned out that the "E's" stood for different middle names. As it developed, the telephone call was for the other Charles E. Heck.

There are many coincidences that occur in this world but what are the chances that two Charles E. Hecks, neither related or known to each other, would be among six people in a small bar on a weekday afternoon and be called to the telephone. I still list it as one of the oddest occurrences that I have ever run into.

Cumberland Division Eats

By Ray Lichty
October 2001

I don't know why, but when I think of areas of our railroad, I think of places to eat. The Cumberland Division is no exception to this general rule.

At Cumberland, there are two places that come to mind. Moons and Naves. Both were popular for their generous helpings, family style, of home-cooked, ordinary food. Nothing fancy. Just good. Ken mentioned the Fort Cumberland Hotel. That was the only place anywhere, as I remember, where three of us in the Training Program could share a room and save money. Saving on the cost of the room left more money for eating. The Allegheny Inn was the other hotel frequented by lowly-paid trainees. As I recall, that's the only hotel where, if you left your door open for a cross breeze, the hotel's cat would come into your room and sleep on your bed.

There were great "beaneries" everywhere. Some, I remember, were at Paw Paw and Keyser, West Virginia. There was an especially nice place on Route 50 at Redhouse, Maryland.

Ken also mentioned the buckwheat cakes. Preston County was famous for them and had a festival each year in their honor. The Kingwood Motel remains as my favorite spot to enjoy this treat, at any meal.

Just down the road at Mrs. Howard's in Rowlesburg, buckwheat cakes were always available for breakfast. There, they were prepared in the real "country" fashion. The batter was made with a sour starter and kept that way, always using some of the leftover sour batter to prepare the next. This wasn't just a "hint" of sour. This was really "sour", but oh, so good. Mrs. Howard fried her buckwheat cakes so thin they were almost in a crepe style and she only fried them on one side. It's a good thing we didn't have cholesterol back in those days. She would have been outlawed.

We used to work hard, with long days, but we ate good!

More Cumberland Division Tales
By Ken Roloson
October 2003

As Traveling Freight Agent at Cumberland during the late 1950s, it was not uncommon for me to be called upon to furnish 'taxicab Service' for various individuals and/or other departments at the direction of the Division Freight Agent (Boss).

"Woody" Gurley was the local Dodge dealer and my landlord, as I resided in one of his apartments. He persuaded me to purchase a 1957 Dodge Four Door Hardtop with dual mufflers, fins and a huge V-8 engine, with 16,000 miles, which had been traded by an executive of the Kelly Springfield Tire Company. I found out later that it got about 12 miles to the gallon but that was no problem as intermittent gas wars brought the price of gas down to as low as 16 cents a gallon at the Esso Station on Martins Mountain on Route 40 just outside of Cumberland. Unknowingly, I was all set for things to come and was able to furnish 'first class taxi service' to enumerable 'free loaders.' This was in addition to my duties as Traveling Freight Agent.

The first customer was a tall skinny guy from the Engineering Department in Baltimore (can't remember his name, thank goodness) who wanted to go to Petersburg, West Virginia, on the South Branch Subdivision to stake out a warehouse location there. He had arrived the night before on #5 and checked into the Algonquin Hotel in Cumberland. I was to pick him up at 7 AM but at 7 AM he was still in bed, sleeping off a hangover. I knew about his problem in advance and was prepared for it. I finally got him up and got some coffee and cereal into him. We then took off for Petersburg just like nothing happened.

Upon arrival at Petersburg, after introducing him to some local people at the site, he immediately went to work with his equipment and did his job well. I had been told that he was one of the best engineers in the department and he certainly showed it on that day. I drove him back to Cumberland where he had to stop at the liquor store to replenish his supply of 'miniatures' for consumption on Train #12, at about 8 PM. He was a nice guy and very appreciative of my taking care of him. Most drunks are usually that way.

During the late 1950s, the Passenger Traffic Department was in the process of being down-graded and some of their personnel were being transferred to other departments. It was during this period of time that I met Joe Gaynor who had been appointed Industrial Representative and I was asked to show him around on the Cumberland Division. Joe went on to become General Industrial Agent for the K&IT RR at Louisville and eventually would end up as president of that railroad.

Ross Conlon's job in Passenger Traffic was eliminated and he was transferred to the Coal Department in Baltimore. He called me one day and asked if I would meet him on arrival of #11 and take him up to the Bedford Inn at Bedford, Pennsylvania, (30 miles) where a coal convention was taking place. He was a very personable individual and confided to me that he did not know one lump of coal from another but he was doing his best under the circumstances.

Most of the people were kind and appreciative of 'Ken Roloson's Taxi Service,' but there were a few lumps.

I received a wire from A. L. Sherry, Perishable and Livestock Agent, at Pittsburgh, who demanded that he be met on arrival of Train #8 on a certain day; driven to Moorefield, West Virginia, to make one call; and returned to Cumberland in time for #5 the same day. This raised the temper of Division Freight Agent Larry Brown to the point where he instructed me that under no condition was I to make any commitment to these 'free loaders' without his personal authorization, despite the fact that Al Sherry was one of his personal friends. This was the same guy who would double-park on Charles Street (late 1930s) come into the District Freight Office and argue with DFA Ed King and also make phone calls.

Another interesting trip involved the retired Chief Engineer of Phillips Petroleum Company. Phillips called him back to work on special projects. He came into Cumberland the night before and I picked him up at the Fort Cumberland Hotel--destination Martinsburg, West Virginia, where the Washington Gas Light Company (utility) had track storage arrangements for the storage of tank cars of Liquefied Petroleum Gas in our Cumbo, West Virginia, yards. DFA Brown approved this trip, so there was no problem. Upon arrival, he made his inspections of the valves, etc., on each tank car; there were about 20 tank cars on track storage at the time. At one point, he insisted that I get up on one of the cars with him and he would show me how to close off a leak. I really did not want to know. Also, this was not part of my job description as Traveling Freight Agent at Cumberland. However, I went along with it to show that I was really interested. Mission accomplished! I returned him to Cumberland where he went west on #5 that evening. He was a fine gentleman and I really enjoyed his company on that day back in 1953.

At that particular time, the B&O was paying the fabulous rate of 6 cents a mile on private automobiles used in company service; so I said to myself, "Fill 'er up" and have a good time with that 'gas hog' of a car.

Down and Out at Third!
By Gifford Moore
April 2008

Working in Baltimore on special assignment from Monday morning until Friday afternoon required "special arrangements", because I lived in northern Ohio. Each Sunday evening, I would board the Baltimore and Ohio Railroad #10 or #18 in Akron and climb into an upper berth for the journey. Returning on #17 on Friday afternoon was the procedure to get home Saturday morning.

It was a warm, summer Sunday afternoon at our church picnic at the Waterworks Recreation Park in Munroe Falls, Ohio, right alongside the B&O's mainline, when a bunch of men and boys, me included, decided a scratch softball game was in order. We rounded up a bunch, chose sides (in the normal fashion with the bat) and it was "Play ball".

At my turn at bat, I swung twice and missed. Then I got a hold of the next delivery and off it went. I rounded first, storming to second. I rounded second and I heard a voice holler "Throw it to third!" As I chugged my way to third base, I decided in a brilliant flash of base running skill, that I would use a hook slide into third base. Down I went in an awkward manner. I knew as much about hook sliding as I did pole vaulting. My left leg somehow twisted

A sleeping car has been a part of rail travel nearly since the beginning of the railroads. Pullman's "open section" cars became the most common and were often referred to simply as upper and lower berths. During the day there were two non-reclining facing seats that folded down at night to form the lower berth. The upper berth was pulled down from above the window by the  *porter. Lower berths were more expensive as they had easier access, a better ride and the passenger could see out the window. Curtains provided privacy from the car's aisle way.*

and I heard a dull snap; then I immediately felt extreme pain and swelling. I was out at third and really 'out' of commission and down for the next eight weeks.

My wife and others helped me to our car and we went home, where I put my leg in ice water. We decided to go to the emergency section of St. Thomas Hospital in Akron. There, after X-rays, I said to the doctor, "Can you put a bandage or cast or something on it? I have a train to catch this evening." He replied, "Fella, you're not going anywhere this evening. You have a broken leg, the distal end of the fibula, and you're going to be on crutches for quite a while." And so I was for about seven weeks.

At home when I called my boss, Victor 'Vic' Pierpont Gairoard, and told him, he almost came through the telephone. Well, I got pretty good at getting around on crutches. And what's more, I went back to work in Baltimore on crutches and with my left leg in a big cast, with the same traveling routine as before for six weeks. After a while, healing allowed me to graduate to a cane for two or three weeks.

Have you ever tried to climb into an upper Pullman berth on crutches and with a big cast on your leg?

Take Me Out to the Old Ballgame

By Frank Dewey
April 2009

Growing up in Washington, Indiana, put me equidistant (169 miles) between two major league baseball clubs—the St. Louis Cardinals to the west and the Cincinnati Reds to the east. The B&O took advantage of this by operating baseball excursions each summer out of Washington to one or the other or both locations. The excursions were usually operated on a Sunday and scheduled so there was a double-header at the ball park.

Flyers for the trip started to appear around town a month before the trip. Hanging from a string at barber shops around town is where I remember seeing them. I would bet they could also be found in the bars around town but I was too young to frequent those locations. The ones I remember were printed on yellow newsprint with red printing and prominently showed a drawing of a batter and catcher at home plate. Also on the flyer were listed other attractions such as the world famous St. Louis Zoo and the Coney Island amusement park in Cincinnati. At the bottom were printed a schedule of the train operation and a notice that tickets for the train and baseball game could be purchased from the local B&O agent.

My oldest memory of a baseball excursion was one that I did not get to ride. My sister and I were deemed too young, so my mother stayed home while dad went with the "boys" to St. Louis. On his return, he was filthy dirty but happy as a lark. He explained his appearance to my very unhappy mother who was going to have to clean his clothes. He said that the train was pulled by a steam engine and, on the way back, he got a ride in the cab of the locomotive. That might have been dad's last trip on an excursion without supervision.

Hidden deep in my railroad artifacts, or what my wife calls the 'train junk', was this flyer for a baseball excursion from Washington, Indiana, to St. Louis. This was the typical format, printed with red ink on yellow paper the consistency of newsprint, for all flyers that I remember. Several weeks before the trip, these flyers would appear all over the towns, in barber shops, bars and about any other store that would allow it, where the train was scheduled to stop. Similar ads would be printed in the local newspapers.

The flyers were probably printed in the B&O's print shop. The fine print at the bottom indicates that they came in a pack of fifteen with a string through the hole at the top. To take one, just pull it off of the string.

Most of the excursions out of Washington were scheduled, like this one, when the Cardinals were playing the Reds. Such a trip would attract fans, of both teams, located close to B&O's St. Louis mainline. This trip was a little different than others that I went on in that it is only for one game. Normally, the trips were scheduled to attend a doubleheader so you were sure to get your money's worth.

Frank Dewey collection.

My dad worked for Uniroyal as an industrial engineer. Uniroyal was the former United States Rubber Company. They had their clothing division in Washington. There was a plant downtown that made lightweight raincoats and housed the administrative offices. Another plant was on the east end of town on the south side of the B&O tracks at SE 21st Street. That plant made rubber-coated rainwear, parka and topcoats, and even deep sea diving suits. At one time, the east end plant got inbound coal via the railroad to fire their heating plant.

Dad was a railfan! His father was a lawyer in Des Moines and started him watching trains as a kid. In fact, I have Volume 1 of Trains Magazine hardbound that my grandfather got when the magazine first started in November, 1940. I think that my dad was somewhat jealous of my being able to work on the railroad.

Dad would drive my sister and me down to the Washington depot where we would watch passenger trains. We probably went there most often. We would be there for the arrival of 1 & 2 and 3 & 4 many weekends. If dad were at work, we might even ride our bikes down to the station to see what was going on or to pester the agent for timetables. Washington is where the passenger engine crew was changed, the car knockers walked the train and attached or removed the back-up hose for the move into and out of St. Louis Union Station and the locomotives were watered. That always meant there was quite a bit of activity when a passenger train was in the station.

Freight trains and switching were usually observed at the "Relay" down at Shops. We used to sit at the "Relay" at Shops for hours watching the 1600-series 0-8-0 switch engines go back and forth. In the days of assigned cabooses, it was always fun to watch the westbounds come into Shops. The headend would stop at the "Relay" to change headend crews and then the train would depart like it was leaving for good. As the rear end approached SW 10th Street, the conductor would close the angle cock on the caboose and pull the coupler pin. The train would go into emergency but still would not stop until the rear was somewhere just west of the yard office. Meanwhile, the conductor would be controlling the speed of the free-wheeling caboose with the hand brake to allow it to slow down enough that a gap was large enough from the rear of the train for a switchman on the ground to throw the switch to enter the yard. The caboose would then glide on down past the yard office and, if all went well, would drift into the caboose track and couple onto the cabooses already in the track. Meanwhile, a yard engine with the new crew's caboose would move out to the main to couple onto the now-stopped freight train. Shortly thereafter, a fusee would be thrown high in the air from the caboose to signal the headend to highball. Of course, being the B&O, nobody had radios, so hand signals were the only communication.

When I was young and steam was still being used to switch the yard, there were typically switch engines working on both ends of the yard. There was an afternoon city switcher for local industries and one or two switchers working the car shops. As I remember, there were a total of nine engines a day working the Shops yard on weekdays.

We would also go to the roundhouse to see if anything was going on. The roundhouse had 27 stalls and took care of 1600-series 0-8-0 switchers, some 2700-series 2-8-0 local engines that were normally used on the lines north and south of Flora, the 4500-series 2-8-2 engines used on any mainline freight still using steam, and the 5200-series 4-6-2 passenger engines that were used on trains 29 and 30. Towards the end of steam, there was one President-class pacific that was assigned to Washington—the 5314. In fact, that was the last engine I saw in steam as it had been lowered to working freight service on the Gypsum Local that ran in turn service between Shops and the gypsum plants outside of Shoals, Indiana. My, how the mighty had fallen!

My first ride on a baseball excursion was a trip to St. Louis with mom, dad and my sister. Upon arrival at St. Louis Union Station, we stepped outside and caught a street car to go to the St. Louis Zoo. That was my first ride and probably last ride on a street car outside of a museum. The Zoo was fantastic and I still remember seeing the monkey show where the monkeys were more like children and the elephant show where one elephant shaved the beard of another elephant sitting on a stool—you had to be there to understand.

Another early trip was taken to Cincinnati, again with the

whole family, to visit family friends. After that, I guess I was finally old enough to enjoy a baseball game; and dad started making the baseball excursions a father-son affair. By then, the trains all operated to Cincinnati. The demographics were slightly better for the eastbound trip than the westbound. Between Washington and St. Louis, the only town of any size was Vincennes with a population of about 18,700 (according to the Form 6). Lawrenceville (6,500), Olney (8,500), and Flora (5,474) were not major population centers.

Going east, the train would first deadhead from Shops to Vincennes, about 19 miles, to tap that population center and then operate east with a stop in Washington (13,000—but a lot with railroad passes), Loogootee (2,424), Shoals (1,339), Seymour (9,630), and North Vernon (3,583). As I remember, the trains stopped picking up passengers after they got fairly close to the destination since folks living there could get to St. Louis or Cincinnati quite easily by car.

The old Crosley Field was close enough to Cincinnati Union Terminal that it was an easy walk. There were usually several other baseball excursion trains that would arrive about the same time as we did, so there was a large crowd making the walk to and from the park. I remember seeing trains listed on the arrival/departure board from Chillicothe and Huntington. I am sure they also came from other locations.

Old Crosley Field was nothing like the modern parks. Needless to say, the grass was not artificial. It sat less than 30,000. There were seats that had blocked views behind the steel beams holding up the upper deck. There was a laundry across the street from the outfield that always had the windows open to vent out what must have been stifling heat and a robotic tin-man advertisement for a plumbing supply company on the roof of a building beyond center field. The size of the park seemed enormous at the time for a boy from a small town in southern Indiana.

I remember one trip in particular. It was special for Washington in that the Reds were going to honor Charlie Harmon. Charlie was a small town hero for Washington. Anyone who knows anything about Indiana knows that basketball is

KING. Charlie was the forward for the Washington High School Hatchets in 1941 and 1942 when the Hatchets won the Indiana State Basketball Championship. Charlie was a natural athlete and went on to play professional baseball. Unfortunately, he was ahead of his time and started out in the Negro League. By the time he had been picked up by Cincinnati, he was past his prime. However, he played for several years with the Reds and the event to honor him was his last year. I think most of Washington was at that game.

The excursion trains were not small operations. Normally, they had 18 to 22 cars. One car had a full-length counter and served drinks and sandwiches. The early trains often had some non-air conditioned cars but later trains were all air conditioned or at least the air conditioning was working when they started out. I remember one of the St. Louis trains was so large it had to double out of the St. Louis train shed. The last train to Cincinnati had 22 cars and some of them were old Pullman cars being pressed into service as coaches. They were very popular on the late night trip back since the sections could still be made into beds. These were not high speed operations since usually the long trains were powered only by two freight units. In fact, the first time I saw Geeps was on one of the excursions. Those engines (B&O 911 and 912) were permanently assigned to the St. Louis Division after their appearance on the excursion.

As I remember, the last excursion was one to Cincinnati the summer of 1964. It was a 22-car train that was packed. After that, dad and I went on one more baseball excursion to St. Louis but that was on a charter bus. It was just not the same.

Ball Park Excursion Flyer

By Frank Dewey
October 2009

In the April, 2009 issue of *News & Notes*, I had an article *Take Me Out to the Old Ballgame* about the baseball excursions operated on the St. Louis Division out of Washington, Indiana, to St Louis and Cincinnati.

In that article, I made reference to the yellow and red flyers that would appear around town advertising the trains. I seemed to think that I might have one of the flyers somewhere in my railroad library (also known as 'train junk' to the wife).

While looking for material for an article about family trips on passenger trains (which appears in this issue of *News & Notes*) I found the flyer, included with this article, for what I remember as being the last excursion offered out of Washington. Take note of the low cost of both the round trip train fare ($6.00 Washington to St Louis) and the seats at the ball park ($2.25 for reserved grandstand). Also, note that even though this was seven years after the last operation of steam on the B&O, the logo chosen for the flyer shows a steam engine along with the diesel locomotive.

Chapter 16   Travelling on the Varnish

My First Train Ride

By Pete Hartley
January 2003

It was the summer of 1908 or 1909 and I was five or six years of age. (I was born September 1903.) A trip was being made from our farm on Cow Run, Jackson County, West Virginia, via horse-drawn wagon to Ravenswood, a distance of 12 miles, to purchase some furniture from Harpold Bros. Hardware. I was permitted to accompany dad, mother and brother Hoyt on this mission.

The route took us through Cottageville, our closest access to the railroad (B&O) that ran from Ripley to Ravenswood. Mother and I were dropped off at Cottageville station, an old 36 ft. boxcar partitioned into an office for the agent and a waiting room equipped with a coal burning stove and a couple of benches. From there, all excited, I saw that smoking locomotive round the bend and with bell ringing and steam hissing grind to a halt. Mother helped me up the steps into the wooden passenger coach where my bulging eyes revealed the beautiful red velvet seats and the oil-burning lights hanging from the ceiling.

Something should be said about that railroad line. Originally known as the Ripley Mill Creek Valley Railroad, it began operation in 1888, giving Ripley and that Jackson County area rail connection with the outside world. The B&O acquired the line sometime later and operated it for many years. Bill Walker, a congenial gentleman, was conductor on the line's passenger trains for years and the road was locally known as "Bill Walker's Railroad".

I never dreamed on that eventful day of my first train ride that during the ensuing fifty years I would ride many miles on trains with amenities far more elaborate than those available on my first ride: dining cars, Pullman sleepers, club cars, all air-conditioned, on such feature trains as B&O's Capitol Limited, National Limited, Royal Blue, and the Burlington's California Zephyr.

That "boxcar" station and the railroad which gave me that memorable first ride are only memories to the very few remaining former patrons. Someone expressed it well with these words: "The song is ended, but the melody lingers on."

Riding The Rails Part II
Baltimore to Philadelphia - Steam

By Ken Roloson
January 1999

About six months after "recovering" from my Freight Train Adventure (1938) from Bay View Yard, Baltimore, to Cumberland, Maryland, I decided it would be quite a thrill to ride a passenger steam locomotive from Mt. Royal Station to Philadelphia.

Again, I went through the process of executing a liability release and obtaining a "letter of authority" from Assistant Vice President M. W. Jones, to ride the locomotive cab of Train #504, the Marylander, from Baltimore to Philadelphia. This train, along with the Royal Blue, was a comparatively short train as it carried no through cars to and from the west at Washington. Consequently, these two trains were the fastest on the railroad. At that time, the line was double track, jointed rail (no CWR), speed limit 80 MPH for passenger trains and protected by Automatic Inductive Train Stop system, which required the engineman to physically acknowledge a stop indication before entering the restricted block. Failure to do so would bring about an automatic brake application

I arrived at Mt. Royal in plenty of time in anticipation of this "once in a lifetime" trip. Incidentally, the conductor on this train was Bob Poore, father of former RABO member Roland (Barney) Poore.

The train emerged from the smoky Howard St. Tunnel with two electric locomotives on the point. The momentum of the train carried the two "motors" through the third rail gap at the station and it stopped after re-engaging contact with the third rail just east of the station. Upon approaching the locomotive cab, the engineman was already on the ground inspecting the engine. I showed him my "letter of authority" and climbed aboard, introducing myself to the Fireman, who indicated where I was to sit. The engine (P-7 #5518 - President Garfield) was surprisingly clean, in sharp contrast to Q-4, #4632, on my previous trip to Cumberland. As the Fireman was busy with his duties inside the cab, I glanced around the cab interior and spotted a framed sign, which said, in effect, "TO ALL ENGINEMEN OF PASSENGER

Ken Roloson got his engine-cab experience on the 5318, one of 20 P-7-class Pacifics especially built in 1927 for the hotly competitive Washington-New York service. The ultimate in B&O's passenger steam power, all originally were painted olive green with gold striping, and were named for U.S. presidents. In this 1938 scene at Glenwood, Pa., the 5318 still carries its original livery and name -- "President Garfield" -- on its cab.

Walter Tesky photo, H. H, Harwood, Jr., collection.

TRAINS, viz. The train will be handled in the following manner: (1) Safe operation will prevail at all times; (2) The train will be handled with the comfort of the passengers considered; (3) Every effort will be made (in consideration of 1 and 2) to keep the train "on time". It was signed by Vice- President-Operation and Maintenance. These were beautiful locomotives and 20 of them were built, in 1927, by Baldwin Locomotive Works in Eddystone, Pennsylvania, for high speed passenger service between Washington and Jersey City.

With all passengers loaded, the air whistle in the cab indicated that the train was about to start, being handled by the electric locomotive engineer, called a Motorman. Power was applied by the motors and the train slowly moved over the Baltimore Belt Line on an ascending grade. We passed under the North Avenue

Bridge over Jones Falls and into the double reverse curve before entering several short tunnels: Maryland Avenue, St. Paul Street, Charles Street and Greenmount Avenue. The electrified trackage terminated at Waverly Tower (Clifton Park) with a pocket track between the eastbound and westbound mains. The motors were uncoupled 'on the fly', as the motor Conductor suddenly appeared and pulled the coupler pin, the two motors racing ahead and darting into the pocket track. The leverman in the tower realigned the switches quickly and the steam engineman got the train moving at a rapid rate of speed. This entire operation took place within a very short period of time on a "split second" basis and I thought it was fantastic -- just like playing with Lionel Trains. Herb Harwood's book "The Royal Blue Line" has some interesting photos of this operation.

In the engine cab, we were now gaining speed, rapidly, and I was beginning to hold on very tight. At first it was rather frightening but I was becoming accustomed to it, despite the fact that my internal organs were taking a beating. We hit the Bay View curve at a high rate of speed which gave me a funny feeling, wishing I were back on the ground.

The next point of interest was the track pans at Swan Creek, Maryland, where we slowed to approximately 45 MPH, the Fireman dropping the tender scoop at precisely the right moment. This put about 4,000-5,000 gallons of water in the tender without stopping the train. The scoop automatically returned to its former position when the end of the track pan was reached. This was a keenly interesting operation for one not acquainted with it.

This East End of the Baltimore Division was a "curvy" piece of railroad and the engineman was very proficient at his job of getting the train over the line and maintaining the schedule. At one point, we approached a dirt road grade crossing and saw a gravel truck heading for it at a high rate of speed. The engineman had the whistle on continuously and he and the fireman exchanged stern glances. We were doing about 80 MPH at the time. At the last minute, the truck slowed down and stopped at the crossing with smiles exchanged between the two men. They were lucky in this particular case. We approached and crossed the double-track Susquehanna River Bridge at reduced speed and noted Garrett Island in the middle of the river. This island was named for former B&O President John W. Garrett. We came upon another track pan in the vicinity of Newark, Delaware, (Harmony, Delaware) and the same procedure was used in replenishing the water supply in the tender. Before this run was over, there would be two more track pans- one near Yardley, Pennsylvania, on the Reading, and the other in the vicinity of Bound Brook or Middlesex, New Jersey, on the CRR of NJ. To my knowledge, these were the only track pans on the B&O. PRR and NYC had numerous installations on their high density lines.

We made the first station stop at Wilmington, Delaware, with on-time arrival and departure. The rest of the trip to the 24th & Chestnut Streets Station in Philadelphia was uneventful. I enjoyed the opportunity to take this trip and thanked the engine crew upon my arrival in the "City of Brotherly Love". I was a little on the dirty side but not quite as bad as the trip to Cumberland. I returned on the next passenger train to Baltimore.

On several occasions, I rode diesel cabs on the railroad. They were more comfortable but not as "thrilling" as riding a steam locomotive at high speed. The coming of the diesels made the Baltimore Belt Line electric operation, as well as the track pans, obsolete and they were removed in due course. Incidentally, the Baltimore Belt Line electrification was the very first main line electric railroad in the United States.

Birthday Party on the Train

By Frank Dewey
January 2006

I think I came about my interest in railroading genetically. Both my grandfather and father were fascinated by trains even though neither one worked for a railroad. My father gave me my first Lionel train on my second Christmas but would not allow me to play with it alone until I was in my early teens. Who do you think that train set was for?

My early memories of being around trains included many long hours, usually with my father, at the passenger depot in Washington, Indiana, were I grew up watching either the National Limited (trains No. 1 and No. 2) or the Diplomat (trains No. 3 and

No. 4) stopping to change engine crews and water the engines and cars. There were also hours spent at the railroad yards at the west end of town. On the railroad, this was known as "Shops" but most of the locals referred to the location as "The Relay."

A favorite memory of my introduction to railroading took place on my seventh or eighth birthday. Dad was friends with one of the local B&O Railroad policemen named Huck Berry (really). With Huck's help, my father and mother planned a birthday party for me, my sister and about a half-dozen of my friends.

On the day of my birthday, we all went to the Washington depot to catch Number 1, the westbound National Limited, for the eighteen mile trip to Vincennes. At first, our group settled into the big reclining seats in one of the coaches. Shortly after the train started to glide out of the station, a member of the train crew, the Stewardess, and Huck Berry came along and herded us toward the front of the train where they started giving us a tour of the workings of a passenger train. First, we looked into the baggage compartment of the combine. There, also, was a quick glimpse into the Railway Post Office car just ahead of the combine but we naturally were not allowed in there. Then, we worked our way back through the combine to see where the dining crew had dormitory space and the Coffee Shoppe Lounge that served light refreshments to the coach passengers. Next came the two long distance coaches and the one local coach. These included amazing things like toilets that flushed onto the speeding rails below, seats that reclined at the push of a button and the always child-fascinating water fountain with those little folding paper cups. We ended the tour in the dining car just as we pulled into Vincennes. There was just enough time for a quick look into the crowded kitchen and souvenir copies of the children's menu.

During the lay-over in the Union Station at Vincennes, we ate fried chicken out of the box lunches that my mother had made—this was long before KFC. I remember my mother had visited all three of the shoe stores in Washington the week before the trip to get enough shoe boxes so that ever member of the birthday party had their own boxed lunch. Lunch was completed with a birthday cake. Amazingly enough, none of the other passengers in the waiting room seemed to be really bothered by the party even though my mother had to entertain us all with games like "Pin the Tail on the Donkey". I guess that was sort of a test of the Chucky Cheese idea, just years ahead of its time.

Finally, it was train time for Number 2, the eastbound National Limited. This time we were herded to the rear of the train for boarding on the observation car. We must have driven the poor Pullman porter nuts as everyone had to try out the porter call buttons. As soon as the train left the Vincennes station, the Pullman Conductor and B&O Stewardess took control of our group. As we worked our way forward through the sleeping cars, the Pullman Conductor and the porters explained the various types of accommodations. They showed us the rooms set for daytime use and then made up some of the berths to show us how they worked at night. By the time we were back in the dining car, the train was arriving back in Washington. The steward in the dining car gave us all those brown B&O pencils that came with erasers like passengers used to write out their meal orders and a small B&O note pad.

Several days after my birthday, I received a letter with a Baltimore and Ohio Railroad return address. It was from the St Louis Division Superintendent (I am not sure, but I think that would have been A. H. Woerner) apologizing for not knowing that we were going to have a special party on board the train. He said that if he had known, the railroad would have been able to do more. I have no idea what they could have done to improve on the trip that we did have.

After thirty-five years of working on the railroad and lots of train rides, I think that ride was one of my fondest. I just wish my parents had thought to take a camera as the mental pictures are getting harder to remember after all of those years.

The Philadelphia Phillies and the B&O

Ken Roloson
January 2000

During the Carpenter (duPont) ownership period, the Philadelphia Phillies used the B&O RR whenever they could in their travels to and from most National League cities. This took place before the move of the New York Giants to San Francisco and the Brooklyn Dodgers to Los Angeles and other expansions that took place in both the National and American Leagues.

The B&O Passenger Traffic Department in Philadelphia was quite active in obtaining and servicing this source of revenue, over the years, under the direction of W. Preston Cox and Leo Drumheiser, Division Passenger Agents. The key man in these movements was Charlie Meister, Passenger Representative and a native of Cumberland. He personally took care of all the team's "wants" and usually accompanied them on most of the trips. To hold this business was quite an accomplishment considering the B&O's time disadvantage to and from the West from Philadelphia, as compared to PRR direct service. The entire relationship (success) was based upon the personalized service and attention provided by the B&O RR and Charlie Meister.

The Phillies management was so impressed and satisfied with Charlie's proficiency and attention to detail that they made him an offer of employment; and after considerable thought, Charlie became the Traveling Secretary of the Philadelphia Phillies organization at considerable increase in salary over and above what he was getting at the B&O.

This relationship lasted for many years--even after the advent of jet aircraft and the league expansion that followed.

Another example of "Local Area Management" on the Baltimore and Ohio Railroad.

Bussing, Railroad Style

By Ed Willis
April 1998

In the mid 1960s, I was Assistant Trainmaster at Mt. Clare Yard and Dave Crawford was Trainmaster at Washington's Eckington Yard.

The Passenger Department decided that the Budd cars operated between Baltimore, Brunswick and Washington were being wasted during their long layover at Washington Terminal. Therefore, they contracted to run excursion trains with school children from Silver Spring to the B&O Museum at Mt. Clare.

Mr. Crawford accompanied the trains to Mt. Clare and I would take the trains to the museum. On arrival, Mr. Crawford assigned

Nicknamed "Budd cars" or "RDCs" (for Rail Diesel Car), these self-powered stainless steel passenger cars were first introduced by the Budd Company in 1949. Powered by twin underfloor diesel engines, they could be run singly or together in full trains. B&O was an early buyer, and acquired a small fleet to replace steam-powered commuter trains in Baltimore, Washington, and Pittsburgh. They proved highly successful and survived well into the MARC era. Here, a 4-car Budd train out of Brunswick pulls into Kensington, Maryland, to pick up Washington-bound commuters in 1972.

H. H. Harwood, Jr., photo.

me to look after the school children and he looked after the teachers and teachers' aides.

Everything was going along fine until one day we had two school busloads of children from Baltimore. When we were loading the excursion train for the return trip to Silver Spring, the Baltimore school teachers thought this train was part of their tour and loaded their children on the train. No one caught the mistake until the teacher from the Baltimore school bus asked when they would return because they had to have the children back at their school in time for their dismissal. After this was discovered, Mr. Crawford had to arrange for bus transportation to return those children from Silver Spring to Baltimore.

Just another challenging day on the railroad.

Recollections - Mt. Royal Station and the Howard Street Tunnel

By Ken Roloson
April 2000

Mt. Royal Station, its "rocking chairs" and tower clock, was a household word back in the "good old days" on the B&O in Baltimore. The station was built back in the 1890s in connection with the construction of the Howard Street Tunnel and the creation of the electrified Baltimore Belt Railroad from Camden Station to Waverly, Maryland (Clifton Park). This was the first electrified main line railroad in the United States at the time and it more than served its purpose during the period it was in operation.

As everyone knows, B&O passenger trains to New York terminated at Jersey City and passengers and their baggage were transferred to "Baltimore & Ohio Train Connection" busses, operating via ferry, to various destinations in New York and Brooklyn. Baggage was delivered to passengers at their final destination. If you rejected the Pennsylvania Railroad's "mass transit" operation to Penn Station in New York, the B&O was "the way to go" to and from New York City. A first class operation but expensive to the Company and it was reluctantly discontinued in 1957. I can recall at the time of the discontinuance, Mr. J. W. Phipps, Jr., Vice President-Traffic (former RABO member) received a phone call from a lady who used our service often to and from New York. She objected to the discontinuance, stating that on the B&O she "could always get a seat" (the PRR often had standees on their trains). Mr. Phipps replied, "That was the reason the trains were taken off" - too many empty seats.

In addition to the passenger trains (eight a day in each direction), plus commuter trains to and from Washington, Mt. Royal was host to numerous freight trains between Potomac Yard and Jersey City and the western trains, such as NY 94, to Philadelphia and Jersey City. Many of the freights were double-headed and required four electric locomotives on the ascending grade from Camden Station to Waverly Tower, operating on the outside track through Mt. Royal Station where the Third Rail was

Most big cities had one or more suburban stations to add flexibility for the travelling public and to attract the wealthy urban passengers. Baltimore was no exception but, like many others, the cities expanded to encompass what was earlier considered suburban. Mt Royal Station was such a place. Built in 1896 at the north end of the Howard Street Tunnel, it gained fame for its rocking chairs in the passenger waiting room. The station was closed in 1961, three years after the service to New York was terminated. Jervis Langdon, Jr., arranged the donation of the building to the Maryland Institute College of Art in 2009. To this day, CSX freight trains lumber past the beautiful facility whose train sheds have been retained.

B&O Railroad Historical Society collection.

continuous. As the tunnel was built in the 1890s when 36-ft. box cars were the norm, many of the newer cars would not clear the tunnel, necessitating a float operation between Locust Point and Canton, with resulting delays in service. In 1936, a 'gauntlet track' was built in the tunnel, which alleviated some of the problems at the time. Subsequently, the tunnel was single-tracked; but to this day, the tunnel cannot accommodate the largest 'double-stack' trains, placing CSX at a definite disadvantage in trying to attract North-South traffic under the Conrail acquisition.

In 1937, I bid a stenographer's job in our Washington, D. C. office at the fabulous rate of $5.15 per day. But, I had to commute from Baltimore. I purchased my first car, a 1933 Pontiac coupe, straight eight miles to the gallon but gas was 7 gallons for a dollar, so that was no problem. The problem was getting it to start. I parked it on an incline at Govans Presbyterian Church. Drifting down hill, by the time I reached York Road it would start, and off I would go to Mt. Royal Station to catch the 7:15 AM train to Washington. On the return trip 6:25 PM arrival at Mt. Royal; sometimes the car would start and sometimes it would not, which necessitated a streetcar trip home. This commuting business was ruining my social life in Baltimore, so after about five years, I bid a rate clerk's job in Baltimore

I often frequented Mt. Royal just to watch the trains and have many fond memories of my visits there.

Your Sins Will Find You Out

By Roland Jones

July 2001

In the early 1950s, as a member of the B&O Railroad Police Department, I worked as a Road Patrolman, 7 PM — 5 AM. My territory was the Belt Line, which covered Mt. Royal Station to Bay View Yard, including all buildings, sidings, Huntingdon Avenue Tower and Waverly Tower. When time permitted, I met all passenger trains that stopped at Mt. Royal Station.

One night, as an eastbound train stopped, the Jersey Central Conductor, Andy Meeks, called me to remove a non-paying rider who seemed mentally disturbed. As I followed Andy through the dark train, I noticed a couple duck down behind the seat. I turned my flashlight on them and recognized that they were B&O employees, both married to someone else, taking a trip to New York together. Had they sat still, I would never have seen them. I won't give their names since in those days there were many employees with 'relative ability' and some of the relatives may still be living.

I did remove the non-paying female passenger and it developed that she was a 'walk-away' from a Washington, D. C., mental hospital.

Riding the Rails "On the cheap"

By Ken Roloson
July 2001

Having accumulated the required service for a trip pass on the B&O (which I believe was six months), I decided to take a trip on the railroad by myself in 1937.

I did not want to be bothered with any kind of luggage, so a small paper bag filled the bill, containing tooth brush, tooth paste, two pairs socks, two handkerchiefs and a small washcloth. Shaving was no problem because, at age 20 1 shaved about once a week and I would not be gone that long.

Traveling light has its advantages, so I began my trip from Govans in Baltimore on the #8 trolley to Preston St., transferring to the #21 trackless trolley which dropped me off at Mt. Royal Station where I boarded a connecting train to Washington. My three trip passes were: Baltimore-Chicago; Chicago-St. Louis (Alton); St. Louis-Baltimore, The Alton Railroad at that time was part of the B&O System. My schedule involved #9 (Chicago Express) leaving Washington at 1:00 PM and arriving at Chicago at 7:00 AM; the Alton Limited leaving Chicago 11:10 AM arriving St. Louis 5:20 PM; B&O #12, (Metropolitan Special) leaving St. Louis 10:20 PM, Cincinnati 7:15 AM, Cumberland 8:20 PM, Washington 11:50 PM - connecting train to Baltimore (Camden) arriving 12:48 AM.

You will observe the schedule involved a four-hour layover at Chicago and approximately five hours at St. Louis. This was not a sightseeing trip in the strict sense of the word but an educational train ride over the main lines of the B&O RR, traveling in coach.

I recall, in looking back, that all of those passenger trains operated on time and they carried mail and express, which was standard operating procedure on the B&O (AMTRAK, please note). After all, Daniel Willard was still the President of the railroad and a late train had to have a good excuse.

Train #9, the Chicago Express, carried coaches and Pullmans along with the 'head end' traffic previously mentioned. My mother had prepared a sandwich so that took care of lunch the first day. Dining cars in those days did not operate through. The car on # 9 operated from Washington to Pittsburgh and another car from Garrett, Indiana, to Chicago. Having a ravenous appetite at this particular stage in my life, eating in the dining car was the "next best thing to being in Heaven". Two meals on #9; one on the Alton; and three on #12. Dinner on the second day was in the St. Louis Union Station. #12 left St. Louis at 10:20 PM and had no dining car until Cincinnati. The trip from Cincinnati to Cumberland was in daylight hours and an interesting segment of the journey, particularly over the West End of the Cumberland Division which would be my territory as Traveling Freight Agent 18 years later. Most of the cash I had with me was spent in the dining cars-"Living High off the Hog" as they say. I spent a lot of time in the combines talking to deadheading train crews and picked up a wealth of information. All in all, it was a great trip. I had a good time but will have to admit it took me a couple of days to rest up on my return.

Conquering a Roomette Bed

By Robert L. White
July 2001

I must tell a story on myself, even though it is quite embarrassing. Actually, I wrote this story a couple of years ago but held it back for reasons which will be evident to you.

This goes back to the days when we rode B&O passenger trains for business purposes. I traveled only on insured losses. Even in those days, we had insurance deductibles and I didn't get to travel a lot. You could say I was an inexperienced traveler by train. Some of you will, no doubt, even say I was a "dumb" traveler by train, after you hear my story.

This was my first trip in a roomette car. As you know, a roomette is a compact private traveling space with a pull-down bed. For daytime travel, it had a comfortable seat with a nice window for travel viewing. In the corner, there was a wash basin with running water and a toilet. When it was time for bed, you pulled the bed down. The bed consumed most of the space and came to rest on top of the wash basin.

On my first trip, I sat up rather late, going over some of the details of the loss I was about to investigate the next day. Then, it was time to prepare my bed. I washed up, brushed my teeth and

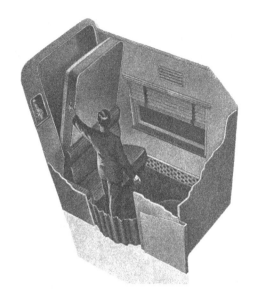

The sleeping car roomette made first class overnight space much more affordable for many people. However, it brought with it many challenges to be overcome. This Pullman Company illustration shows the passenger pulling down his bed for the nighttime set-up. Shown in the cutaway is the curtain that was zipped closed when the bed was pulled down. It permitted the passenger to open the room's door and back into the car's aisle as the bed took up the entire width of the room. This process had to be reversed to provide access to the toilet under the bed. Not an easy or pleasant arrangement, especially in the middle of the night. Bill Howes Collection.

dressed for bed, garbed in my boxer shorts. When I tried to pull the bed down, however, I found there was only about six inches of space between the bed and the edge of the door. How could anyone get this bed down? After a number of unsuccessful tries, all the time chastising myself saying, "If the fat lady across the aisle can do this, Bob White can do it". I worked out a plan. By extending one leg high, straight up, and flattening myself against the door (a move Barishnikov would have been proud of) I achieved my goal. I fell into bed and dozed off immediately.

When I awakened, early, I decided to slip my trousers on so I could open the door to put the bed down, hoping no one would see me. I turned the handle and peeped into the aisle. What a pretty sight I saw. All of the other roomettes had neatly zipped canvas curtains which permitted occupants to zip up and back out into the aisle, without exposing themselves, to pull their bed down.

I didn't tell the guys I was traveling with what I had done and in fact no one has known until this story what a dummy I was on my first trip in a roomette. Anyhow, subsequent travel in a roomette was much easier and certainly less stressful.

(Editor's note: Since the toilet was under the bed, good thing he didn't have a call from Mother Nature during the night!)

Christmas Eve in the Howard Street Tunnel
By Ken Roloson
January 2002

The Philadelphia Freight Traffic Department in 1949-50 was a good -sized organization, headed up by John W. Hartzell, General Freight Agent. Mr. Hartzell was a flamboyant-type person and liked the better things in life. He decided to throw a big Christmas party on Christmas Eve at the office in the 24th & Chestnut Sts. passenger station.

In looking back (50 years) it is my recollection that he had it catered, financing it through an assessment against the expense accounts of the Sales personnel. Rule G was "suspended" for this affair on railroad property. In addition to members of the Philadelphia Freight Traffic organization and their wives, various people from the local Operating, Passenger, Traffic, and Station Service Departments were invited, including M. B. Van Pelt, Terminal Superintendent; W. B. Weis, Terminal Trainmaster; and his Chief Clerk, Dan DeBenevil; W. J. Edgette, Terminal Agent; and others. Mr. Hartzell, on occasion, was not held in the highest esteem by his superiors in Baltimore and they were conspicuous by their absence at the party. Also, in attendance was Ed Swindt (not sure of name or spelling), Road Foreman of Engines, East End, Baltimore Division, and this gentleman is the subject of this story.

John Hartzell always said that a Manhattan was not a real Manhattan unless it was made with Canadian Club, so Ed and I 'tackled' a few of them. I mentioned that my wife and I were going down to Baltimore for Christmas on No. 5 at 2:20 PM. As he was riding the Diesel, he invited me to ride in the cab with him. Question: How about the wife? Charlie Meister, Passenger Representative, was on his way home to Cumberland and offered to assist her with the luggage and presents aboard one of the Pullmans on the rear of the train.

No. 5 on that particular Christmas Eve was a pretty long train, about 15 cars or more with three units. Swindt and I made our way down the platform to the head end and climbed aboard. I was feeling a little wobbly, as I recall. Met the Engineer and Fireman, the Engineer relinquishing his seat to the RFE who operated the train to Baltimore. I can't recall where I sat (if I did) and the rays of the sun coming through the cab window were not contributing to my well-being. The train handled very well and I noticed the speed indicator topped 100 MPH in the vicinity of Van Bibber, Maryland. Speed limit for passenger trains was 80 MPH!! What a thrill, even though I was not feeling the best.

We made our way down through the Belt Line and into the Mt. Royal Station train shed; but as the train was exceptionally long, Swindt pulled a considerable distance into the Howard St.

Howard Street Tunnel is a major operating feature of the Baltimore Terminal. This photo looks at the Mt Royal Station or east end of the longest tunnel on the B&O (still true for CSX). The station's current owner, Maryland Institute College of Art, has retained the train shed but the passenger platforms have been removed.

Tunnel, well beyond the planking between the rails of the station. At that time, the tunnel was double-tracked with a gantlet track (installed in 1937) between the two tracks. As Swindt was going on to Camden, I thanked everyone in the cab for the ride and prepared to climb down off the engine.

I was warned to be careful once on the ground and watch out for the third rail. It seemed like I was a long way inside the tunnel; I was somewhat scared but made it back to the station where my brother picked us up and drove to my mother's home in Govans, where I began a period of recuperation from the events which had transpired.

All of the people in this story, including my dear wife, have passed on.

Some individuals have insinuated that I have "stretched the truth" in some of the articles I have written for RABO *News & Notes*. This is to certify that the aforementioned account is "the truth, the whole truth and nothing but the truth". In fact, I probably have left out a few of the details.

B&O Blows Smoke in Cleveland
By Herb Harwood
April 2009

N&N Editor's Note: The genesis of this article was an extended exchange that took place on the B&O Yahoo internet discussion group concerning B&O's passenger operations in Cleveland Union Terminal (CUT). (The B&O Yahoo site on the internet is a location where those interested in all things B&O, especially modeling, can exchange stories, ask questions and get answers.) In this case, someone brought up a question as to how the B&O passenger trains, in the steam days, operated in and out of CUT, where steam was not permitted. Then, like many such internet discussion groups, the subject took on a life of its own and widened to include other aspects of B&O's Cleveland passenger operations. I was able to get the resident RABO Guru on all things Cleveland, Herb Harwood, to chime in on the discussion and afterward, I added some material to Herb's response and asked some questions that led to a general article on CUT and B&O's relationship to it. Everyone is invited to check out the B&O Yahoo site. You may find it interesting. Visit

Cleveland Union Terminal was unusual in that the entire facility was below street level, with no externally visible station structure as such. The area above the station was occupied by commercial buildings of different types, including the landmark Terminal Tower office building, Hotel Cleveland, Higbee's department store, and other office buildings. Electrification was clearly necessary to make the plan work. This aerial view shows the layout as it looked when opened in 1930. The passenger platforms are under the large vacant area in the center, with the coach yard at the right. B&O's tracks can be seen at the right, at the river level below the complex.   H. H. Harwood, Jr., collection.

at http://finance.groups.yahoo.com/group/Baltimore_and_Ohio. Here is what Herb had to say:

The Yahoo discussion 'thread' apparently started when somebody asked whether B&O ever operated steam into CUT after it began using the terminal in 1934. Like all such discussions in this very active group, many others chimed in, some informed, some not, and some wandering off the immediate subject into other aspects of CUT operations.

To put this discussion in something resembling perspective, CUT was jointly owned by the New York Central, its (then) Big Four subsidiary, and the Nickel Plate, and opened in 1930, initially serving only its owners. B&O was the first tenant, arriving in 1934 after abandoning its still-surviving 1898 stone station in the "Flats" immediately below CUT at Canal and Columbus Roads.

CUT was electrified from the beginning and, in fact, a local ordinance prohibited steam within the station area. NYC's passenger trains changed power at Collinwood, just east of Cleveland, and at the Linndale suburban station on the west side, and were hauled through the terminal by CUT's large, austerely handsome "motors" drawing 3000 volts d.c. from overhead catenary. (Their 2-C+C-2 or, in steam terms, 4-6-6-4 wheel arrangement, was the original model for the Pennsylvania Railroad's famous GG-1. Indeed, the CUT electrification and its locomotives really were designed to be integrated into a planned, but never consummated, NYC mainline electrification between New York and Chicago.) The Central's flagship 20th Century Limited famously disdained CUT and Cleveland altogether, stopping only to change crews at Collinwood; several other premier trains also bypassed the terminal at various times during the 1930s and '40s.

By the time B&O entered CUT, its Cleveland passenger services were down to two trains each way--a connecting train that handled through sleepers to the east via the CT&V and Akron Junction and what Clevelanders (or at least those who rode it) called the "Wheeling Plug" (officially Nos. 58-59), a meandering Cleveland-Wheeling local service. In order to catch the Akron business, the "Wheeling Plug" also ran via the CT&V line to Akron Junction, rather than the CL&W route via Lester and Sterling, Ohio. After pausing at the old wooden CT&V Howard St. station in Akron, it then climbed around a long-gone loop track at Akron Junction to connect with B&O's westward main line, made another Akron stop at the Union Station, then proceeded west on the main line to Warwick, where it joined the former CL&W route to Massillon and Holloway, Ohio, and Wheeling. During the 1930s, the eastern connection consisted of Cleveland-Akron trains 34-37 (later 33-34) that carried coaches as far as Akron's Howard St. station and sleepers destined for either Baltimore or Philadelphia (depending on the period), which were switched on or off mainline trains at Akron Junction.

The early 1940s brought some significant improvements, though. First off, a new Baltimore-Cleveland daylight train, the Washingtonian (Nos. 21-22) was created in April, 1941, as a joint B&O-Pittsburgh & Lake Erie-Erie service, which actually entered Cleveland as an Erie train and used whatever Cleveland station the Erie happened to be using at a given time (see comments on the Erie below). Shortly after, wartime pressures led to trains 17-18, the Cleveland Night Express, established in May, 1942, as a direct all-B&O Baltimore-Cleveland service, replacing the old Cleveland-Akron connecting trains and carrying through coaches and sleepers, which also incorporated light dining services. (As before, Akron passengers used the Howard St. station.) Nos. 17 and 18 proved to be Cleveland's principal link to Washington for businessmen, politicians and government employees and remained so through much of the 1950s.

In order to get into the terminal, B&O had to perform some operating gymnastics that required a switchback and a steep grade from its track in the Cuyahoga River valley to the CUT line on the hillside just above. The track used was B&O's already-existing freight interchange with the Nickel Plate, which at this point paralleled the CUT line along the hillside before turning west. To reach CUT, a westbound B&O passenger train, for example, would pass what was called Nickel Plate Junction on the B&O line in the valley, stop in the clear, then back up the hill to the NKP connection. It then reversed direction and, using a short stretch of NKP trackage, proceeded west again to a CUT connection near E. 14th and Broadway, where B&O power cut off and a CUT electric "motor" picked up the train for a run of about seven blocks into the terminal. The B&O engine then returned over the same switchback route to B&O's W. 3rd St. engine terminal at the north end of its Clark Ave. yard in the 'Flats'.

Passenger steam power generally consisted of unglamorous older Pacifics, although in the late '30s the 'Wheeling Plug' was briefly blessed with the lightweight experimental 4-4-4 Lady Baltimore--largely as a desperation move by the operating department, which could find few other uses for the pretty but slippery little thing.

As far as I know, B&O steam never operated into CUT itself-- and, if it ever did, it was only for some special circumstance. B&O did, however, run steam on excursion trains from Cleveland, including several railfan specials; but all of these started from a loading place near the B&O freight house in the 'Flats' west of the old Canal Road passenger station. The last and most famous of these was the "Last B&O Mainline Steam" trip to Holloway on May 17, 1958. Another notable excursion of the 1950s-era was a diesel-powered 10-car special for B&O's Cleveland-area employees and their families to Chippewa Lake Park, south of Medina, Ohio, on the former CL&W line, in August, 1957. Looking back, this train represented a last hurrah of the old B&O, when it had enough Cleveland employees to warrant a train of this size, and when strong vestiges of the old Dan Willard "B&O Family" tradition still existed. (Incidentally, the Chippewa Lake amusement park, once one of the most popular in northern Ohio, at one time had been owned by Oscar Townsend, an early CL&W director and major stockholder.)

There was only one regular exception to CUT's "no steam" rule but it was not for the B&O. When the New York Central inaugurated its streamlined Cleveland-Detroit Mercury in 1936, the train operated on an extra-fast schedule and, to save time, skipped the Linndale station and engine-swap stop. Its steam power was attached at CUT, but the train was spotted so that its engine (a breathtakingly ugly streamlined ex-Big Four K-5 Pacific) would be in the open. This operation continued for several years after, before CUT resumed its pristine all-electric status.

Nickel Plate's through Buffalo-Chicago trains exchanged power near E. 40th St. and W. 38th St., but the same road engine handled them at each end. While the train was stopped at CUT, the through power would run over the NKP's own line (used for all freight) and pick up the train from the electrics at the other end. (Cleveland was not a division point on the NKP, so the train and engine crew also ran through.)

Full dieselization (or so it was thought) ended the CUT electrification in 1953 and the big 'motors' eventually migrated east to be rebuilt for 600-volt third-rail operation out of Grand Central. But during the winter of 1954-55, the Central ran into some power shortages, and suddenly steam materialized within the terminal (and without benefit of clergy) on several main line and Big Four trains. In addition, both the NYC and NKP sneaked steam into CUT for baseball specials and excursions, the last being some Nickel Plate specials in 1957. (Well, steam was hardly "sneaked" in, since the engines put on glorious smoke shows as they attacked the stiff westbound grade out of the terminal from a dead stop. The Cleveland smoke inspectors tuttutted, but the show went on.)

CUT's second tenant, the Erie, did not enter the terminal until 1949, after it had dieselized its passenger service. Before this, it chose to remain in its old 'Flats' station at Canal and Columbus Roads, just across from the old B&O station. Ever frugal, the Erie wanted to avoid CUT's high terminal charges and felt that it could justify maintaining the ancient structure because of its relatively high volume of mainline connections, joint Erie-P&LE Cleveland-Pittsburgh trains and Youngstown locals. Originally, too, there was no direct track connection between the Erie and CUT, although the Erie's line came close in the vicinity of E. 40th St. When the Erie finally started using CUT, a new connecting track was built from a point west of E. 34th St. to the nearby Erie line, primarily on unused grading and bridges originally intended for the Van Sweringens' planned four-track rapid transit line. Afterward, the old Erie station survived many years as a popular restaurant and, in fact, outlived all CUT passenger services.

True to its adamant 'not invented by us' philosophy, the Pennsylvania Railroad stayed out of CUT, although a connection was graded for it as part of the original terminal construction. The Pennsy stuck with CUT's predecessor, the now-moldering 1865 Union Depot on the lakefront, until it became seriously decomposed; afterward, it cut back its remaining services to its more heavily-used E. 55th-Euclid Ave. station.

C&O, of course, never ran its own trains into Cleveland, although it did operate through sleepers out of Cleveland for its mainline points, primarily for its headquarters employees and for patrons of the Greenbrier and Homestead resorts. C&O office cars were regular residents in the Nickel Plate's small coach yard, located on the site of its old passenger station off Broadway near E. 14th St. Traditionally, an NYC/Big Four train handled the C&O cars to and from a connection with C&O's Washington-Detroit Sportsman at Columbus; but as trains were progressively cut off in the 1960s, they were shuffled to Fostoria (via NKP) and then Toledo (via NYC).

The 'Wheeling Plug' died shortly after World War II, leaving Nos. 17-18 as the only B&O trains using the Union Terminal. Diesels kicked steam off the runs in September, 1951, eliminating the engine change, and the trains soldiered on into the 1960s as its clientele slowly vanished. Nonetheless, and although it underwent several train consolidations east of Pittsburgh, it was upgraded with lightweight sleepers, including an ex-C&O 10/6 car that replaced its classic but clunky heavyweight open-section Pullman. B&O's last Cleveland service finally expired on January 4, 1963, by then reduced to a forlorn, half-forgotten three-car train.

As for CUT itself, it struggled on in ever-diminishing circumstances until Amtrak's advent on May 1, 1971. In the meantime, not only had the B&O gone, but all remaining former Nickel Plate services (by then Norfolk & Western) ended in 1965. On the eve of Amtrak, a total of only nine Penn Central trains entered the terminal--2-1/2 round trips on the ex-NYC Chicago line and two round trips on the one-time Big Four. The next day, all were gone, leaving Cleveland with no intercity train service. Well, not quite. Surviving all its prestigious peers, else--the New York Central's vaunted 'Great Steel Fleet,' the Nickel Plate's comfortable (and cheaper) New York, Chicago, and St. Louis services, and, of course the B&O--was a single moth-eaten Erie Lackawanna commuter trip to Youngstown. That one struggled into the Conrail era before being put out of its misery on January

17, 1977, leaving only local rapid transit trains to scoot along the CUT right-of-way--including, ironically, the line to the airport. But I suppose that the upside to that sorry story is that you can still take a train from CUT to almost anywhere in the world-- provided that you're willing to change modes at the airport.

Taking the B&O to Texas

By John Arledge
January 2012

Bill Howes's article in the October issue of *News & Notes* regarding the last trip on the B&O's Capitol Limited brought back memories of some of the train trips I made in the early days of my career on the B&O.

I grew up in Texas; and in May, 1950, after graduation from high school, I came to Baltimore. In June, I obtained a position of Office Boy in the B&O's Baltimore Regional Accounting Department. Over the next few years, prior to getting married, I made several train trips back to Texas to visit relatives, primarily to Midland where I had last lived before coming to Baltimore.

As I recall, I was at first only entitled to a half-rate pass on passenger trains and, even after becoming eligible for a full rate pass, was restricted from the so-called 'crack trains'. I rode coach at first; the B&O from Baltimore to St. Louis, and then on the Missouri Pacific and Texas & Pacific Railroads to Texas for what were normally two-day trips. For example, I could leave Camden Station in Baltimore around 5 PM on a Friday and not get to Midland, Texas, until around 4 PM Sunday. It was a long coach ride.

In January, 1957, after my marriage and a two-year stint in the Army during the Korean War, I obtained an officer's position in the B&O's Labor Relations Department in Baltimore. Thereafter, my positions entitled me to a full rate pass on all trains and Pullman cars. I could also ride on locomotives.

Around that time, for trips between Washington and Fort Worth, the B&O and the Missouri Pacific had entered into an arrangement whereby a bedroom car was placed on the B&O's National Limited in Washington and was transferred to the Missouri Pacific's Texas Eagle at St. Louis. You could get on a

Although painted and lettered for the Missouri Pacific's "Eagles," the sleeper "Cascade Drive" was actually a B&O 10-roomtette, 5 double-bedroom sleeper that was part of the equipment pool used for through service between Baltimore, Washington and various Southwestern cities. Perhaps this was the car in which John Arledge rode.

H. H. Harwood, Jr., photo.

National Limited coach around 5 PM at Camden Station in Baltimore and, on arrival in Washington, transfer to the Missouri Pacific bedroom car. The National Limited arrived in St. Louis around 1 PM the following day. The Texas Eagles left St. Louis about 5 PM so, upon arrival there, you could get off the bedroom car, walk around downtown St. Louis, get something to eat and, when you returned to the railroad station, get back on the bedroom car which was now on the Missouri Pacific's Texas Eagle bound for Texas. You could stay on the bedroom car until arrival in Fort Worth the following morning. The car was taken off at Fort Worth and you could move into a coach for the trip on to Midland, for example. On the return trip, the bedroom car was put on at Fort Worth and switched out in Washington. I had relatives in Fort Worth; and when my wife and I made these trips, they would come down to the train station to visit for the one hour it normally took to complete the switching out of the bedroom car. My wife and I made many trips to Texas under this arrangement in what we thought was the height of luxury.

Chapter 17   A Snow Job

The Emperor's New Clothes

By Walt Webster Jr.
July 1996

In 1963, the Engineering Department underwent one of its many major reorganizations. This particular one abolished the Regional Offices. I was Regional Engineer, Construction, in Cincinnati and I, along with others, was reassigned to a new position in Baltimore. Through the efforts of General Manager Conley in Cincinnati and then Assistant Chief Engineer Collinson in Baltimore, an extra Pullman car was added to the National Limited of Friday afternoons, Westbound and Sunday afternoons, Eastbound. This was to facilitate our commuting until we could successfully relocate. In addition to myself, Art Dase, Charlie Weber, Bob Breiner, Bob Cassini, Jack Dunseth and Bill Smith were regular commuters.

Many tales could be told about these trips but the one I am relating is particularly memorable.

On one Sunday morning, the news reports were giving a warning of a winter storm coming from the west. The predictions were accurate and it started snowing before noon. By mid-afternoon, it was evident that we were experiencing a major storm. Of concern was the ability to reach the train station to catch our train. A call to the dispatcher revealed that the National Limited was expected to be about two hours late. Not wanting to subject my wife to driving in this storm, I called the cab company for a taxi. I was informed that the company wasn't responding to suburban calls and that only a small portion of their fleet was cruising in the downtown area.

Although I had plenty of time, I decided to leave immediately. I mounted chains on my station wagon and, with my wife and children, departed for Cincinnati Union Terminal. There was no traffic; and with the traction afforded by the chains, we had no problem in traveling there. I was still apprehensive about my wife returning to our home in West Hills. After a reasonable time, I called and was relieved to find that she had returned without incident. After a wait, I boarded the train which proceeded to the Clifton Street Station where the other commuters boarded.

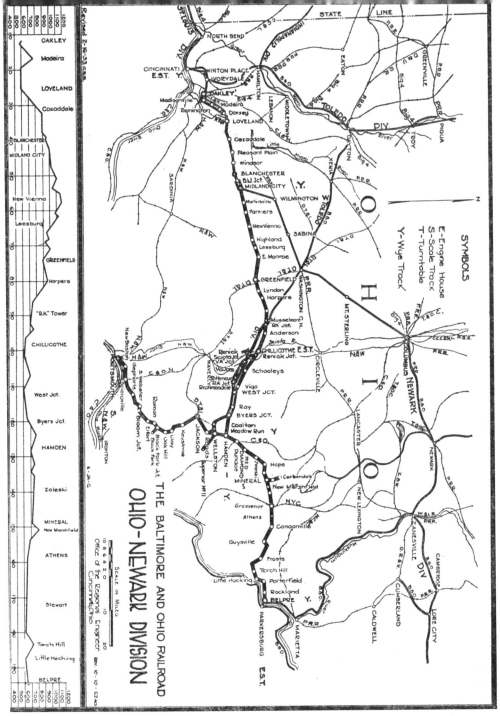

Ohio-Newark Division October 25, 1964, employee timetable map showing the Parkersburg and Chillicothe Sub-Divisions' main lines and other branches.

Ray Lichty collection.

285

In the Club Car, our discussions centered on the storm which was keeping pace with the train. On this trip, I had been assigned to a bedroom with Jack Dunseth. Jack left the Club Car early. As we approached Chillicothe, I went to my bedroom. When I opened the door, I was greeted by Jack wearing his pajamas, felt bedroom slippers and his overcoat. The unusual ensemble promoted me to inquire why he was wearing his overcoat. Jack said that he was going to detrain at Chillicothe and make a telephone call to determine if his wife had gotten home without problems. I warned him that the train wouldn't remain long and that he could not depend on the scheduled 20-minute station stop.

Upon arrival, Jack opened the platform door and proceeded to the outside telephone booth. It seems that Bob Breiner had a similar idea and reached the booth at the same time. Always the Virginia Cavalier, Jack yielded and told Bob to precede him. After Bob had finished and Jack had closed to doors to the booth, the whistle blew and the train departed. Bob made the door on the

The Chillicothe, Ohio, station was jointly used by the B&O and the Norfolk & Western who's clear tracks can be seen crossing the B&O in the foreground. This postcard view looks east on both rail lines. The station was also the B&O's Ohio Division headquarters whose offices included the train dispatchers for the division. Built in 1871, the station was destroyed by fire on February 8, 2012.

fly, leaving Jack stranded in the phone booth on a snowy train platform dressed in his pajamas, felt slippers and overcoat.

I was concerned about my stranded friend but I reasoned that Jack knew his way around the Railroad. Even though he was not dressed for success, I knew Jack would figure out a way to get to Baltimore. Since there was nothing that I could do, I went to bed. I had just about gone to sleep when I was aroused by a knock on my door. I was handed a telegraph message from Jack requesting that I pack his clothes and give them to the porter to leave them at the station at Cumberland, Maryland. It seems Jack was going to catch a freight train that was following the National Limited and I guess he was a little concerned about his traveling attire.

Was the incident over? No! Before we departed Washington, DC, I was handed another message from Jack. It seems his wardrobe was still incomplete. He was advising me that, although he had the rest of his clothes, I hadn't given the porter the shoes that he had placed in the compartment for the porter to polish. I envisioned poor Jack, dressed now for the weather except for a pair of felt slippers peeking out from his trousers. He requested that I take them to the Superintendent's office. Sure enough, I recovered the shoes from the compartment, and I might add that they were unpolished. But somehow, I don't think that bothered Jack when he finally retrieved them.

To Catch a Train

By Jeanne Bailey
July 2008

During February of the winter of 1958, my husband, Glyn Bailey, a Traveling Auditor for the B&O, was scheduled to head off by train for an audit in Cincinnati, Ohio, after a weekend at home. Glyn traveled a lot during those days but was always able to come home on weekends.

It started snowing sometime during Friday night and snowed all day Saturday and Saturday night. By Sunday morning, we were knee deep in snow with snow still coming down and our street a complete snowdrift of beautiful white pillows of snow. Since we did not have the weather-warning systems we now have, this huge storm was a surprise. You called family members and friends to inquire how they were making out; how much snow had accumulated where they lived; and hoped our food supplies were plentiful, to get us through.

The radio (we didn't have a TV) advised that all public transportation, i.e. streetcars, in Baltimore City, Baltimore County and Northern Anne Arundel County, had ceased operating. All major roads into and out of Baltimore City were blocked by snow. Plows were struggling to open them. Ambulances transporting patients to St. Agnes Hospital, our nearest hospital, were able to get as far as the bottom of the hill at the hospital but apparently not up to the Emergency Room door. Somehow, sleds mysteriously appeared to carry patients from the ambulances to the Emergency Room. Doctors, nurses and vital hospital personnel worked on and on until another doctor or nurse made it to the hospital to relieve them. I seem to recall many of them stayed at the hospital and slept there until they were once more on duty.

Outdoors, our road was a magical fairyland--Wonderful if you could stay indoors and enjoy the serenity and beauty of the world. But, Glyn had to catch a train late Sunday afternoon to arrive at work on Monday morning in Cincinnati. Wonderful friends, Harry and Melba, who lived about two blocks from our home, made it to our house through the drifts. Between the four of us, we managed to dig out and uncover our car. However, where do you go when everything is knee deep or waist high in snow? We could hear the snow plow struggling on Frederick Road, our main artery to Baltimore City. What to do!!!

Since we had the shovels, good backs then and no arthritis, we decided to shovel, shovel and shovel. We shoveled to the end of our road, a distance of about 100 feet. Then we started on the cross street and dug our way up that street about a long block to the next cross street. There, we discovered a truck had managed to get through. Hooray! If we could get the car there and follow the truck tracks to the main road, perhaps we could get to Baltimore.

Back home we trudged. After something to eat and hot tea to warm us, Glyn and his suitcase, Harry, Melba and I got into our car, crossed our fingers and took off. We finally managed, after much trying, to get ourselves and the car to Frederick Road. What a sight-- one narrow lane fully snow-covered but passable and it was still snowing. We decided to go for it to get Glyn to Camden Station and the train to Cincinnati. After some hairy moments during the seven-mile drive and a long time getting there, Glyn made it to the train at Camden Station.

The three of us managed to struggle back to Catonsville. Once there, we discovered the road into our development drifted shut and impossible to drive through. We left the car on Frederick Road, hoped for the best and fought our way through snowdrifts to our house.

Everything remained paralyzed for several days as Baltimore City and Baltimore County struggled to free everything from this monstrous snowstorm. About Wednesday of that week, the Police advised me I would have to move our car. A small store lot had been cleared so that cars could be moved there. Since our development was still snowbound, I climbed through the drifts once more and managed to move the car. Frederick Road was still a big fat mess but they were bringing a streetcar with a snowplow attached to clear the rails. Hospitals were still struggling with personnel and patients arriving and being discharged. We did not seem to have any problems with telephone or electric wires and everything was still white and beautiful.

Saturday morning, I collected our car from the store lot and was able to drive to Camden Station to pick up Glyn on his return to Baltimore. We made it home through the still snow-clogged streets as people were still shoveling and snow was piled high everywhere. Our nearest grocery and pharmacy were now open and life was again right in our little world.

And that was how Glyn got to and from work during a snowstorm in 1958.

Baptism of Snow

By Jim Sell
October 1997

I wonder how many are still working who remember the BIG SNOW of 1950, on Thanksgiving Eve and Thanksgiving day, at Parkersburg.

I had just been appointed Night General Yardmaster at Parkersburg and was apprehensively trying to get my feet on the ground when, on Thanksgiving Eve, just as I was going on duty at 7:00 P.M., it started to snow. It snowed unusually hard and very steadily. When the crack eastbound freight, No. 88, arrived, there was about a foot to a foot-and-a-half of snow on the ground. No. 88 had 55 minutes Terminal Time and it made the Superintendent very unhappy if that time was not met. Because of the heavy snow, we had to double the Parkersburg reduction off the train and then double the fill-out onto the train. A wind had come up and it blew snow into the switch points and it was necessary to sweep the points each time a switch was used. No. 88 was in the Terminal for two hours. And, yes, I heard about it.

From then on, it was downhill. Murphy's Law kicked-in and whatever could go wrong, did go wrong. Switching was almost impossible. As I remember, we derailed the lead wheels of five or six cars because of snow between the switch points and we accomplished almost nothing that night.

We had called out trackmen to sweep switches and they worked hard but the snow was falling so fast and, because of the wind, they couldn't keep up with it.

No. 30, an express train, arrived about 3:45 A.M. with the firebox frozen and it was necessary to change engines. The only one we had available was the Monongah Division Local's engine. It took over an hour to get 30's engine to the shops and the Local's engine to the depot. In the meantime, No. 3 was waiting to get into the station. Delays; delays; delays!

I do not know just what happened but the roundhouse crew intended to turn an engine on the turntable and somehow they missed lining up the table and the man running the engine mistook a signal and they ran the engine into the turntable pit. I heard later the man running the engine said he couldn't see and moved the engine on what he thought was a voice command.

When my quitting time came at 7:00 A.M., I could not get home. I walked to and from work and lived about two miles from the office, so I slept on the Terminal Trainmaster's desk. It snowed all Thanksgiving Day and little or no railroading was done, as some crews couldn't get to work and the snow and wind filled the switch points making switching cars almost impossible.

On Thanksgiving night, the National Limited left the depot 30 minutes late, around 10:45 P.M., and, half-way between the station and the yard office, the train parted between the dining car and the sleepers. The engineer kept blowing the engine whistle to get someone's attention. The switchtender at OB Tower noticed the train was not moving and he called me and the Night General Car Foreman. It took both of us a while to get to the train, as the snow was now 32 inches deep. After we got to the train and saw that the train had parted and had torn off the steam connections between the diner and the first sleeper car, it was necessary to wade through the snow to the shops to get materials to make repairs. It was a defective coupler anti-creeper device that had caused the train to part. I noticed a man in low-cut shoes, trousers, pajama tops and an overcoat along the train. He said to me, "I am the Operating Vice President of the Union Pacific Railroad and I will help you put the train together when you are ready." He did too! I thanked him and we shook hands. I forget his name but he knew what he was doing and was a big help. The National Limited left Parkersburg almost three hours late. The General Car Foreman told the Chief Dispatcher what had happened and that is the last we heard about it.

In the meantime, No. 94 was waiting at the stockyards in Belpre. 94's consist included 22 loads of livestock that would normally have been set off there at the stockyards for feed, water and rest. The tracks at the stockyards were impassable. I told the conductor to bring the stock to Parkersburg; but, first, I asked the stockyard people to load as many sacks of feed as they could on 94's engines. Then, I phoned the local fire department and asked them to bring a hose to the depot. When 94 arrived at the depot, we took the sacks of feed off the engines and put them on baggage carts and fed and watered the stock by having a yard crew pull the stock by the hose and carts of feed. The stock never did get rested at Parkersburg. Fortunately, the station platform was reasonably well-cleaned by the trackmen.

The railroad purchased many, many shovels from the local Ames plant and hired many men to shovel snow onto flat cars to be dumped off the right-of-way. If ever there was an unsuccessful project that was it. Anyone who applied was hired but darn few worked and fewer flat cars were loaded. Lots of snow went unshoveled and many shovels disappeared. Railroading did not return to anywhere near normal for some time.

I can't write everything that happened--crews going on the law; derailments caused by the snow and wind; killing steam engines because we could not get them to the shops to be watered; etc. Nor do I remember everything but when it was over and the 36 inches of snow had mostly departed, I figured my feet had hit the ground and whatever else happened while I was Night General it couldn't be as bad as my 'Baptism of Snow'.

Chapter 18   The Biggest Characters

Police Story

By Bob Wheeler
January 2001

A few years ago, when Maurice E. Good took over the Police Department, he had already developed a vocabulary that no one in the Police Department had any trouble understanding. They knew what he meant when he spoke. One particular day, Mr. Good was talking to one of his Captains about his well-being. A short time later the Captain made an appointment with his family doctor for that afternoon. The Captain arrived on time and was examined by the doctor. While the doctor had him bent over the examining table, he said, "I don't care what your boss, Maurice Good, said. I fail to find any lead in your butt."

Cumberland Division Notes, Then and Now

By Ken Roloson
October 2001

Interesting tales about the Cumberland Division in the old days keep cropping up in the author's aging mind, particularly during the period 1955--1960 when I was Traveling Freight Agent there. Ted Klauenberg was the Superintendent when I arrived in October, 1955, and he was succeeded by R. J. (Ray) Cannon a couple of years later.

My boss, Larry Brown, Division Freight Agent, directed me to keep an up-to-date list of office cars and to whom they were assigned in the event we were called upon to ride any of these cars over the Division. Note that I refer to them as office cars and not private cars. I had the cars listed on an index card which I carried in my wallet.

On several occasions, Larry Brown was called upon to ride the cars of President Roy B. White and Vice President-Traffic J. W. (Bill) Phipps, Jr., over the Division between Harpers Ferry and Grafton, West Virginia. This involved driving your car to either Harpers Ferry or Grafton and retrieving it later,

An interesting and frequent visitor on the Division was Wilbur

At the time Ken Roloson was checking office cars, the B&O had 13 such cars assigned to various top officers. Shown here at Camden Station in Baltimore, No. 97 was typical of the breed. Pullman built it for the B&O in 1923, and over the years it was upgraded with air conditioning, new trucks, and other improvements. It was one of the last of its noble fleet when retired in 1969, and, happily, still survives under private ownership. Unfortunately, others have not been spared and have come to an inglorious ending on a scrap heap somewhere.

H. H. Harwood, Jr., photo, c. 1960.

Galloway, General Manager Eastern Region, whose car usually came up on #11 and was set off on the boiler track, just east of the station. The station redcap was usually instructed to tidy up the station platform, picking up cigarette buts and other trash, to get ready for Mr. Galloway's arrival. Joe Gross, Assistant Trainmaster, usually drove down to Paw Paw, West Virginia, to ride the car to Cumberland, making sure that Mr. Galloway was up and dressed for arrival of the train in Cumberland. On one particular occasion, George Dove, General Freight Agent at Baltimore, to whom Larry Brown reported, came up to Cumberland to spend a few days in the territory and his trip happened to coincide with one of Mr. Galloway's trips. George Dove, as everyone knows who knew him, was a great showman. Some have said that he should have been in the circus. George said to me, "Ted Klauenberg and Wilbur Galloway are having a meeting on the car on the boiler track at 10:00 AM and I want you and Larry to be there." We had no alternative but to comply. The meeting was primarily about Klauenberg's operating people and what they did not do that they should have done, etc., etc. This was my first time to indulge in a scotch on the rocks at 10:00 AM, a far cry from the 'after 5' criteria. As we were not invited for lunch on the car, George, Larry and I retreated to the Fort Cumberland Hotel where George Dove called my attention to a spot at the far end of the bar where the floor tile was worn. He said, "This is where Max Freese usually stood." Max Freese was a former Division Freight Agent at Cumberland who had a "little problem". and Traffic officials in Baltimore decided the best solution was to have Max Freese switch jobs with Mel Gemmill, Division Freight Agent at Parkersburg. Gemmill eventually retired as DFA at Cumberland and was succeeded by Larry Brown.

Getting back to the office cars, the Division grapevine had a pretty good idea when these cars would appear. The yard at Hancock, West Virginia, stored covered hopper cars for use by Pennsylvania Glass Sand Corporation at Berkeley Springs, West Virginia, on the Berkeley Springs Branch. When word was received about an office car on the Division, the Hancock Yard crew would move half of the covered hoppers up the branch and out of view. If they did not do this, the officials would invariably attempt to reduce the number of assigned cars to this customer's pool and, based on previous experience, create a car shortage and increased trucking of sand.

Wilbur Galloway was a lover of buckwheat cakes, especially the kind made from Preston County, West Virginia, buckwheat flour, allegedly the world's finest. On many occasions, the flour was trucked from Kingwood down to M&K Junction where it was placed on Mr. Galloway's car.

The interlocking tower at Miller (Cherry Run) West Virginia, was closed on September 24, 2000; and 58 days later, the tower at

West Cumbo was eliminated, During the year 2000, signal crews worked to install electro-code signaling on the 60 miles of track between Orleans Road, West Virginia, located at the east end of the famed Magnolia Cut-off, and Harpers Ferry, West Virginia. As part of the project, the traditional color position light signals are being eliminated in favor of the Seaboard-type search light signals. Four additional manned interlockings will be eliminated by mid 2001. Low Grade track #4 was one of the reasons for the West Cumbo tower's survival. This single track was known as the 'Cherry Run Low Grade' and was signaled for eastbound traffic only. During the late 1950s, an unfortunate head-on collision occurred in a cut on this line, a very disastrous derailment with fatalities which was difficult and costly to clean up. This line and other tracks are now signaled in both directions and interlocking control and all communications are being transferred to Jacksonville, Florida. Until its closure, West Cumbo was known for its peaceful location and the friendly people who worked there.

The tower at Miller (Cherry Run) is being moved in pieces and reassembled (February 2001) at the Martinsburg, West Virginia, Roundhouse Museum complex. The West Cumbo tower was demolished on February 27, 2001.

The writer wishes to acknowledge the February, 2001, issue of Railpace magazine and the February issue of Cinders, the monthly publication of the Philadelphia Chapter, National Railway Historical Society, for some of the information used in this article.

Kesler's Curve

By Jim Sell
January 2003

Ken Roloson's article *The Magnificent Magnolia Cut -off* and Ray Lichty's *Waters' Ways*, both in the October issue of *News & Notes*, were especially interesting to me because I could relate to many of the locations in the areas noted in the articles. My mother's family, the Keslers, had settled in the Paw Paw, Green Spring, Magnolia and Okonoko areas of West Virginia as early as the seventeen hundreds. My great, great, great grandfather, John

Kesler, purchased a farm between Paw Paw and Magnolia near Flora Falls (named for John's wife's family). Magnolia was named for Maggi and Nora Norton (Magnora). The Nortons were close relatives of the Kesler family. Timothy Norton settled there in 1802. The farm was passed down through the Kesler family for generations. When the Western Maryland Railway was being constructed, they obtained a right-of-way through the farm from my great-grandfather. The railroad followed the river and there is a big curve in the river at the farm; consequently, a big sweeping curve in the track. This curve has long been known as Kesler's Curve.

My great grandfather was an eccentric who did not believe in banks. He buried his money in earthen pots under fence postholes. Some railroad workers happened to dig up a few of these pots and, I guess, word eventually got out that the family who owned the farm was wealthy. Sometime later, when the railroad was operating, the crew of a passing freight train saw the big Kesler house on fire. They notified the volunteer fire department at Magnolia. When the fire department arrived, they found my great-grandfather had been murdered by axe blows to his head. (The murderers were never found.) My mother's uncle, Bill Kesler, took over the farm and rebuilt the house and operated the farm.

I can remember, as a young boy when we lived in Cumberland, my parents would take us children to the farm on the Fourth of July for a big Kesler family picnic. A big gang of relatives would be there. Some I knew and some I didn't know. There were so many of them. The ladies would try to out-do each other with their cooking —chicken, homemade bread, apple butter, pies, preserves, etc. etc. etc. I can remember a large tub of home-grown watermelons in ice cut from the Potomac River during the winter.

After everyone had stuffed themselves, most of the children would go off to play. I would stay to listen to the "old folks" reminisce. It was a special time for me. My grandfather's mother told stories of the Civil War. How her family hid what they considered valuable in the cistern on the farm and walked the C&O towpath to Cumberland fleeing the advancing Confederate

Army. One of her sisters told of her son who had gone over the mountain (I don't know where) to get a side of beef. On his way home, carrying the beef on his shoulder, he was attacked by a mountain lion. Rather than surrender the meat to the lion he fought it — mostly by kicking it. He managed to save the beef. His mother said, "I spent most of the night patching him up." They told stories of fish pots in the river, hunting, farming, etc. Mostly, they reminisced remembering their ancestors. This was of great interest to me. I also remember that mother's uncle Bill had horses on the farm. My mother, her uncle Bill and others would have horse races. My mother was a good rider and she enjoyed it. Uncle Bill died when I was about 10 or 12 years old and that was the end of the picnics. It was, however, a time of my life I would like to live over. My mother and father have also passed on and I have lost touch with her people. I don't know what has happened to the Kesler farm or if the Western Maryland still has tracks there or if Kesler's Curve is still part of the railroad. I must still have relatives in the area because there were many of them.

Opportunity Knocks

By Carl S. Kadron
July 2004

In the early 1960s, my boss, Henry Diegelman, Director of Taxes, received a telephone call from the Real Estate Department. They requested assistance from the Tax Department on the sale of a piece of B&O property in West Virginia. The potential buyer wanted to meet with us to shape the transaction to his best tax advantage. Norm Murphy was handling the sale and I was assigned to assist him on the tax aspects.

The buyer, James Lowe, came to Baltimore and met with Norm and me. We retired to the Chesapeake Room of the Lord Baltimore Hotel for lunch. Over a delicious crab cake lunch we discussed the proposed real estate transaction. Mr. Lowe outlined how he envisioned the structure of the purchase of the property. I reviewed the tax aspects that he proposed and found no adverse effects to the B&O. Norm Murphy also had no problems with the proposed sale.

During our lunch discussion, Mr. Lowe told us that at the time he had four hardware stores and planned to expand in the Mid-Atlantic and Southeast regions of the country. The company, Lowes Companies, Inc., had gone public with its stock by an Initial Public Offering at $16.00 per share. At the time of our meeting, the stock was selling for about $20 per share. Mr. Lowe suggested that Norm and I should purchase one or two hundred shares of his company's stock because he thought his expansion would be successful.

Opportunity Squandered

Neither Norm or I took Mr. Lowe up on his suggestion. I'm not sure Norm or I could have afforded $2,000 for the shares at that time! And, there was the possibility of a conflict of interest. But what would have happened to our personal fortunes if each of us had bought 100 shares?

Well, the stock has split ten times since 1966 - mostly two for one. If Norm and I had each purchased one hundred shares back in the early 1960s, we would each now have 40,400 shares. On May 18, 2004, the stock was selling for $58.27 per share. So, our holdings would have been worth $2,354,108 to each of us today.

Granted, the $2 million profit is purely speculative. It assumes that we would have held the shares for 42 years. In reality, we could have more than doubled our money anytime after 1966. We have all seen the success of Lowes Companies, Inc. They now have 982 stores in 45 states. Mr. Lowe's proposed expansion in the 1960s was very successful indeed.

Another Stevens

By Andy Koerner
October 2008

The July, 2008, issue of *News & Notes* included Ray Lichty's comments about the unfortunate passing of Donald H. Stevens. That article, appropriately, mentioned Don's father, John F Stevens, and his illustrious great-grandfather, who was also John F. Stevens. What was not mentioned was the man in the middle of those two railroaders, Donald French Stevens, Don's grandfather. Donald French Stevens was also a B&O railroader and kept Don's string of four generations of railroaders intact.

Ray also mentioned in that July issue of the newsletter that I

Left: Marias Pass Rededication July 10, 1991. Right: John Frank Stevens. It should be otherwise but John Frank Stevens is not a household name on the B&O. Stevens made his reputation as a railroad pathfinder when he laid out the route for the Great Northern Railroad across the Rockies at Marias Pass, Montana, and Stevens Pass in Washington state. He had done significant work earlier in finding routes for the Canadian Pacific Railroad across the Rockies and the mountain ranges west, thereof. Stevens is also credited with designing the Panama Canal and improved the Trans-Siberian Railway for the Russian government. His connection to the B&O was as a personal friend of Dan Willard and served on the B&O Board. He and his wife lived in Baltimore in the mid 20s. His Great-Grandson, Don Stevens was an Assistant Director in the Chessie Finance Department and a RABO member.

began service with the B&O in 1937 (before Ray celebrated his first birthday) as a Machinist Apprentice at the Mt. Clare Back Shop. To be more precise, in October of 1936, about ten of us from Baltimore including Bill Dadd, who eventually became General Superintendent Motive Power and Equipment, and Pail Nigh, who became supervisor of the welders at Mt. Clare, were sent to the Cumberland Back Shop as special apprentices and machinist apprentices.

In February, 1937, I was called back to work in the Mt. Clare Erecting Shop. In July of 1937, I was furloughed and was one of the first to receive U. S. and Maryland Unemployment Compensation, which had just started in 1935. I still have my Compensation Claim Card.

Then, I returned to the railroad in November of 1939. That is when I first worked in the B&O Central Building when I took on the position of Order Writer in the Purchasing Department.

As I recall, in the year of 1943, I learned of a secretarial position opening in the office of the Vice President-Operations and Maintenance. I was able to secure that position in the VP's office on the 5th floor. I was the Secretary to Donald French Stevens. He was the Assistant to the Operating Vice President. The Operating Vice President during that time was W. C. Baker. That was during the period of time of the end of WW II. At that time, Col. Roy Barton White was presiding as President down on the 3rd floor.

Interestingly enough, the main part of Donald Stevens' job was dealing with the draft board offices to exempt our vital employees from the draft in WWII. You might think that was the managers of the company, which it was; but the bulk of this activity was to keep the vital Engineers and Conductors "Working on the Railroad". There was a great shortage of qualified T&E employees who knew the territory because of the overall war effort. The logic of the need for such qualified workers was a big part of the reason for his success with the various SSS draft offices in keeping such folks on the job. Mr. Stevens worked very closely with Col. Paul K. Klacious in these SSS matters. The colonel was headquartered in the Fifth Regiment Armory, not far from Mt. Royal Station.

Another of Mr. Stevens' assignments was the official greeter of foreign and important national dignitaries visiting on our railroad. Mr. Stevens was quite the diplomat; and when a VIP was traveling on our railroad or visiting, he was on hand.

I remember being with Mr. Stevens when the Archbishop of Canterbury, Geoffrey Francis Fisher, arrived in Union Station in DC.

(Fisher was the Archbishop of Canterbury from 1945 to 1961. He presided at the marriage of HRH The Princess Elizabeth and later at her coronation in 1953 making her Queen Elizabeth II.)

Mr. Stevens was always the perfect gentleman.

To my knowledge, it was perhaps late in 1946 that Mr. Stevens retired. When he retired, I went to the Safety Department where I was Secretary to George W. Elste and worked in that capacity until he retired.

I then went to the Insurance and Safety Department, working for Clarence Dawson, and did some secretarial work during that time for RABO member Bob White.

When the C&O took over, I worked in the Safety and Fire Prevention Department under Roger Cassidy.

Not being satisfied with the job and because I was very high on the Union seniority list (we had to join), I bounced around in various departments until I went into Data Processing where I worked under Jack Campbell and Will Koerner.

Of course, as to John Stevens, the father of Donald French Stevens, there are a number of books relating to his escapades with the Great Northern Railroad, the Panama Canal and the Russian railroad system.

The Stevenses were a notable railroad family for sure!

A Railroad Titan of My Time

By Keith Rader
April 2010

I just finished reading Bob Withers' article in the last *News & Notes* where he quoted Mr. Arthur W. Conley and called him "Ike". I worked for Mr. Conley for several years and I don't recall that he was referred to as "Ike" in my presence, although others have such recollections. Ironically, on many occasions I have said that he was an 'Eisenhower'. He was fair and more than understanding of the problems being experienced by others. It was said on the Western Region, "We bow to the east three times a day but only as far as Cincinnati." He was regimented and well-respected for his mannerisms and style. He was a master of delegating; a master of correspondence; and a master of time. If Mr. Conley scheduled a meeting, you could set your watch that the time scheduled never changed. He was a General in statue.

ARTHUR W. CONLEY, a B&ORR titan, was a Crew Caller at Peach Creek, West Virginia. Afterward, Arthur became Yardmaster, Trainmaster, Superintendent, General Manager and, in his final months, Chief Operating Officer during the C&O/B&O Merger.

When Arthur was a Crew Caller, his job was to inform crew members when they were needed for service. Telephones and cars had been invented; however, for a lowly Crew Caller, even a bicycle was a luxury. Arthur was instructed to notify an Engineer that he was needed for train service. He knocked on the Engineer's door but did not receive an answer. When he returned to the Crew Caller's office, he told the Crew Dispatcher that he was unable to notify the Engineer he was needed for work, there was an exchange of a few unfavorable words. "Get your skinny rear back up that hill and don't come back without notifying that man we need him!" More determined than ever, Arthur rapped on the door but still received no answer. Recalling the instructions he had been given, he entered the man's home, went to the bedroom and pulled back the sheets. What do you know; no Engineer; just his wife. The crew member he wanted had anticipated a call and was already at the Crew Caller's office.

Later, when Arthur was Yardmaster, O. E. West, who was Chief of Yard Operations, visited Arthur's' terminal. Mr. West had conceived a method using symbols (something like shorthand) to identify the destination for a carload of freight. For example; X46 stood for Philadelphia, X48 for New York, etc. These symbols were used on their switch lists when cars were being classified or bunched for their final destination. Mr. West insisted that each track in the classification yard have a permanent place for a specific classification. He observed that track No. 7 was not being properly used. "The cars on No. 7 do not belong on that track", he said. Arthur promptly, being eager to satisfy his boss, directed the Yard Foreman to couple No. 7 and pull the cars back behind the hump. "When you get there call me", he said. When Arthur received the notification from his Yard Foreman that he had completed his task, Mr. West had left on his way back to Baltimore. "OK", Arthur said, "He's gone and you can shove those cars back down into No. 7. It's OK now."

On another occasion, Arthur was Trainmaster at Needmore Yard at Dayton, Ohio. It was early morning and in reviewing the past night's performance, he was at a loss as to why nothing had departed on time. It was near 8:00 AM and he would soon be hearing Superintendent Batchelter's gruff voice on the phone. "What can I tell him", he thought, reaching for his pipe. Yep--the phone was ringing and before he got the receiver to his ear, he could hear the growl.

"Hello ! Hello ! Hello ! darn phones don't work half the time!" he yelled before hanging up. An hour later, the communications people who had been summoned by his Superintendent showed up in numbers to fix the system that mystically had repaired itself. Everything was quieter now and the atmosphere was back to normal.

Now the shoe is on the other foot and Arthur is General Manager at Cincinnati. A similar situation occurs with Eric Howard now holding the position of Trainmaster at Dayton, Ohio. When Eric heard that Mr. Conley was on the phone, he expected the worse. But Eric is confused. Mr. Conley is asking

A. W. "Art" Conley is a perfect example of the 'old school' successful railroader. His first railroad job was at age 16 as a yard clerk. He worked his way up serving as Superintendent of the Toledo and Cumberland Divisions before becoming the General Manager at Cincinnati. His last position was as the Chief Operating Officer in Baltimore. A good operating man who dealt fairly with his people, he was held in high regard by those who worked for him and those for whom he worked.

B&O Magazine photo.

personal questions and is not mentioning anything about the previous night's poor performance. "Eric, have you met my daughter, Julie," he said. "Oh yes sir, Mr. Conley", Eric replied. "Then could you do me a favor"? "Oh, yes sir, Mr. Conley, what is it you need?" "Go to my house and pick her up and take her to Needmore Yard, so she can straighten that place out." No response; all was quiet.

I had just completed a system train classification study for him and shared a ride on the office car to Cumberland, Maryland. It was his birthday and he was on the way to our headquarters in Baltimore to become Chief Operating Officer during the C&O/ B&O merger. He said that he felt like a pregnant woman. "I have nine more months to work before retirement and they want me in Baltimore", he said.

Mr. Conley's General Manager position at Cincinnati, Ohio, was filled by Mr. A. W. Johnston. That was the beginning of another era!

Car-Pooling Deluxe

By Gifford Moore
January 2009

In the early 1960s, I was working for the Baltimore and Ohio Railroad (B&O) at and out of the B&O Central Building in downtown Baltimore. It was a 25-mile commute each way from Carroll County, Maryland.

Living close by on the same road were three good friends and neighbors: Gordon Volkers and Maurice Good, with the B&O (and RABO members) and Anton "Bud" Endler, with the Baltimore Gas and Electric Co. (BGE)—who also worked in Baltimore with a similar commute. In fact, our homes were two on one side of the road and two on the other in a square configuration, so to speak, within sight of each other.

One day Maurice said, "The pastor at my church has his old car for sale at 100 bucks. What say we buy it jointly and use it to drive to work?" Not knowing fully what we were getting into, we agreed.

Each of us kicked in 50 dollars, $25 to buy the car and $25 to take it to a garage for inspection, repair, tune up, whatever. Bud

Endler volunteered to be treasurer and we agreed to give 15 dollars every two or three weeks to cover insurance, gas, oil, parking and other miscellaneous charges. We thought it would be a good thing as it would release our family cars for our wives to use during the work week.

As I recall, licensing, registration, and insurance turned out to be somewhat hilarious. "What? You want four names on the title? Do I hear you right? You want four names on the insurance policy? There's not enough room on the certificates for all that information!" But, it was accomplished and we were off and running. Sorta!

The "old girl" burned oil, mightily, and had rust spots. Its color was, well, dark, and we never painted it. I think we washed it a time or two. It had a big hole in the floor in the back seat which we covered with cardboard or plywood. And it ran a little noisily—but it ran.

The hole in the backseat floor actually came in handy on occasions. Most Fridays, someone would go to the Lexington Market and buy fresh-roasted peanuts. On the way home, we would shell the nuts and throw the empty shells out through the hole in the floor! It wasn't littering as the shells were biodegradable.

We took turns driving our "bomb" and usually parked in Baltimore at the B&O's Camden Train Station when space was available, trying to scrounge free parking where we could and only parked in a costly lot when absolutely necessary. On occasion, we would go to the airport when one of us was leaving town or coming in.

When things were quiet and normal, we left downtown about 5:30 PM, and would wait until 5:45 for each other. After that, "you were on your own" to get home, although that seldom happened.

We agreed to leave the car parked on weekends in one of our driveways and took turns, rotating it each weekend. We all had keys. The car was always within sight of someone and was used on weekends for a variety of trips: shopping, to the nursery, for church and Sunday school and so on. Maurice even used it once to fix his backyard for a lawn by dragging some kind of sod-breaking contraption like a harrow behind it.

So this car-pooling concept worked. In time, we had enough in our treasury to get another Chevy, similar to the first, which I believe we gave away to some kid in Sykesville. Our investment, individually, was modest and I believe the others would agree that it was an interesting and enjoyable part of our lives.

In 1966, I left the B&O and went to the Lehigh Valley Railroad. With tongue in cheek, I said to the others, "I'd like my 25% ownership returned to me." "No way", was the answer. "How about one tire or its equivalent?" "Ha, ha", was the next answer. Then, seriously, I said, "At least take my name off the title, the registration and the insurance." That was done. It was a great activity: practical, economical, enjoyable. Yeah, verily!

Clowning Around

By John Arledge
January 1999

Dick Kraft's B&O Bio on T. J. Klauenberg, in the last issue of RABO *News & Notes*, reminded me of an incident that took place in the early 1960s when Ted was Assistant to Vice President of Operations at Baltimore. I was sitting in the office of my boss, Manager of Labor Relations R. L. Harvey, waiting for the arrival of some labor union officers to begin a grievance conference when there was a rap at the door and Ted Klauenberg stepped in. He proceeded to explain that he had testified the day before in a court case in Baltimore and wanted to give Mr. Harvey the pertinent details. Mr. Harvey told him to go ahead, advising his secretary to have the union officers wait a few minutes should they arrive.

Before launching into the details of his testimony in the suit against the railroad, Ted said that when he first took the stand, the court reporter requested that he state his name and job title. Ted related that he was Theodore J. Klauenberg, Assistant to Vice President of Operations for the B&O Railroad. The clerk reporter then said, "And your last name is spelled C-L-O-W-N- - - ?" at which time Ted interrupted stating, "No it's not Clownberg, it's Klauenberg, K-L-A-U-E-N-B-E-R-G!"

The clerk reporter recorded this and then said, "And your title,

Mr. Klauenberg, is Assistant Vice President?" to which Ted answered, "No, it's Assistant to Vice President."

Ted said the court reporter sort of grinned and asked, "Mr. Klauenberg, just what is the difference between an Assistant Vice President and Assistant to Vice President?" Ted responded, "About $30,000 per year."

A Few Tales Concerning "Uncle George"

By George Bull
April 2004

I worked for George Dove for a few years and would have to say there were several happenings during those years that I have not forgotten.

I always called Mr. Dove "Uncle George" as I didn't feel at ease calling him George and he did not want me to call him Mr. Dove. After all, he was a big shot and I was a peasant. So, it was always "Uncle George" and he called me "Georgie." Working for "Uncle George" was an experience not forgotten, as he was different.

I remember when he first came to Baltimore as he succeeded Harold Williams. He then referred to himself as a "General" (General Freight Agent). In the early 1960s, he was promoted to head up the new Piggyback Department and, after a few years, President Langdon brought in Ernie Wright as Vice President and Mr. Dove was in charge of sales.

Uncle George generally left Baltimore every Monday for either St. Louis or Chicago. One of my jobs was to take him to the airport. Upon arrival, he insisted I accompany him to the VIP Room of TWA. Uncle George would then consume five quick "JBs and water", following which I would escort him to the ramp for boarding. He would take my arm and away we would go.

Then, one day he stated, "Georgie, I want you to see the airplane." The security officer thought otherwise but anyone who knew Uncle George would not have been shocked by his insistence that I see the airplane. I finally told the man, "Look pal, do I look like a criminal? Let me see the damn plane and I promise—on my mother's grave—I'll be right back." He let me

Prior to the Staggers Rail Act of 1980 which deregulated the railroads, much of the railroad selling work was based on the personalities of the members of the Sales Department. A perfect example of such a salesman was George Dove. He started with the B&O in 1918 in the freight office and spent his entire career in the Sales Department. He worked in Pittsburgh and Chicago before moving to Baltimore as General Freight Agent. He then was promoted to the developing market of piggyback. George was notorious for being sure his customers, away from the office, had an adult beverage close at hand and George was sure they didn't drink alone. Actually, a customer wasn't even required for George to enjoy a stiff drink or two or ....

B&O Magazine photo.

go and Uncle George took me right to the plane and introduced me to several lovely young ladies—TWA girls. When I returned, I told the guard, "You see, I told you I would be right back."

Hard times fell on TWA and the VIP Room was not always open. So one Monday, upon our arrival at Friendship, we had to go to the bar and pay for the drinks. Still, Uncle George had his usual five "JBs and water", and while he was consuming them, he kept telling those around him that he was a "General" on his way to Yokahoma and I was his pilot. He must have said it a half a dozen times.

Now, I had been to Yokohama, years before, during the "Big One". Just before boarding the plane Uncle George had to use the bathroom and one of the fellows at the bar asked me if I had been to Yokahoma recently. I didn't want to embarrass Uncle George and I told the gentleman, "Not for several years." The fellow then told me of the innumerable changes that had taken place. I thanked him for an update and assured him I would look forward to my visit to the new Yokahoma. With that, TWA Charlie came in and begged Uncle George to board the plane. He took my arm and away we went.

As was generally my practice, I watched as the plane disappeared and then I returned to my car. You must keep in mind that while Uncle George had consumed five, I had two so my next stop was always at a Deli on Washington Blvd. I would purchase soup, a sandwich, Tasty Cake, coffee and a paper. Then, I would head for a nearby cemetery, have a quiet, peaceful lunch, read the paper, doze for about 15 minutes and generally left the cemetery about 1:00 PM—ready to "hit 'em".

Uncle George was really a nice guy, if he liked you, and I am glad he treated me very well. After he had his five JBs and water, he could be a little tough. I often think of the TWA pilot who thought I was "Uncle George's" personal pilot. Little did he know I was a "drummer" who represented the finest railroad in the country— "The Chessie System". Also, little did he know I visited Yokahoma in 1945 aboard the USS Bancroft DD 598 a week or so after WWII ended.

One final remark about "Uncle George". If you ever met him—you never forgot him!

One More Uncle George Tale

By George Bull
July 2004

My friend, George Dove, retired in the early seventies. From time to time, not too often, my other friend, Wally, would call and inform me Uncle George was coming down and wanted to have lunch. At that time, I was still a piggyback salesman but not reporting to Stan Christovich so it wasn't as easy for me to get away for an extended period. Of course, I drove the car and had the membership to the Governor's Club, I also knew the bartender rather well and "JB and water" consisted of at least eight ounces of alcohol and one-half ounce of water. For a number of years, Uncle George showed up two or three times a year and his last trip was one to be remembered.

I received the Monday morning call from Wally Havener--The

"General" was coming down and Wally and Howard Johnson would meet us at the Club. The four of us arrived about noon and Bill the bartender was happy to see us. Uncle George started off with a glass of buttermilk, followed by five "JBs and water" (heavy ones). A little later on, he ordered a large glass of tomato juice. Being retired for several years, he couldn't handle what he could previously and then it happened! He made a dash for the men's room but he didn't get two steps from the table. He threw up all over himself and all over the Governor's Club. It was bad and everyone was embarrassed. My friend Wally told me he and Howard had to leave and instructed me to take care of Uncle George. Needless to say, I really didn't appreciate Wally's instructions. For one thing, I was not reporting to the Piggyback Department any longer and I was thoroughly disenchanted with the turn of events.

Uncle George had to be cleaned up because eventually, following a five o'clock meeting with Wally at the Lord Baltimore or Danny's, he had to go home. I had heard there was a cleaner on Baltimore Street The Block whereby they would take care of accidents such as this in a matter of an hour. Uncle George and I drove to The Block only to find just about everything closed—it being Monday. Not knowing what to do, I brought him into my office as I had a bottle of Carbona Cleaner in my desk. There, the 'General' was sitting behind my desk in his sleeveless undershirt while I worked on his shirt, tie and suit coat. I managed to do a pretty good job, although I could not get the wrinkles out. I then told him to follow me to the washroom for further cleansing. He quickly stated it was unnecessary and I politely told him to shut up and I was tired of farting around with him for four hours or so. I also told him if my new boss had become aware of such "goings on", I would no doubt be collecting unemployment by the end of the week.

I delivered Uncle George to Wally and Howard at 5:00 PM and that was the last I saw of him until I visited him at Union Memorial Hospital the day before he died. There was only one George Dove and my last visit with him was indeed sad. Mr. Dove was not the dapper 'General' he displayed for so many years as he was reduced to a very humble exit. Down deep, he displayed compassion and, while he was tough, he sure loved the railroad and remains a legend with lots of us. Of course, so do his friends Wally and Howard Johnson—two more great fellows.

Jim Sell's Last Railroad Home

By Norman Murphy
July 2007

In my well-paid position as the "Chief Proofreader" of *News & Notes*, I have the opportunity to be one of only two persons (N&N Editor Ray Lichty is the other) who see the numerous contributions to *News & Notes* before publication and distribution of the newsletter. When I read Jim Sell's comments, titled *My Second Home,* that accompanied The Parkersburg news article he sent Ray regarding the B&O's historic contributions to the economy of Parkersburg, fond memories of my first contacts with Jim immediately came back to me--particularly those that involved Jim's "last railroad home".

At several locations, the B&O owned houses to insure local managers, possibly moving on short notice, would have a suitable residence. At Grafton, West Virginia, the company provided a house for the Division Superintendent at a very favorable monthly rent.

James J. Sell collection.

That "last railroad home" was a three-story, frame dwelling (with dirt basement) owned by the B&O and known as 301 McGraw Avenue in Grafton, West Virginia.

Historically, the McGraw Avenue dwelling was "reserved" for lease to the Superintendent of the Monongah Division headquartered at Grafton. The annual rent?? $1.00 per year!! Any taxes were assumed by the B&O; utilities were the responsibility of the Superintendent.

In the early 1960s, Jim was promoted to Superintendent of the Monongah Division, succeeding RABOer Ray Pomeroy. Jim deferred taking possession of the McGraw Avenue dwelling until that summer so as not to disrupt the school year for the Pomeroys.

At that time, my primary real estate responsibilities involved the leasing of B&O properties. And it just so happened, our office had recently embarked upon a systematic and comprehensive program of reviewing the thousands of active, "old" leases on record in the department--with the obvious objective being to increase the B&O's income from rental of surplus properties and thus improve the company's "bottom line". Therefore, it "fell" upon me to inform Jim that his McGraw Avenue rent would no longer be the $1.00/year paid by his predecessors but, rather, would be at market level. At that time, I had not yet had the opportunity and privilege of meeting Jim personally, so I was really worried about how a newly-promoted Division Superintendent would react to such type of news and the fact it was being given by a low echelon real estate agent. Not to worry!! No problem!! The new rental (I recall it being $80 or $90 per month) was accepted gracefully and without rancor.

Jim retired in August of 1978; and, shortly thereafter, he and his wife, Vigdis, purchased the McGraw Avenue property. The dwelling was beautifully and substantially improved and upgraded by them over the years and they continued to reside there until they moved (in 1995, I believe) to their current home in sunny Arizona. Jim had to relocate many, many times during his railroad career and 301 McGraw Avenue ultimately turned out to be the place that he and Vigdis called home the longest.

And one more little Sell/Murphy anecdote from the 1960s. From his many telephone conversations with me, Jim had become aware that my wife and I vacationed in Bermuda each year. At the end of one of those conversations, Jim said he and Vigdis had often discussed a possible Bermuda vacation and he asked me for some information regarding where we stayed in Bermuda. After hearing me "spout off", he asked me to go ahead make reservations for Vigdis and him for a certain time period. My response: "But Jim, you haven't even seen Cambridge Beaches!" His reply was somewhat along these lines: "That's OK. I trust you. If it's good enough for you, it's good enough for us." I made the reservations and held my breath. (Remember—I still had not met Jim personally.) The Sell post-vacation report: "We had a fabulous time and loved Cambridge Beaches!" I breathed a lot easier.

I ultimately had the good fortune to meet Jim and Vigdis. What a great couple! No wonder they have so many RABOer friends who always wish them continued good health and happiness. I hope Jim gets his wish to celebrate with Vigdis on her 94th birthday!

Youngstown Stories

By Mark Craven
July 2008

My wife Doris and I lived in Youngstown, Ohio, on two separate occasions in the 1960s.

The Division Freight Office was located on the second floor of the Passenger Station with a fairly long driveway from Mahoning Avenue. The railroad bridged Mahoning Avenue, with the station located west of Haselton Yard and east of Ohio Junction. The tracks through the station were at the second floor level. A pedestrian tunnel went under the tracks on the first floor with steps at either end so passengers could reach either platform. Not more than 50 yards away and parallel to the driveway flowed the Mahoning River, a river that never froze due to its many detours through the various steel mills.

The above description sets the scene for these two stories.

A Hunter's Lament

Although this man has passed on to a better life, he will not be called by his given name.

The Passenger Station had a large lawn on either side of the

The Youngstown station at track level. The street access was a floor down. This view is looking west, railroad direction.
E. H. Weber photo, H. H. Harwood, Jr., collection.

driveway which was cut regularly and bordered by trees along the river and a stone wall bordering the tracks from the station to Mahoning Avenue. Coupled with the grain that sifted out of hopper cars as they went by, the area became a regular feeding and resting area for pheasants. One of the employees of the Division Freight Office was a hunter. He knew how good pheasant tasted and wanted to put one on his dinner table. He knew that firing any kind of gun was out of the question and he wasn't that good with a slingshot; however, each day he saw the flock of pheasants feeding on the lawn which kept him scheming about getting one. He didn't even consider what Ohio Fish & Game would think about taking a game bird out of season.

Finally, the idea came to him. He would bring his fishing rod to work, bait it with some kernels of corn and drop the line from the second story window to the lawn below. All he had to do was wait until one of the birds found the corn, got it in its craw and then it was just a matter of reeling it in, twisting its neck and it would be ready for the pot. This plan seemed a good one but was not completely thought through. Can any of you readers see the error in judgment before reading on?

The day finally came; the pheasants were out there feeding; it was lunch time and there were hardly any people around. The line was baited and dropped out the window. It wasn't long until one of the birds found the corn and ate it. Our friend was already tasting the roasted bird, so he started to reel it in.

Well, all hell broke loose! As you could expect, the bird was not coming willingly and someone who witnessed this event said everybody in Youngstown heard the commotion before he got that bird to the second floor and silenced it.

Needless to say, one sacrificed bird assured the others a safe haven.

Not Every Snow Bank Has A Silver Lining

It was a cold winter morning with more than a foot of snow on the ground and I was coming down Mahoning Avenue from the west side. Looking up ahead, there were bright lights along the tracks on either side of the station. My immediate thoughts were a derailment but getting closer, I could see there were no railcars and no signs of heavy equipment. The driveway into the station had many parked vehicles and even some TV vans.

After finding a place to park, I went into the station, cornered one of the passenger clerks and asked him what had happened.

One of the night passenger trains had carried some silver coins from the Federal Reserve for the local banks. The night clerk had moved the baggage wagons into position and had loaded them, then had to wait until the train's departure before bringing the wagons across both mains. There was no tractor so the wagons had to be hand-pulled and pushed to get them across the tracks and to the freight elevator that would take them to the first floor.

When the train departed, they started to move the baggage wagons across the tracks. This was not the smoothest crossing and the wagon with all the silver coins got hung up. The baggage men were trying to get the wagon moving when one looked up and later said, "All I could see was this big head light coming at me, so I yelled and started to run. Wham! When that engine hit the wagon it started raining silver!"

Some $50,000 dollars in silver hit the platform and the snow-laden roadbed.

Before I arrived, some of the Passenger Department personnel had picked up quite a bit of the silver and turned it over to the government agents in charge of the recovery. The shoveling and sifting of the snow and soil continued; and in the end, I was told, all was recovered but about $2,000 which was believed to be in the ballast.

Fortunately, no one was seriously injured. One good thing happened. A few days later one of the baggage handlers was seen driving a nice new tractor pulling a couple of baggage wagons.

A Railroader Who Knew Operations
By Van Vander Veer
October 2000

My first encounter with C. T. Williams was shortly before my conclusion of the Engineering Management Training Program at Engle on the Cumberland Division. We were laying rail on #2 track and a car drove up and a very excited individual jumped out stating we had to finish the rail laying at once to avoid train delays.

The more this individual talked, the less work was being performed by the trackmen. So, I finally went up to him and stated, "If you will stop your yelling and leave here, we will get the rail installed and not delay the trains!" He looked at me, turned around and drove off. After he had gone, the Foreman told me that was C. T. Williams, the Division Superintendent. However, C. T. always appreciated an individual who stood up for himself and thus, by pure luck, I enjoyed a very pleasant relationship with C. T.

The message line was a great way for many railroaders to listen in and find out what was going on the territory. Both the Operating and Engineering Departments used the message line for instructions to the field or to inform some poor individual that he was causing problems on on the railroad. One day, C. T. was giving a newly-appointed young Trainmaster the devil for not having a good operation and this discourse went on for some time. Finally, a very loud voice came on the message line and said, "Tell the General Manager to go to hell." There was silence for a short period of time and C. T. demanded to know who said that. Only after C. T. retired, did the person who said those words mention it again to C. T. stating, "You were too hard on the young Trainmaster." "Yes," C. T admitted, "I could have been just a little too outspoken."

When I was Division Engineer on the Pittsburgh Division, we were programmed to lay new rail on the Main Line Subdivision between Sand Patch and Meyersdale on number 1 track. I requested Earl Johnson to reverse the trains for number 1 track to number 2 track to give the track forces uninterrupted track time and try to set a record for rail laying. Earl said it was ok if C. T. Williams, General Manager, agreed. I then told C. T. how important it was to lay the rail, avoid excessive cost, and actually minimize train disruption.

I believe my statement "We would set a new record for rail laying and he could 'needle' the other General Managers on how to lay rail" finally convinced him to say "yes." The first day, we did a great job and far exceeded our expectations. but the Time Saver trains westbound did take a delay and the VIPs in Baltimore told C. T that could not happen again. Thus, only then did C. T. tell me he was sorry but we had to lay the rail under traffic. To this day, I believe C. T. was sincere in his effort to help and felt that we should have continued our plan for the rail-laying program.

C. T. was a great railroader and I was always happy to have him ride over my territory in a high-rail vehicle. We enjoyed many conversations about railroading, especially those problems associated with field operations.

C. T. Williams

By Ray Lichty
October 2000

Dick Hosmeyer's "Letter to the Editor" asked for some stories about C. T. Williams. Chester was quite a character and such a strong personality was certain to generate a lot of stories. I'll respond with a few.

My all-time favorite is the tale about Bob Guess when he was working as Chief Dispatcher at Akron. Chester was General Manager at Pittsburgh. One evening, Williams called Akron and

Starting as a yard clerk at New Castle, Pennsylvania, Chester Williams became the Superintendent of the Newark, Chicago, Akron, Pittsburgh and Cumberland Divisions and General Superintendent. His last position was as General Manager of the Eastern Region headquartered in Baltimore. Chester was a typical boss of his time. Aggressive; ruled with an iron-fist; impulsive; quick tempered; he often was unreasonable in his demands but nothing he wouldn't have expected from himself. His reputation proceeded him and he was proud of it!

B&O Magazine photo.

Bob answered the phone. Williams asked, "Who's this?" Bob replied, "Guess." Williams responded, "This is Chester Williams. Who is this?" Bob, now knowing what was happening, then answered, "This is Robert Guess, sir." Chester retorted with, "You have a clever name, young man. You had better be careful how you use it!"

When I was Assistant Trainmaster at Wilmington, Delaware, Chester found out that Judy and I owned a house trailer. He was intrigued with the idea and told Bill Johnston, who was Superintendent at Baltimore, that he would like to put our trailer on a TTX car. That way, if there was a problem during the night, he could have an engine attached to it and send us to wherever the problem was located. Then, when I got up in the morning, I would be on the job.

Speaking of being on the job, when the vacancy developed for the ATM at Wilsmere Yard in Wilmington, Jack Humbert, who was in the Power Bureau in Baltimore, told C. T. Williams I was the man for that job. Chester liked Jack and respected his recommendation.

Chester called me and the entire conversation went something like this; "How would you like to be Assistant Trainmaster at Wilsmere?" "That would be wonderful." "Fine, the job is yours." "When should I report?" "Yesterday!"

At the September RABO meeting, this request for C. T. Williams stories was discussed. Allan Baer and Maurice Good told about the time that a Time Saver had a bad derailment on the Pittsburgh East End. Chester brought his office car to Rockwood and parked it on a siding. He stayed there until the derailment was cleaned up. But, the most interesting part of this story is that while he was there, he arranged for meals to be served the T&E and wreck train crews on his car.

Also. at the September meeting, Al Gibson told of two incidents. One occasion, Gibby was in the Mechanical Department at Willard, Ohio, and Chester was Superintendent at Garrett, Ind. The hump retarders at Willard were operated by steam. Gibby had been unsuccessful in getting a car of coal spotted and the boiler started to lose pressure. Gibby ordered the retarders turned off. Within minutes, C. T. Williams called from Garrett and wanted to know what in the world Gibby thought he was doing. Gibby explained that he could not get the car of coal spotted. Williams slammed down the phone. Within a couple of more minutes, the Willard Trainmaster called and said, "We're coming in to spot a car of coal."

On another occasion, Chester told Gibby, "You're an ornery SOB." Gibby replied, "So are you!"

Oh, the good old days. Things were different then and people were different. I don't think our new society allows for such personalities. That may be a mixed blessing.

Reminiscences

By James E. Sell
October 2000

I never worked directly for Mr. Williams but I did have a few occasions to meet and talk to him, particularly when the merger committee (B&O-C&O) was working in Chicago. I remember one occasion when he and Mr. Bertrand met with the committee in Chicago and Jim Alvord and I gave them a synopsis of a consolidated yard we were going to propose. Mr. Williams asked a lot of questions and we answered them. Mr. Williams shook his head and said, "I think that will work."

After the meeting, they invited some of us to lunch on Mr. Bertrand's car. At lunch, Mr. Williams reminisced about some of his experiences. The only one I remember was one he told about riding from Pittsburgh to Chicago with then President R. B. White. As they were riding over the Akron-Chicago Division, Mr. White pointed to some leafy vegetation growing in the ditch alongside the track. He said, "That is kale and, oh, wouldn't it be nice to have some of that." Mr. Williams said, "When the President makes a wish, it is up to you to see that it is fulfilled."

When he got back to Pittsburgh, he sent his chief clerk to a grocery store for six cans of kale. Together, they took the wrappers off the cans and then took some wrapping paper and hand-printed "KALE" on the paper, glued the paper on the cans and sent it to Mr. White, "From the Akron-Chicago Division."

I have heard many stories about Mr. Williams and his demanding character but, fortunately, I never experienced that side of him.

More C. T. Williams

By Al Gibson
January 2001

I was General Foreman in Willard, Ohio, from 1942 until 1946, when I had my first conversation with Chester Williams. He had just been promoted to Superintendent of the Chicago-Akron Division with headquarters in Garrett, Indiana. I was advised that the third trick engineer in charge of the boiler ordered coal through the Trainmaster's office. Our shop boilers

Roy B. White used office car 902 (then numbered 904) during his tenure as B&O's president, and it was most likely that he was riding in it when he set off a minor scramble to accommodate his casual wish for kale. The car itself had a distinguished past, having been built in 1929 as the "Ranger," privately owned by Eleanor "Cissy" Patterson, a member of the Medill newspaper dynasty and owner of the 'Washington Times Herald.' B&O bought it in 1942 and immediately assigned it to White, who had just succeeded Daniel Willard at the B&O's helm. After this photo was taken, it was modernized and eventually sold to a private owner. Reputedly, it still survives in an immobile state.

H. H. Harwood, Jr., photo, 1966.

furnished steam heat for the station offices, restaurant, dispatch office and the roundhouse. We also provided steam for the eastbound hump retarders.

When I arrived for work, the first trick engineer said, "Mr. Gibson, we need coal bad, I only have enough to bank the boilers to keep them alive." I called the Trainmaster's office and told John Krause, "If we don't get coal now, we'll be out of business." About that time, the phone rang. It was Chester. He said, "Do you know that the hump is shut down?" I said, "Yes sir, but I don't have enough coal to keep these boilers operating." Then, the other phone rang. The Trainmaster said, "Gibby, get the track cleared. I'm delivering a car of coal. When all this is done, we're back in business."

I later heard that the General Manager from Pittsburgh told the Trainmaster that he better furnish coal when the roundhouse orders it. I think we handled the problem fast and properly, but whether it pleased Chester or not, I didn't really know.

My second conversation with Chester was about the time we received the T-3 locomotive, which was built at Mt. Clare Shop and was designed by our own Mechanical Engineer's office. They were from the Q-1 locos which had 64" drivers. The boiler was lengthened by applying a new section. Because of this, we had to replace the old frames in order to take care of the 74" wheels. Passenger locos had 80" drivers. Freight locomotives had 64" drivers. The T-3 was designed to be used for both passenger and freight.

Getting back to the conversation with Chester, I received a call from my Superintendent of Motive Power saying that they were going to test one of T-3 locos and it would arrive at Willard with the test car on Friday. I was to get all the equipment applied to start the test on Monday. This gave me part of Friday, Saturday and Sunday to get it ready. We had to add a coal bucket to the tank, which held two hundred pounds of coal. Then, we had to apply a thermostat to the smoke box which recorded the inside temperature. We also had to add a telephone in the cab which allowed us to converse with the test car. When the coal was dumped, it was recorded by phone to the test car.

About that time, the phone rang again; it was Chester. He said he wanted to get another trip west. I said, "Mr. Williams, if you do, it will be too late for us to equip all of the materials needed to make the test run Monday." He told me that he was going to call the engine. I immediately called my Superintendent in Pittsburgh, Mr. Reece, and told him that Chester wanted to make another trip west, and that he would have the engine back in time. I told him that I would not be able to have the engine ready for Monday. A little later, Chester called and said, "Boy, did you call Mr. Reece?" and I replied, "Yes, I did." He said, "Do you know who you're working for?" I said, "Yes, too many people." He said, "You're a little cocky today!" and, I said, "No more than you are." He then said, "Alright, hold the engine." I let it be known that he couldn't always have his own way.

Memorable Moments in Pittsburgh
By Keith Rader
April 2010

1961-1963, those were the days on the B&O when men were men and we were all aware of the difficult tasks each of us had to overcome. The Baltimore and Ohio Railroad was a low profit railroad during the early sixties. The railroad found it necessary to cut management's pay 10% across the board but we still had a sense of humor. When Jervis Langdon came aboard in 1961 as our new President, he gave back our 10%, saying it would never happen again as long as he was our President.

It was New Year's Day in the 'Steel City' of Glenwood, Pennsylvania. Big John Kalfus, Jr., General Chairman for the trainmen, was having a beer at the Homestead Bar. His childhood friend Phil Fonner slips in behind him and slyly picks up John's beer and takes a sip. John begins by stuttering, followed by some not-too-kind words. When John attempted to un-tangle his size 13 from behind the brass rail, he broke his leg. The headline on the local newspaper highlighted, "All was not quiet in Steel City on New Year's Day". Earl Johnson was the B&O Superintendent at Pittsburgh. Earl, John and Phil had schooled together. I was the Terminal Trainmaster at Glenwood and Mr. Johnson called asking if I could pick up four or more copies of the newspaper for his book of memoirs.

I received a call from a rendering plant located on the east side of the Allegheny River Bridge wanting to flag our track while the wrecking ball tore down their facility. I informed them that it would require a qualified railroad flagman to protect them while they were doing this work.

A few days later, I received a call from the B&O Operator on the bridge. A suspicious person with a fusee and red flag was doing something on the bridge, he said. My first thought was that the rendering plant had decided to flag for themselves to save the cost of our charging them for our flagman. I immediately called our railroad policeman asking him to meet with me on the bridge. The railroad policeman thought we may need a city police officer on the scene; and when I arrived, they were both there. We approached the suspicious character on the bridge and asked for his credentials. "I am the B&O Bridge Inspector", he said. We were all embarrassed but you can be sure that inspector will notify the Operator the next time he makes an inspection.

Our General Manager was Chester T. Williams who had a loud bark but a soft bite. He became a legendary figure in short time.

Chester had previously been at Pittsburgh as Superintendent when John W. Thorton was Chief Train Dispatcher. At that time, there was a labor shortage. Thorton went into Superintendent Williams' office to inform him that he had a man outside who he thought would make a good Train Dispatcher. He wanted to promote him to that position. Mr. Williams said, "Well, John, why don't you promote him?" John replied telling his boss, "He only has one arm and I wanted to tell you that first." "Get out of here John", he said, "That is not a handicap. Some of those you have now don't have any heads!"

We quickly learned that our new General Manager was known to be a stickler for telephone etiquette.

On one occasion, General Manager Williams made a call to Glenwood Yard. Everyone was very busy. The only person who had time to stop the ringing was A. R. Woods, the Monongahela Connecting Railroad Yard Clerk, who had stopped by to pick up supplies for his interchange office. When Woodsie picked up the phone, he calmly said hello. The caller was General Manager Williams asking as to who he was addressing. "A. R. Woods, sir", he replied. Mr. Williams followed with, "What is your capacity?" "Oh--about two gallons", Woodsie said. "My name is Williams, I am your General Manager", he said, and then the lecture began.

Martin O'Toole was the 2nd shift classification clerk. When the phone rang, Marty picked up the receiver saying simply, "Hello". Mr. Williams followed with, "Who am I talking to?" Marty mistook the voice to be his hunting buddy and replied, "If you don't want to talk, hang up and get off my phone." The following day, the Crew Caller went to Marty's residence and summoned him to Mr. William's office. Nothing resulted in any disciplinary action when the cards were put on the table, just some constructive instructions.

General Manager Williams called Selby O'Neil, the Trainmaster at Willard, Ohio, on the phone. Supervising the terminal at Willard was a tough assignment and Selby was one of the few who could master the job. The reports showed that things had not gone well the night before and Mr. Williams was seeking answers for his superiors in Baltimore

Selby hesitated, and then replied, "Well, Mr. Williams, we had a cloud burst and the rain washed all the numbers off the switch lists. We had to stop the hump and make out new switch lists." All was quiet on the line. "Selby", the boss said, "did you ever use that excuse before?" "No, sir", he replied. Mr. Williams said, "Don't ever use it again." Loud bark; no bite.

A similar situation takes place and Selby is fumbling his reports looking for an answer. Not finding it, he laid down the phone and looked out the window. Finally, he thought he had delayed long enough and he picked up the receiver. "Hullo-hullo." Mr. Williams said, "Where did you go?" Selby and Chester were both pro's, Selby was Irish Catholic and he knew Mr. Williams was protestant. "Well sir", he said. "I was watching out the window and an ore train, passing on the main, just pulled the protestant end out of one." That was good enough to get him off the hook.

Conductor Potter, a grouch of sorts, dubbed "Powder Puff" to match his initials, had a red signal; the train ahead of him was in distress. He listened to the Conductor ahead explaining, on the train wire, his problem to Mr. Williams and the Train Dispatcher. Potter then began telling everyone what he thought they were doing wrong. Mr. Williams said, "Do you know who you are talking to? I am the General Manager." Our grouchy conductor said, "Do you know who you are talking to?" The reply was, "No." "I am G. D. glad of that", Potter said, and quickly hung up.

Mr. Williams was chastising the Glenwood Crew Caller. The yard crew at the Try Street Passenger Station had a one-hour delay waiting on one of its trainmen. "Well, Mr. Williams", the caller said, "it is like this, I have to call the Pittsburgh Operator and she calls the Connellsville Operator who calls Trainman Haines's neighbor. Mr. Haines does not have a phone. His neighbor notifies Mr. Haines he is on call by putting a lantern in his window. But Mr. Haines never sees the light."

As I was the Terminal Trainmaster at Pittsburgh, Mr. Williams instructed me to hold a formal hearing and do something about Mr. Haines being tardy. My subordinate was a hard worker and was liked by all his fellow workers. Additionally, he was a poor man with a large family and I wanted to help him. At the hearing, I asked if we would be expecting a repetition. "Yes, sir, Mr. Rader", he said. "You sure can." It was obvious he did not know the definition of "repetition". We voided his reply telling him he can't say that.

When President Kennedy was shot, I heard the news in my car, while I was waiting on Terminal Agent Mark Sturges. Our beloved General Manager had just been operated on and we were donating to his blood bank. A few weeks later, my phone rang at Glenwood Yard. Having been schooled on the proper way to answer a telephone, I answered, "This is Keith Rader, Terminal Trainmaster." After a moment of silence, I heard a familiar voice. Mr. Williams said, "Rader--I knew I would get your blood eventually and I am calling to say thanks."

Another memorable moment was when General Manager Rayburn, who followed Chester Williams in that job, called asking me to meet with him and a gentleman from the real estate department at Allegheny Yard the following morning. Fielding Lewis was his name, taken from a Civil War General, I was told. Mr. Rayburn requested a tour of the yard, which covered a two-mile stretch from the Allegheny River Bridge to the Western Penitentiary, all on the west side of the Allegheny River. We had a few customers there including a produce merchant who rented our old freight house, H. J. Heinz, who was on strike most of the time, and the penal institution that received an occasional carload of goods. In addition, we had a hundred or more storage cars in Alleghany Yard needing heavy repairs. Pittsburgh was known system-wide as the location of Glenwood Shops. It seemed that whenever any terminal on the system wanted to get rid of a bad order car they would bill it to Glenwood. We held those cars awaiting repairs at Allegheny Yard

We did not have a repair program at the time because of lack of funds. But that didn't matter. If it meant chaining a car, even one that maybe should have been scrapped, to the rear end of the local, they somehow got it to Pittsburgh.

At the end of the day with Mr. Rayburn and Fielding Lewis, I was asked what would happen if they decided to close Allegheny Yard. "Nothing", I said, "if you find me a place to store these shopped cars." "Don't ever, ever tell that to anyone else", Mr. Rayburn said.

Six months later, the yard was sold for three million dollars to the city and the *Three Rivers Stadium* was born. That was a lot of money for a poor railroad.

Shortly afterward, I was moved to an assignment in Baltimore and the three million dollar sale made a happy ending for my days in Pittsburgh.

One of B&O's handsome EM-1 articulateds, the 7629, is working hard hoisting a westbound coal train up the grade and through the twisting curves of Swine Creek Hill, south of Middlefield, Ohio, on B&O's Lake Branch. A sister EM-1 is helping on the rear. The train's consist is destined for an ancient McMyler coal dumper at Fairport Harbor, on Lake Erie near Painesville, Ohio.

H. H. Harwood, Jr., photo, 1956.

INDEX

APPENDIX
Railroad Company Abbreviations

Baltimore & Ohio Railroad (B&O)
Owned or Affiliated Railroad Companies

A&S	Alton & Southern
ACL	Atlantic Coast Line
B&OCT	Baltimore & Ohio Chicago Terminal
B&S	Buffalo & Susquehanna
BR&P	Buffalo Rochester & Pittsburgh
C&N	Columbus & Newark
C&O	Chesapeake & Ohio
CH&D	Cincinnati Hamilton & Dayton
CNJ	Central Railroad of New Jersey
CRR	Clinchfield
CSX	CSX Corporation
CSXT	CSX Transportation
CUT	Cincinnati Union Terminal
FM&P	Fairmont Morgantown & Pittsburgh
L&N	Louisville & Nashville
MHB	Municipal Harbor Belt
O&M	Ohio & Mississippi
PM	Pere Marquette
P&LE	Pittsburgh & Lake Erie
P&W	Pittsburgh & Western
RDG	Reading
RF&P	Richmond Fredericksburg & Potomac
SAL	Seaboard Airline
SC&M	Strouds Creek and Muddelty
SIRT	Staten Island Rapid Transit
TRRA	Terminal Railroad Association (St Louis)
WTC	Washington Terminal Company
WM	Western Maryland

Other Railroads

AT&SF	Atchison Topeka & Santa Fe
B&A	Baltimore & Annapolis

BN	Burlington Northern
CB&Q	Chicago Burlington & Quincy
CNW	Chicago North Western
CR	Conrail
CRI&P	Chicago Rock Island & Pacific
CTN	Canton
ERIE	Erie
MP	Missouri Pacific
NYC	New York Central
NYS&W	New York Susquehanna & Western
N&W	Norfolk & Western
PRR	Pennsylvania
SLSF	St. Louis-San Francisco
SOU	Southern
SP	Southern Pacific
TP	Texas Pacific